THE DAY TRADER'S
MANUAL

Wiley Finance Editions

Financial Statement Analysis
  Martin S. Fridson

Dynamic Asset Allocation
  David A. Hammer

Intermarket Technical Analysis
  John J. Murphy

Investing in Intangible Assets
  Russell L. Parr

Forecasting Financial Markets
  Tony Plummer

Portfolio Management Formulas
  Ralph Vince

Trading and Investing in Bond Options
  M. Anthony Wong

The Complete Guide to Convertible Securities Worldwide
  Laura A. Zubulake

Managed Futures in the Institutional Portfolio
  Charles B. Epstein, Editor

Analyzing and Forecasting Futures Prices
  Anthony F. Herbst

Chaos and Order in the Capital Markets
  Edgar E. Peters

Inside the Financial Futures Markets, 3rd Edition
  Mark J. Powers and Mark G. Castelino

Relative Dividend Yield
  Anthony E. Spare

Selling Short
  Joseph A. Walker

The Foreign Exchange and Money Markets Guide
  Julian Walmsley

Corporate Financial Risk Management
  Diane B. Wunnicke, David R. Wilson, Brooke Wunnicke

Money Management Strategies for Futures Traders
  Nauzer J. Balsara

The Mathematics of Money Management
  Ralph Vince

Treasury Operations and the Foreign Exchange Challenge
  Dimitris N. Chorafas

Fixed-Income Synthetic Assets
  Perry H. Beaumont

Option Market Making
  Allen Jan Baird

The New Technology of Financial Management
  Dimitris N. Chorafas

The Day Trader's Manual
  William F. Eng

THE DAY TRADER'S MANUAL

THEORY, ART, AND SCIENCE OF PROFITABLE SHORT-TERM INVESTING

William F. Eng

Wiley Finance Editions
JOHN WILEY & SONS, INC.

New York • Chichester • Brisbane • Toronto • Singapore

I wish to dedicate this book to my mother, King,
whom I call every Mother's Day.

Charts appearing in Chapters 1, 2, 7, 8, 9, and 11,
and in the Case sections from Part Three of this book are
adapted from THE MASTERCHARTIST PROGRAM, Roberts-Slade,
Inc. Reprinted by permission.

In recognition of the importance of preserving what has been written, it is a
policy of John Wiley & Sons, Inc., to have books of enduring value printed on
acid-free paper, and we exert our best efforts to that end.

Library of Congress Cataloging-in-Publication Data:
Eng. William F.
    The day trader's manual: theory, art, and science of profitable
    short-term investing / William F. Eng.
        p.   cm.   Wiley Finance Editions
    Includes index.
    ISBN 0-471-51406-3
    1. Stocks. 2. Futures. 3. Options (Finance). 4. Investments–
Case studies.   I. Title.
HG4661.E54 1993
332.6–dc20   92-14732

Printed in the United States of America

10 9 8 7 6 5 4

Preface

I've written *The Day Trader's Manual* to fill the need for a book on modern-day trading methods. In the past, day traders have had to educate themselves about current developments in the markets, trading hardware and software, and trading techniques. This book is designed to make it easier for traders to learn what they need to know to trade more intelligently and profitably.

Although all traders can benefit from this book, every trader will benefit differently. For every 100 ideas contained in these pages, the beginning trader might learn and understand 80; the other 20 will probably be too advanced for him or her to immediately grasp. The more experienced trader, who is conversant with the rudiments of day trading, might merely review the 80 basic ideas and concentrate on mastering 10 of the 20 advanced ideas. Finally, the complete trader will read, understand, and master all 100 ideas. As an experienced generalist, the complete trader will be capable of integrating all the information offered into a total trading plan.

It will be worthwhile for you to learn as much as you can from this book, no matter what your background; but ultimately, all 100 ideas are necessary for successful trading. As an experienced trader, I can tell you that if even one key concept escapes you, that one will someday—given enough time in the markets—prove to be the Achilles' heel that will cost you money in a trade. This Achilles' heel, if not dealt with, will be the ultimate cause of your trading failure.

Merely reading this book, however, is not enough. You'll need to combine the ideas in this book with your trading experiences, personality, and style to transform the insights here into valuable working tools. I hope that reading *The Day Trader's Manual* will start or extend an educational process that will make you a more successful trader.

William F. Eng
Chicago, Illinois
October, 1992

Contents

PART ONE

THE THEORY OF
DAY TRADING

1

Time, Price, and the Day Trader

This section is the first of three parts to this book. This chapter offers the reader a theoretical framework in which the day trader can apply currently applicable trading techniques to a smaller-scale trading scheme: daily trading. The counterpart to studying the methods is a section that will explore the various techniques as applied to various stages of the markets themselves. First, the techniques are thoroughly analyzed; then they are applied to defined market stages.

Can currently used trading techniques that are applicable only to daily bar charts analysis be applied validly to shorter time frames? It is my contention that this is possible; additionally, the section on chaos theory and pattern fractionation and how they apply to day trading will reinforce this contention.

WHAT IS DAY TRADING?

Day trading is the process of making trades during the course of the trading day with the intention of making short-term profits. (This is the most succinct definition of day trading that this book will give.) With the advent of 24-hour trading and global trading opportunities throughout the trading day, the effective trading day can be extended beyond the conventional time period in the trader's local community. From this starting point of trade execution, the trade itself can extend to position trades, where the trades are carried forward beyond the day on which the day trades are initiated. Or the trade started at the beginning of the day can be closed prior to the day's trading activities; that is, it can conclude itself as a day trade.

It seems logical that the execution of the day trade at the opening price and the ending of the same trade at the close will give the trader the maximum *length of time* to carry the position. Two initial prerequisites for profitability in any market are that there must be positions taken—as opposed to no positions—and that those positions must be maintained for as long as possible. One way to increase potential profitability is to leave the trade on for as long as possible because this increases the opportunities for profits. Of course, there is the other side of the coin: Increasing the time for the maintenance of a trade can also result in greater market losses.

The above statements are made on the underlying assumption that the position is profitable for the duration of the trade. (If the trade is profitable and the day trader decides to close out the trade prior to the close of the day, the day trader eliminates any possibility of continued profitability by eliminating any market positions: The day trader's potential for additional profits would have been reduced to zero probability by the act of closing out the trade. At this point, open trade profits or losses become *realized* gains or losses.)

The act of allowing the profitable trade to stay open for as long as possible is merely a *mechanical* way to manage the position. It requires no additional thought processes. As this is the most mechanical way to increase the opportunities for profits, it does not give a hint of what is critical to profitability: the range of prices traveled during the period the markets are open from the opening trade to the closing trade, that is, the opening and the closing price, as differentiated from (1) the opening of the day trade and its closing, and (2) the range of prices, from high to low. In terms of prices covered, the range between high and low prices is a subset of prices through which the market has traveled from opening to closing.

As you can determine, the greater the trading range for the particular markets, the greater is the potential for absolute dollar amount of profits. (Implicit in the greater trading range is the fact that there will be accompanying increased trading volume. Increasing volume does not portend more profitable trading, but it does indicate how easy it is to take profits.) Note, however, that simply having the potential for profits doesn't mean that the day trader will make the profits. Offering the right tools to an inexperienced journeyman carpenter will not create beautiful works of cabinetry, yet on a more mundane level, the right tools are necessary. Successful day trading thus requires, among many other conditions, a wide trading range.

Components of Day Trading: Time and Price

What has been cursorily discussed so far is the range of time and the range of prices. The range of time has been defined as a maximum period as bounded by the opening time and the closing time. Any greater time period than that would encompass a larger time frame, which would move it out of the area of day trading. Every legitimate trader is bound to play by these parameters: No trades can be executed prior to the opening trade and no trades can be executed after the closing trade. Open trades can be carried over in the next trading session, however, for the closing of the trade.

Thus, the limiting factor that defines the scope of day trading distinctly is the limit of time.

Because the day trader has access to the data of each trade, the issue of length of analysis is important: Should he analyze every trade tick-by-tick, or should he push to get his analyses closer to the daily parameters?

HOURLY TO TICK-BY-TICK CHART ANALYSES

For most purposes, the treatment of trade-by-trade data is most effectively evaluated with five-minute bar charts. Using the five-minute chart as the base, it is easier to extend to daily, weekly, and monthly chart analyses of the same futures or stocks. Most software for day trading analyses provides for this type of analysis. It is much easier to analyze from a smaller scale to a larger scale than the other way around, as the data collected on the smaller scale can be summarized into larger scales.

The use of tick-by-tick charts is valid if the day trader is an experienced Elliott Wave analyst who needs to discover the wave counts as precisely as possible; for all practical purposes, if the off-floor day trader needs to analyze the market action by ticks, she shouldn't be trading at all.

The off-floor day trader mustn't even attempt to analyze the markets on a tick-by-tick basis, for three reasons: competition from floor traders and stock specialists, delays in price reporting, and incorrect sequencing of trades.

Competition from floor traders and stock specialists. Because it is the province of floor traders and stock specialists to make their living trading so close to the vest, the off-floor day trader would be literally trying to compete with them on their level. This can't be done. If it were possible, then there would be no need for memberships on exchanges. Even though the trend is toward trading from off-floor with computers, those who control the programming of the computers will have access to first trades.

Delays in price reporting. Where is the market really trading at while the off-floor day trader is trying to analyze the markets so precisely? Trades executed on exchange floors are reported by the human-machine chain. Early in our survey work to find the most reliable source of data for day trading purposes, our firm instructed a floor member at the Chicago Board of Trade to report all price changes in the Bond and Soybean pits over the telephone. The average delay from the changes reported on the electric boards at the exchange to the time we received the changes on our computers was about 10 seconds. In slow markets, 10 seconds of price-reporting delay seems like forever, though this problem can be resolved very easily: Give limit orders close to the last sale for trade execution instead of market orders. In fast markets, a 10-second delay can actually turn out to be forever; this problem can be resolved only with additional trading capital.

There are also many times when the prices and trades are reported incorrectly: Numbers and markets are miskeyed and trade executions are reported in different sequences. Given some of these considerations, the tick-by-tick charts are useful but can often be misleading.

The day trader would be best off viewing the tick-by-tick charts for confirmation of his trade executions and not using them to evaluate market conditions for future trade executions. The tick-by-tick charts should be used only for price-reporting functions and not value-decision-making tools (see Figure 1.1).

On the other hand the use of hourly charts for day trading takes a bit too long. There are about six hours of exchange-fostered trading in the average market, so reducing the analysis to segments of six hourly bar charts for analysis offers a maximum number of six decision-making points; that is, the trader makes a decision to enter or exit a trade only after the completion of the analysis of one particular data bar. If the day trader needs many decision-making points, the fact that there are only six hourly points drastically reduces the number of potential trades.

If the day trader waits for market action to unfold during the course of the day—waiting until half the day is over is normal—three of those six decision-making points will have passed, allowing the day trader only the remaining three possible trade exit points for the latter half of the trading session. Until the third or fourth decision-making point passes, the day trader will not generally have enough information to successfully enter a day trade. At that point, there will be only two or three more data points left to be charted before the end of the trading day.

Figure 1.1
The upper chart is a five-minute bar chart of the Dow Jones Industrial average. The lower chart is a tick-by-tick chart that is an exploded version of the area pointed out by the arrow in the upper chart. (11/20 @ 11:25 A.M.)

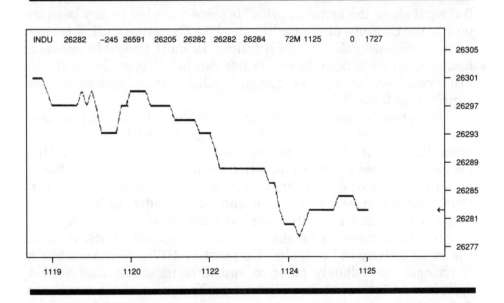

Implicit in this is the reason for exiting a successful trade: Exit only when sell signals are generated, not when the passage of time limits the trading day.

The day trader may exit profitable trades in either of these conditions:

1. Time is up and the day trader has to close out the trades prior to the day's close.

2. The day trader has profits on his trades and arbitrarily decides to close out the trades.

In either case *the day trader would be allowing profits to dictate his trading style.*

As will be seen elsewhere in this chapter, successfully making money in the markets must be based on using both loss-cutting techniques and profit-*taking* techniques. Most experienced traders, however, will tell the day trader that it has been losses that have caused the most damage to their trading, not profits. *Arbitrarily* defined profits are reflections of the trader's parameters. On the other hand, profit, when defined by market action, is a reflection of the market's conditions.

Prices and Price Limits

But what about the factor of price? Is price bounded by any barriers within the confines of the trading day? As far as day trading is concerned, prices, in theory, are limitless. In most tradeable markets, there are no such boundaries: Prices can be all over the ballpark. Price can trade as high as demand will lift it up and as low as supply will force it down.

For practical purposes, however, in the futures markets and some other markets, there are exchange-imposed price boundaries (limits) out of which prices may not trade. Even within this exchange-imposed limitation, price boundaries are lifted after a certain number of days of trading at certain parameters. In effect, the forces of market action will eventually be reflected in the price range, even with artificially imposed limitations of *price* limits.

In stocks, there are no such exchange-imposed limits. Witness the price activity of Jim Walter Corporation (JWC, New York Stock Exchange) immediately prior to and after its announced 5-for-4 split in mid-July 1987 (see Figure 1.2). The price of the stock was $45 at the time of the announcement, whereupon specialists of the stock suspended the stock from trading. This suspension (in effect, a limit bid situation) was not exchange instigated. Within two days

Figure 1.2
Price chart for Jim Walter Corporation before and after a 5-for-4 stock split in July 1987. (Reprinted by permission of INVESTOR'S BUSINESS DAILY, "The Newspaper For Important Decision Makers", July 17, 1981, INVESTOR'S BUSINESS DAILY, INC.)

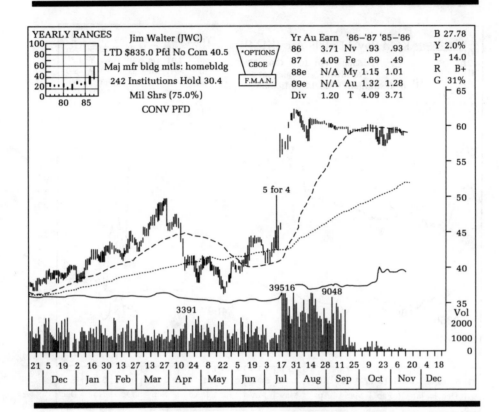

of this announcement, the price jumped to $55 per share. It did not trade between the prices of 50¼ and 54⅞. Prices resumed trading at supposed price ranges where supply was enough to balance out demand.

Another example of the absence of price limits for stocks can be seen in countless issues trading prior to and after the October 19, 1987 stock market collapse. KLM Royal Dutch Air (KLM, New York Stock Exchange) traded to a low price of 22½ prior to that day (see Figure 1.3). From the close of that day, it went to 15½ the next day for a drop of 7 points, or over 31 percent. Then the price rallied to 21 two days later, and sold all the way down to 13½ in the early portion of the next month, November 1987.

The two examples of stock prices activities, extreme though they may be, illustrate the fact that within consecutive days, prices of stocks can be all over the ballpark. In the case of KLM Royal Dutch Air, prices moved violently on an intraday basis. The

Figure 1.3
Price chart for KLM Royal Dutch Air, including the October 1987 stock market crash. (Reprinted by permission of INVESTOR'S BUSINESS DAILY, "The Newspaper For Important Decision Makers", July 17, 1981, INVESTOR'S BUSINESS DAILY, INC.)

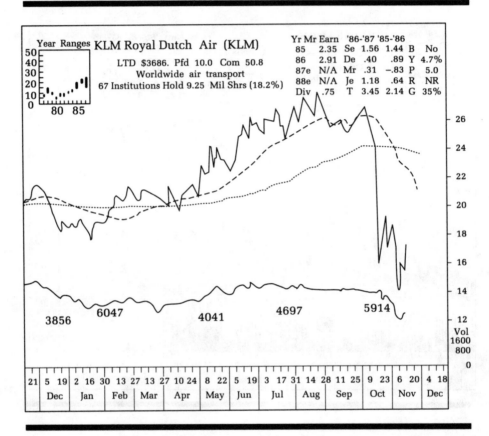

violence of price moves in our current stock market allows for opportunities to make substantial profits through intraday trading techniques.

In the case of futures and commodities, exchange-imposed price limits act regularly to dampen the volatility of violent price moves. In reality, these exchange-imposed limits function more to the benefit of the clearing firms whose clients may be exposed to the limit moves on the wrong side of directional moves. The price limits are not created for the benefit of speculative traders. In limiting the moves to certain ranges, the clearing firms can contact and extract from such clients additional funds to cover mark-to-market losses before the market moves against these clients even more. Having the opportunity to contact clients is certainly better than trying to contact clients for major and financially debilitating losses at a much later time.

Intraday Price Forecasting

Of the two primary aspects of day trading, price and time, price is the dependent variable and time is the independent variable. Price, as critical as it is in defining a trading account's profitability, is held to the time period in which it can fluctuate.

We conclude that once the day's trading is completed, price can no longer fluctuate, but within that day's *time* range, price has the leeway to do anything it wants.

This, then, is our task: to forecast price movements within the confines of the day's time limitations using technical analysis tools. This forecasting will be facilitated or impeded by what has been done prior to the current day's price and time data.

The mere act of day trading precludes any stringent applications of fundamental analysis. Fundamental analysis does not consider the factor of price action to be critical in value analysis. Fundamental analysis considers supply and demand factors with the expectations that these factors will be felt in a final outcome: value, independent of time considerations. Technical analysis takes price data and studies where it came from, where it is, and where it is expected to be in the future, independent of long-term supply and demand influences.

FORECASTING THE LENGTH AND DIRECTION OF MARKET MOVES

The two factors a trader has to recognize is the direction of the market's moves and the length of the market's moves, regardless of whether he or she is a short-term scalper or a long-term investor. These factors fall into the realm of market forecasting and predictions. Despite the fact that it is necessary to trade markets correctly with the right number of positions, and with the correct position management by pyramiding correctly and limiting oneself in regards to extraordinary market losses, the trader needs to know where and how the markets are headed.

A framework for developing a scenario as to probable direction is necessary to help the traders withstand temporarily adverse market moves. For example, believing that the market is bullish while the market is selling off dramatically helps the trader to hang on to existing positions and also to add to positions or initiate new positions at relatively bargain prices. Conversely, believing that a market is bearish while the market develops an intermediate rally will aid the trader in staying short in the bear market. The trader in such cases will be less likely to be scared out of his positions.

A second necessary framework involves knowing when the market's current activity will cease. Whether the markets are bullish or bearish, how long they will stay bullish or bearish is a question the trader needs to have answered. If the trader is sophisticated enough, she will recognize that holding positions in such markets far past their effectiveness will mean opportunities lost. If the trader holds onto longs for a bull move, the trader makes money. If the market remains in a trading range and is about to reverse, merely hanging on means an initial loss of potential profits because the trader overstays the market, and eventually the trader will lose money when the market does reverse to the downside while she is holding onto her longs.

A translation of a book written by Richard Lewinsohn presents some of the issues of forecasting and predictions: *Science, Prophecy and Prediction* (the original edition was in German and was titled *Die Enthullung der Zukunft*). The task of forecasting and prediction in the markets is a subcategory of his stratification of the conditions under which prediction and forecasting can be implemented. Table 1.1 offers a beginning framework for prediction and forecasting analysis.

Economic predictions, the closest that Lewinsohn comes to expositing forecasting skills for traders, is lumped into the realm of inductive statistics. The task of the economist—not precisely the trader but close enough, nevertheless—is to draw conclusions from aggregate data according to probability of occurrences. Economists use induction; that is, they determine the upper boundaries and the lower boundaries of their analysis and forecast for possible occurrences within these upper and lower limits.

In the above delineation of the main aspects of prediction, it is evident that all acts of prediction embody within themselves some elements of other classifications. Especially in the case of traders, the tasks of prediction contain within themselves elements of intuition, deduction, induction, activism, and imagination.

For traders, intuition is required because there must be an intractable belief that a market is bullish before one goes long or that a market is bearish before one goes short. Without this belief, weak-willed or undisciplined traders are easily discouraged from maintaining such positions when market action might temporarily move against their positions.

There have been traders who have maintained long positions well after all profits have dissipated and tremendous losses have mounted, and who have then miraculously recovered such losses and made embarrassingly huge profits. There are no logical reasons to account for this.

Table 1.1
Methods of Prediction

Classification	Basis	Characteristic	Applicability
Intuitive	Revelation	Belief in transcendental inspiration and absolute faith in the validity of the prediction.	Religious prophecy
	Inspiration	Sudden realization of hidden connections.	Many discoveries and inventions
Deductive	Verifiable laws	Deductions of predictions from general principle.	Science, sociology
	Pseudo-laws	Predictions from illogical or antiquated principles.	Astrology, foretelling, palmistry
Inductive	Individual experience	Unsystematic deductions by false analogy.	Works, especially crafts
	Experiment	Generalization of systematised individual investigations	Science, technology
	Statistics	Conclusion from aggregates according to probability theory.	Meteorology, medicine, public opinion polls, economic research, insurance, government
Activist	Individual action	Predictions of voluntary behavior.	Everyday living
	Planning	Long-range and complex objectives; creation of new conditions.	Industry, public finance, armaments
Imaginary	Creative fiction	Utopias, science fiction.	Literature, art
	Unconscious	Visions, based on wish fulfillment and past events.	Dream visions, hallucinations

From Richard Lewinsohn, *Science, Prophecy and Prediction* (New York: Bell Publishing Co., 1961).

The probability of this occurring is not great. Yet, every so often one reads of cases where the underdog makes out like a bandit; unfortunately, it is these spectacular examples that make the trader want to hope against the odds. A good case in point concerns a soybean trader at the Chicago Board of Trade in the early 1970s. As a member he made a passable living trading the beans and brokering customer orders, but he developed an infallible belief in late 1971 that soybeans were going to explode on the upside. He bought and accumulated longs in the bean complex. The strength of his belief left him without any emotion whatever when the market went against him initially. Yet he maintained those longs in the face of such adversity, and soybeans eventually went to $12.90 per bushel. In later cocktail parties he was fond of saying he didn't actually make $40 million in the move, but rather a smaller amount, which was in the neighborhood of $25 million.

On the other hand, there was the case of a stock options trader at the Chicago Board Options Exchange who developed a reputation as a market timing guru. He was written up in a major weekly newsmagazine as having turned several thousand dollars into a million dollars. He developed positions that eventually went against him. So strong was his conviction that when the losses mounted, he went to his friends and several clearing firms to raise money to cover his mark-to-market losses. In a strange twist of fate, every person he contacted turned him down. As a result of the lack of maintenance capital, he was forced to liquidate all his positions. The saving grace for this options market-maker was that the forced liquidation saved him from additional losses.

Deductive and inductive skills are easy for traders to develop. If the market behaves in one particular fashion, then it is reasonable to conclude that such and such result will happen. This is independent of whether or not there is any logical or directly relational basis for these observations. A mere act of statistical correlation is all that is needed to validate such observations. There are countless examples of traders who always wear the same pair of socks, same tie or trading jacket, and so on, for endless days because there had been past successful trading campaigns associated with those particular items of personal wear.

Activism as an element of prediction is similar to inductive reasoning, except that activism is enacted on a smaller scale, and imagination acts as the engine that drives the trader in the face of adversity and elation.

Given the various facets of market predictions, the trader should have no trouble figuring out the direction or duration of markets! Successful trading is not only a mixture of fear, greed, and superstition, but also a mixture of logic and imagination. Because one of the knowns is that markets will oscillate between an unbounded upper range and a finite lower range, the trader must use inductive reasoning. On the downside, the lower range for any market is a zero value—the trader or investor cannot lose more than he or she puts into the markets. On the upside, the trader or investor can make profit on however much the markets move up, but only if the traders or investors are buyers.

The problem of trader failure is not then a problem of the inability to forecast duration and direction of market movements, but more an issue of execution of the decisions arrived at from correct forecasting techniques. In this case, the hammer is not at fault, but the carpenter is. In order to get the right answers, the right questions must be asked.

WHAT CAN BE FORECAST: TIME, PRICE, OR VOLUME?

One of the major elements in market trading is determining ahead of time where price will be. One can use what has transpired as a base of information to achieve this goal, or one can go on the assumption that future events are independent of current events. In the first case, there is a hint of determinism and fatalism: Every event yet to occur in the future is more or less preordained. In the second case, there is the strictest acceptance of a free will: Whatever is yet to happen acts independently of what has happened. Which is correct? My belief is that fate and free will coexist. At times, events can be forecasted with great accuracy; at other times, nothing can be forecasted. What are those times?

A digression here will illustrate this point. We all know that, on any given day, at around noontime most of us would stop whatever we were doing and take about a half an hour to an hour for lunch break. This is about an 80 percent probability. This is fate. However, if one person was driving down the highway at around noontime, another was in a school class, and another was at a hospital, noontime would mark the extension of free will: The driver on the highway would stop by a fast food hamburger restaurant and grab a quick lunch, the class student would trek over to the cafeteria line and pick several lunch items from the steam tables, and the hospital patient would be served lunch in her hospital room. This is the free will, because the three people had it within their control to be situated on the highway, in the school, or in the hospital.

Fate and free will coexist because at the right time, all have to eat, yet the free will exists because it is within the control of the people to be located wherever they wish. My experience is that there are time windows in which forecasts may be made with high probability accuracy, and there are other times during which no forecasts can be made with any degree of accuracy.

If one looks at what is available from the trading day, one will easily see that there are three products generated from trading, regardless of where and when: the times of each trade, the price of each trade, and the volumes associated with each trade.

Of the three pieces of information, the only element that is forecastable is the element of time. In general, neither price nor volume can be determined in advance. (In certain situations, price can be forecast, but these instances are few and far between. Volume can be forecast not in specifics, but rather as generalizations: for example, volume increases in bull markets and decreases in bear markets.)

Time is the only element that can be known in advance. If one subscribes to the belief that time is forecastable, then it is acceptable to believe that whatever has happened in the past will affect some events in the present and which in turn affect some events in the future.

From merely heuristic principles, if one can find some factor that is forecastable, then it is easy to forecast other factors by making those factors dependent on the forecastable event; thus a model of expectations can be developed.

All theories of observation are based on accepted axioms. Without the acceptance of axioms at the core of any belief system, theories cannot evolve; for instance, the mathematics of geometry is based on the axioms that a straight line is made up of two points, two straight lines make up a flat plane, and two flat planes make up three-dimensional space. No one has ever seen two points in theoretical space. Yet there is a belief that such concepts exist, for there is certainly space out there! In the case of market forecasting, the axiom upon which price forecastability is based is derived from the belief that time is forecastable. Once the belief is there, then it is possible to hook up seemingly *unforecastable* events or factors, such as price, volume, and even open interest in the case of futures and options contracts, to a *forecastable* factor: time.

2

Strategies for Profitable Day Trading

What passes for clear thinking in the markets is, for all practical purposes, really muddled logic and disjointed syntheses. This will be obvious after you've read this section.

The objectives of day trading are not unlike the overall objectives of trading successfully in all time frames, from the shortest to the monthly perspectives. In fact, the objectives of successful day trading can even be extended to practical success in everyday living.

In trading, regardless of time frames and price ranges, there is only one overall objective: profits. It seems ridiculous to emphasize this point, but it is amazing to see how traders easily forget this particular fact. Failing this objective, the next objective is to cut one's losses in bad trading situations. Bad trading situations are defined succinctly as those situations in which the trader is losing money.

The first objective allows the trader to make money, or progress in the trading game. The second objective allows the trader to stay in the game, or increase the trader's chances of accomplishing the first goal. In the former objective, that of accumulating profits, one's goal is more offensive; in the case of limiting one's losses, one's goal is more defensive.

Defensive tactics allow one to stay in the game. Offensive tactics allow one to make the profits! If you can recognize these two categories of tactics and how they play into the paradigm of profits and survivability, you are that much closer to understanding what you can do well in the markets.

Given these two objectives, you are now armed with what is required to succeed in the markets.

OBSTACLES TO PROFITABILITY

With the two simplistic approaches to success in day trading, what then are the reasons why the trader cannot make profits as easily as he would desire? The nature of trading itself creates problems and obstacles of which the trader is unaware that will prevent him from achieving success. Especially in the area of day trading, there are several limiting conditions that make the two objectives of making profits and cutting losses more difficult to attain.

By definition, strict day trading requires that trades incepted during the day be closed out at the end of the day. If it is possible to trade the market on an intraday basis, is there any need to carry positions beyond that time frame? One should be aware that carrying any position for more time than is necessary increases the risk to trading capital. Aside from the consideration of requiring more capital for positioning, only profitable positions should be carried overnight and losses should be eliminated immediately; if there are losses, treat them strictly as day trades, but if there are profits, by all means consider treating them as longer-term trades. This is not day trading per se, but use of a little common sense would lead to greater profits.

One limiting condition is the factor of losses. Because the day trader is looking for maximum profits on a daily basis, the losses that are often being created on open trades are rationalized. The day trader has the tendency to justify carrying losing trades beyond the day's time frame. This is contrary to correct trading tactics, regardless of whether or not one is a day trader: Profitable day trading positions must be extended for as long as possible, perhaps even to the next day, whereas losses must be taken as soon as possible. The general rule is that the day trader must not carry losses to the next day.

Another condition concerns the requirement of margin moneys. Because the trades that are executed are not carried overnight, the day trader will not see the impact of margins as limiting the total positions that the trader initiates and carries overnight. With an overnight trade, the brokerage company that the day trader has his or her account with will monitor the money in the trading account and will immediately ask for additional money or close out the losing positions to bring the account up to the correct margin amounts.

This additional backstop of a "Big Brother" that is built into standard trading accounts to watch over the errant trader does not exist in day trader accounts. During the course of the trading day, the day trader can trade large numbers of positions, considerably beyond the ability of the account assets to margin. This is the easiest way for day traders to get into trouble if they don't have the skills to limit their position sizes. For example, several years ago a large scalper in the U.S. bond futures pit got into a trading predicament. He was known to carry huge positions. The clearing house, not clearing firm, sent a representative to the pit to ask him to cover his mark-to-market losses for that early morning's losses, which were about $3 million. Had he carried the position overnight, he would have needed additional funds for margin to cover his overnight positions.

A final condition comes with the territory of day trading. Most of the successful planning of the trades to be made during the course of the day has to be done prior to the opening trades. During the course of the day, the day trader has no time to analyze new conditions. The more mechanical the day trader makes his day trading, the more control he has over his risk situations.

This accounts for the success of the scalper in the trading pits: He has a mechanical scalping method and he doesn't subject himself to the need for constant reanalysis of ongoing developments in the markets. It is difficult to constantly make decisions with newly disclosed information during the course of a trading day. Unless the day trader is a quick study and can absorb new daily information on the fly, he will soon be immobilized with new information. The extreme case occurs when the trader is immobilized from taking action to limit losses with the new information.

The new information received during the course of the day can be either fundamental or technical. Fundamental information will tend to be supportive of major trends of the markets traded. The technical information may or may not be supportive because the day trader can literally vary the parameters of analysis to make the indicators show bullishness or bearishness!

TWO STRATEGIES FOR PROFIT

There are only two ways to implement the profitability objective:

1. Buy low and sell high (or sell high and then buy low).
2. Buy breakouts and sell breakdowns.

To buy low and then take profits by selling high implies that the markets are in trading ranges. To sell high and buy low also implies that the markets are in trading markets.

To buy the breakouts implies that once the market takes out old highs, prices will go higher still, so that one can take profits at higher prices. To sell breakdowns implies that once the market takes out old lows, prices will go lower so that one can take profits by covering at lower prices. The ideal situation is to buy at the low of a trading market, just before it turns into an upside running market. This would reduce the risk exposure to practically nothing. Suffice it to say that there must be, at the least, some movement in the markets one trades in order to make the profits.

DAY TRADING AT DIFFERENT MARKET STAGES

Implicit in the two ways to make profits is the acceptance of two different types of markets: running markets and trading markets. Running markets are those markets that move dramatically from one price level to another. Trading markets are those bound by an upper and lower price range. These categorizations are not new and may seem redundant to the experienced trader, but these price actions are also seen constantly even in the day trader's perspective.

Figure 2.1

Daily bar chart, March Deutsche Mark contract, Chicago Mercantile Exchange. (2/21 @ 8:16 A.M.)

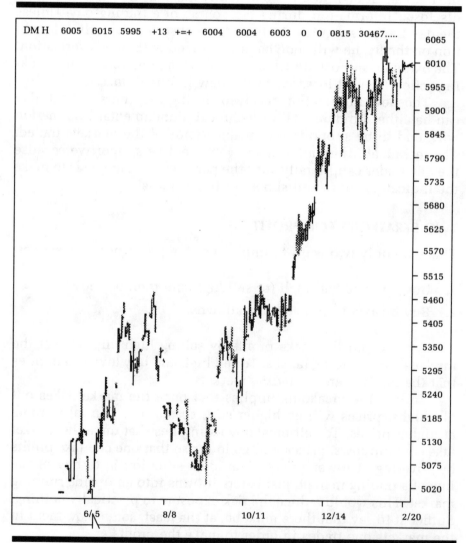

Figure 2.1 is a daily bar chart of the March Deutsche mark (DMH) contract traded at the Chicago Mercantile Exchange. As you can see, the price moved from a low of 50.20 to a high of 60.10, a 9.90 move that took about 3 months. This is an example of a bull move to the upside.

Figure 2.2 is a chart of the June Swiss Franc (SFM) futures contract traded at the Chicago Mercantile Exchange. In this particular

Figure 2.2
Five-minute bar chart, June Swiss Franc contract, Chicago Mercantile Exchange. (4/10 @ 12:50 P.M.)

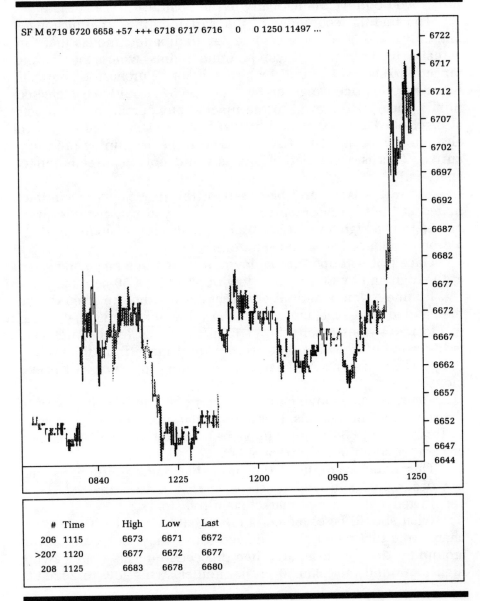

#	Time	High	Low	Last
206	1115	6673	6671	6672
>207	1120	6677	6672	6677
208	1125	6683	6678	6680

example, which was composed of 5-minute bars, the trading range was bounded by 66.77 on the upside and 66.57 on the downside. However, at around the price level of 66.72, the market condition changed and went into a bull market condition. Immediately after 11:20 A.M. of April 10, prices shot up to over 67.17. This took less than 2 hours to happen. On the chart, the critical time point (11:20 A.M.) is marked with an arrow. This chart, which is from my own files, was faxed to a broker who requested the chart at 1:09 P.M. (about 1½ hours after the critical juncture point—or possibly a fractionating point?) of that day.

What would you have given to know that at around 11:20 A.M., prices would move dramatically to the upside?

The trading techniques of the past identified trading ranges and bull markets. There are some day trading techniques that can actually identify the critical juncture points where the trading range markets shift to bull or bear markets. Purchasing contracts between the price range of 66.77 to 66.57 would have created profits once price moved to the upside, but purchasing contracts at precisely 11:20 A.M. would have offered substantial profits, with absolutely no risk! (At 11:21 A.M. CST, a precise timing point occurred. This is a correlation analysis and not a cause-and-effect analysis.)

Figure 2.3 is a daily bar chart of the July Soybean contract traded at the Chicago Board of Trade. As you can see, the price moved from a high level of $7.70 a bushel to a low of about $5.77½, a drop of about $2 over the span of 9 months.

Once price stopped going down, it traded in a range bracketed at the high end by $6.25 and a low of $5.77½, a 50-cent range.

It's fine to know and observe that prices went up, then down, then traded in a range, but what is the value of knowing that prices would move dramatically lower from the $7.79 level? And what is the value of knowing that prices would move from the trading range? Up or down? At what critical timing juncture will prices move?

Figure 2.4 is a moving average chart of a 5-minute bar chart of the Dow Jones Industrials. Please note that prices dropped dramatically from the 2654.70 level into a bear market to a low of 2622.40, or about a 30-point drop in one day.

This is an example of the profitable trading situations that can occur on an intraday basis even in a market that has been considered a standard of market stability: stocks.

What should be observed is the possible fractal nature of this chart. Note that when prices moved lower they found support at around the 2622.40 level and then proceeded to carve out a swing high to around the 2639.50 level, another swing low to 2620.60,

Figure 2.3
Daily bar chart, July Soybean contract, Chicago Board of Trade. (3/19 @ 11:46 P.M.)

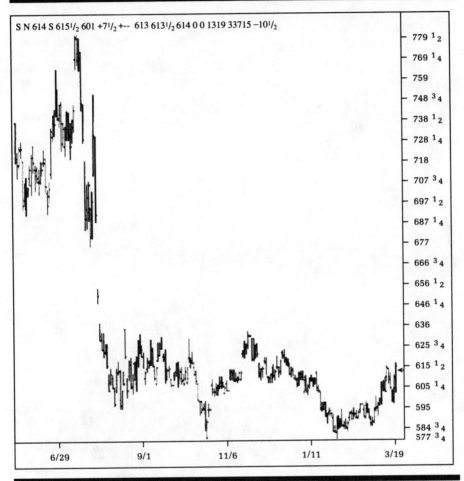

and then another possible swing high of 2639.50 at the rightmost part of the chart. The dimension of the bear market drop led the way to an apparrently *larger*-scaled trading range! Why would this trading range be larger, in relative terms? The trading range is itself about half of the bearish market drop of 30 points. Trading ranges, once developed, should approach some proportional dimension; that is, if the drop is 30 points, the trading range that can be formed afterward should be about an 8-point range or so, not a range that is about 50 percent of the previous bear market move.

The fact that the trading range is of such dimensional scale indicates to me that this trading range was part of a larger-scaled move, perhaps a down move of 60 to 100 points. In a sense, this

Figure 2.4
Moving average, five-minute chart, Dow Jones Industrial average. (11/21 @ 3:57 P.M.)

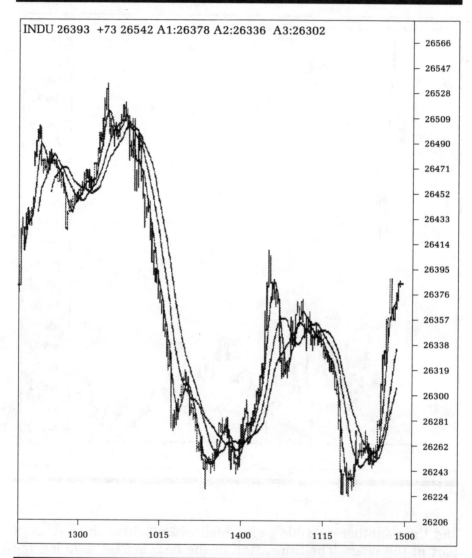

trading range took care of the 30-point down move and also took care of some larger-scaled down move—perhaps this is a fractal bifurcation point?

Figure 2.5 is daily bar chart of the Dow Jones Industrial averages over the span of about 6 months. One of the primitive techniques I use to identify possible trading ranges is analyzing price action with moving averages.

Figure 2.5
Moving average charts, Dow Jones Industrial average. (11/20 @ 3:27 A.M.)

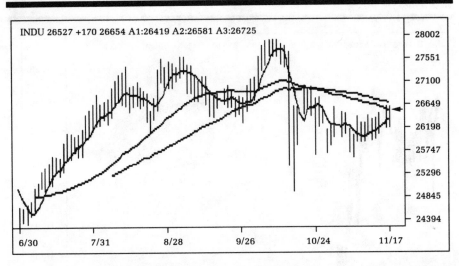

INDU 26527 +170 26654 A1:26419 A2:26581 A3:26725

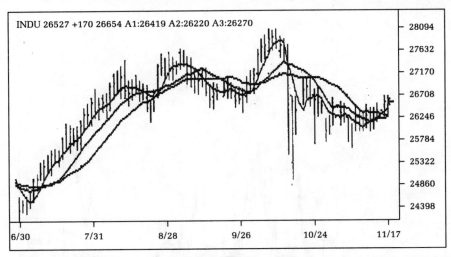

INDU 26527 +170 26654 A1:26419 A2:26220 A3:26270

The strength of moving averages is that they can be used validly as breakout or breakdown signals. Note that in #1 Chart, the moving averages used are 5 days, 34 days, and 55 days; #2 Chart uses 5 days, 13 days, and 21 days. Note that the longer duration charts create more valid crossover signals, whereas the shorter duration charts create more false signals; that is, prices are not sustained in the direction of the breakout or breakdowns that the crossovers would signal.

Figure 2.6 is a 5-minute bar chart of the September S&P contract traded at the Chicago Mercantile Exchange. Here you can see

Figure 2.6

Five-minute bar chart, September S&P contract, Chicago Mercantile Exchange. (8/25 @ 2:05 P.M.)

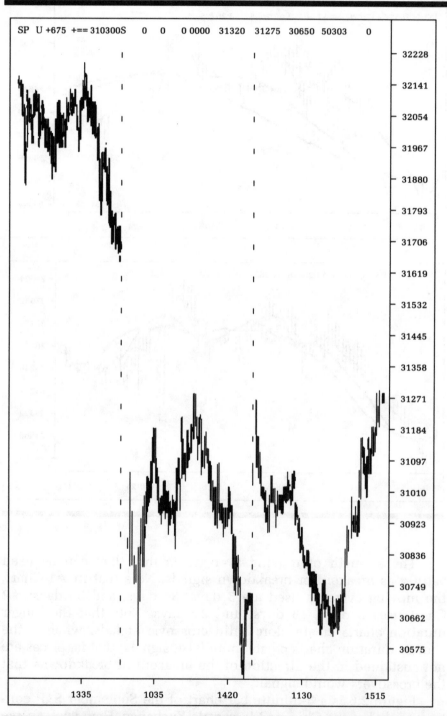

that prices, once they found a support level at around the 305.75 price, traded in a tight range from a low of 305.75 to a high of 312.71.

The author applied the Fibonacci ratio analysis from the previous high swing to the low of the break.

In this example, a substantial portion of the downmove from the 322.28 level occurred overnight since prices gapped about 9 points to the downside. It would have been difficult for the trader to have made a large portion of that range from previous close to the next day's opening. However, there are price pattern behavior observations (which are discussed in the Sequential Patterning section of this book) that can give the day trader clues about the probability of such a move occurring on the next day's opening.

Figure 2.7 is a daily chart of May soybeans traded at the Chicago Board of Trade. I placed it here because in Figure 2.3 an-

Figure 2.7
Daily bar chart, May Soybean contract, Chicago Board of Trade. (5/1 @ 10:41 A.M.)

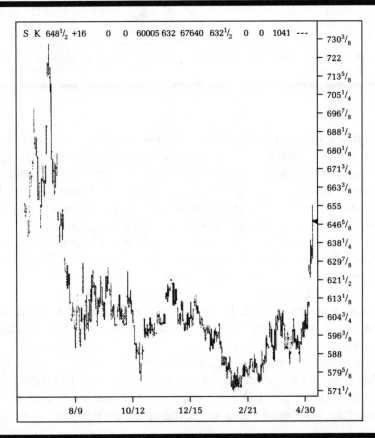

Figure 2.8
Sixty-minute bar chart, December S&P contract. (11/20 @ 5:06 P.M.)

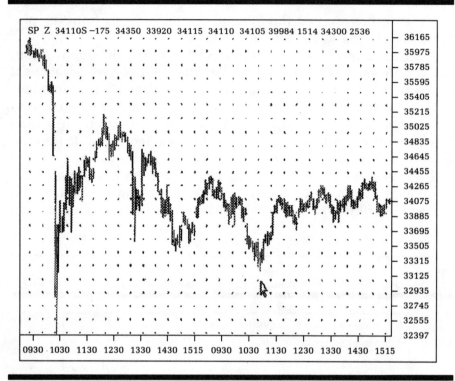

other soybean chart but of a different month (July), it wasn't known whether prices would move up or down from the trading range. One of the questions you were asked to consider was "What would it be worth to know the precise breakout or breakdown point from a trading range?" In this particular example, prices moved up once the breakout point at around the 604¼ level was broached.

The final example of bull markets, bear markets, and trading markets is illustrated in Figure 2.8 with a 60-minute bar chart of the December S&P futures index chart.

Please note the arrow that points to the low of the weakly identified trading range market. Even if a precise point of entry of longs is made at the price level, a bit under 333.15, the next sustained move is not necessarily a dramatic move to the upside. In this particular case, prices traded higher but moved in an upward oscillating fashion. The trader learns here that she can identify important juncture points, but she cannot force the market to move in the direction that she wants and with the momentum that she wants.

COMPARATIVE ANALYSIS OF TRADING
AND RUNNING MARKETS

There are no objective measures for discerning when a running market turns into a trading market and a trading market turns into a running market. In *The Technical Analysis of Stocks, Options and Futures*, I wrote about the various technical analysis approaches to all markets. I categorized the major approaches to market analysis in a chart on the "Behavior of Technical Analysis" (reproduced here in Table 2.1).

The chart contains a starting categorization of the technical analysis indicators delineated from the simplest (upper left-hand corner—moving averages) to the most complex system (lower left-hand corner—William D. Gann techniques).

In addition to the three generic market stages (bull, bear, and trading markets), I have delineated four additional market stages: bull to trading, bear to trading, trading to bull, and trading to bear markets.

These four additional market stages have been observed to exist not necessarily because of precise observations, but because our present-day analysis techniques, primarily sophisticated mathematical techniques dealing with price as the dependent variable, have made it easier to discern their existence. The stage when a market moves from a trading market to a bull market or a bear market was previously unobservable, and therefore potentially unforecastable, without the right analytical techniques.

As an example, when price is analyzed with momentum techniques (oscillators, stochastics, relative strength indicators types, and so on), the collection of dynamic data *can* reveal the transition of the market from a trading market to a bull market. In a perfectly balanced market, where prices are bounded by a high and a low price range, the number of appearances of overbought and oversold indicators should be about even in frequency, regardless of the range of data analyzed. This is exactly why these momentum studies are the most profitable to follow in trading markets; the trader sells on overbought signals expecting the market to sell off and buys on oversold signals expecting the market to rally higher. However, as the market starts to shift from a neutral to a bullish condition, the number of overbought and oversold indicators in a given block of observation periods will shift from about even to that of more overbought signals than oversold.

If and when the market shifts completely to a bullish market, the momentum studies will show *continuously overbought* conditions. At such points of market action, selling into severely over-

Table 2.1
Behavior of Technical Indicators in Market Cycles

	OB = Overbought OS = Oversold	Trading Markets	Trading Markets	
			Bull	Bear
Micro Analysis — Price Sensitive Indicators	Moving Averages pages 35–56	Many false breakouts and whipsaw action	Valid breakouts and continuous confirmation	Valid breakouts and continuous confirmation
	Relative Strength pages 57–74	OB/OS indication excellent	Skewed number of signals to more overbought	Skewed number of signals to more oversold
	Percentage R pages 75–90	OB/OS signals are valid	OB signals invalid. Use modified OS	OS signals give way to modified OB
	Oscillators pages 115–134	OB/OS signals are valid	False OB signals valid if using modified OS	False OB signals valid if using modified OS
	Stochastics pages 91–113	Crossovers OB and OS are valid	Crossovers from OS only are valid	Crossovers from OB only are valid
Hybrid Indicators	Point-and-Figure pages 135–156	False breakouts and whipsaw action	Valid breakouts	Valid breakdowns
	Market Profile® pages 199-229	Normal distribution	Can observe and tell upside breakouts	Can observe and tell downside breakdowns
Volume Sensitive Indicators	Tick Volume pages 157–170	Very good accumulation indicator	Can use to possibly pyramid	Valid signals but because of briefness hard to pyramid
	On-Balance Volume pages 171–197	Very good accumulation indicator	Too long to use to pyramid	Valid but impractical signals
	Bar Charts pages 231–311	Valid, recognizable patterns	Valid, recognizable trend lines, channels	Valid, recognizable trend lines, channels
Macro Analysis — Time Sensitive	Astronomical Cycles pages 339–372	No good	Not applicable	Not applicable
Composite	Elliott Wave Theory pages 373-401	Hard to show beginning and end— just that it is occurring	Can project market to take out previous highs	Can project market to take out previous lows
	Gann Analysis pages 417–437	Whipsaws	Long for the upmove	Short for the downmove

Changing Markets			
Trading to Bull	Trading to Bear	Bull to Trading	Bear to Trading
Excellent behavior	Excellent behavior	Excellent behavior	Excellent behavior
Increasing signals to OB	Increasing frequency of OS signals	Equal number of OB/OS signals from OB skew	Equal number of OB/OS signals from OB skew
Valid signals give way to false OB	Valid signals give way to false OS	False OS to valid signals	False OB to valid signal
Valid signals give way to false OB	Valid signals give way to False OS	False OS to valid signals	False OB to valid signals
Crossovers of OB/OS valid to only OS indicators valid	Crossovers of OB/OS valid to only OB indicators	Only OS area crossovers are valid to both OB/OS valid	Only OB area crossovers are valid to both OB/OS valid
Can project counts to likely tops	Can project counts to likely bottoms	Cannot forecast	Cannot forecast
Can see buildup of buying pressure	Can see buildup of selling pressure	Great appearance of non-trend days	Great appearance of non-trend days
Excellent accumulation indicators	Too late to signal volume distribution	Flattening of OBV breakouts	Flattening of OBV breakouts
Excellent accumulation indicators	Too late to signal volume distribution	Flattening of OBV breakouts	Flattening of OBV breakouts
Reversal patterns valid	Reversal patterns valid	Reversal patterns valid	Reversal patterns valid
Excellent turning points	Excellent turning points	Excellent turning points	Excellent turning points
Probability can be determined that this will happen	Probability can be determined that this will happen	Probability can be determined that this will happen	Probability can be determined that this will happen
Can get one long but whipsawed first	Can get one short but whipsawed first	Whipsaw first then profits	Whipsaw first then profits

and Futures published by Probus Publishing Company, Chicago, Illinois.

bought conditions or buying into severely oversold conditions in bearish markets would result in major losses. At these points, the markets are either in massively bullish or massively bearish conditions. As you can see, an initially correct interpretation of market conditions must be made before correct trades can be executed based on momentum indicators.

3

Day Trading Approaches Defined by Market Action

The conventional approach to making profits in the markets has always been to use the tried-and-true methods of buying in anticipation of potential market breakouts, or in the case of bearish markets, the selling of shares and contracts, or selling call or buying put options, in anticipation of breakdowns. Once a trade is put on in anticipation of the prices rallying higher or selling off, the trader is essentially in the role of the "trade manager." He can do nothing to improve the conditions of his trade. Yet he must pay the most attention to the markets at this point, constantly managing his positions. The correct management makes all the profits; the neglect of position management makes all the losses.

The initial problem in attempting to make a series of correct decisions in day trading is, in a nutshell, to determine by technical analysis techniques *when* the markets are ready to breakout or breakdown, and then to position in advance of these actions.

Fundamental analysis techniques, by their very nature, have been removed from consideration because the validity of these techniques apply more suitably to value analysis, and not price analysis, which is best analyzed by technical analysis. The *when* is definitely flagged in advance by *time* cycles. The *when*, however, has been traditionally flagged by pattern formations and price action, more after the fact than in anticipation of the to-be-disclosed fact.

TRADITIONAL TECHNICAL APPROACHES

The bulk of current-day technical analysis is based on analyzing bar chart formations of price. This practice has its origin in Edwards and Magee's book on pattern formation analysis, *The Technical Analysis of Stock Trends,* first published in 1948. In the book, the patterns formed from the continuous bars were analyzed to disclose potential continuity patterns, reversal patterns, or congestion patterns. This approach was subjective; it relied entirely upon the analyst's ability to "read" a chart correctly. The role of the analyst was to discern when the market moved from any of those stages to the other remaining stages. This discernment was colored by the fact that the markets had to move through a sequential ordering of pattern formations; that is, the markets had to move in this logical sequence: Reversal patterns give way to trend patterns and then move from trend patterns back to reversal patterns. In between these two patterns, consolidation patterns may or may not exist. The probability was that consolidation patterns existed, if not merely to cause the market to pause in its trending action, then to fool the analyst, preventing him or her from making absolutely correct analyses of market action.

The message that Edwards and Magee's book conveyed— that successful trading relied on correctly categorizing price bar chart patterns and then executing such informed decisions—has been carried forth to this day, as the book has been in print for over 40 years and there are many practitioners of the basic chart pattern approach to market forecasting. Is it time to modify the approach?

THE AGE OF VOLATILITY

In the early 1980s the trading environment changed. What was once a valid and viable supposition—that the successful trader has the luxury of spending as much time as was necessary to analyze price patterns before he positioned in the markets—became less so. The markets became more volatile. Please note that the popularity of the conventional bar charting techniques thrived in an environment of relative market tranquility.

Market price behavior shows that at higher prices, trading ranges are greater than at lower prices on an absolute dollar-amount comparative basis and not on a percentage basis. Despite this restraint on percentage of prices, prices do fluctuate widely in absolute dollar amounts. At $2 per share, a 50-cent move on 100 shares is merely $50 gross change. At $150 per share, it is normal to see a month's fluctuation of $10 to $15 per share, which is closer to a 7 to 10 percent variation in prices, of about $1000 to $1500 in gross dollar change on 100 shares of stock. When one compares the fluctuation in the first example, $50, to the fluctuation in the second example, $1000 to $1500, one can conclude that those who successfully trade the higher-priced issue must be able to sustain the variations in their trading accounts. (If the trader were to take the low-priced issue and take on a position 20 times larger, or 2,000 shares, the trader will get a similar gross dollar fluctuation. This is not a viable trading strategy or tactic but a rather weak attempt to mechanically force a similar absolute dollar move in one unit of 2,000 shares to be equivalent to the absolute dollar move of one unit of 100 shares of a higher-priced issue.) It is a fallacy to assume, simply because the dollar amount movements are similar, that the rest of the situation is similar.

If the objective is to dampen absolute dollar price fluctuations, then unfortunately, from the progressions of prices from low to high, policies and regulations of the regulatory bodies and agencies have created the opposite effect. When stocks are trading at less than $5 per share and are listed on the National Association of Securities Dealers Automated Quotations (NASDAQ), no margins are allowed. Stocks priced so low must be bought for the full amount. Once stocks reach over $5 per share and are tradeable on the stock exchanges, they can then be margined at the current 50 percent rate. For every dollar of stock, 50 cents of that amount can be loaned to the buyer for its purchase, or short-sale. Once prices reach higher levels, one would want the margins to increase correspondingly to dampen the naturally increasing price volatility. The margins, however, are maintained at 50 percent, but in one way the effect of margins is decreased tremendously as the prices are increased: Stock indices traded on the futures exchanges magnify leverage even more.

Futures exchanges do not have margins per se, but rather "good faith deposits," which function like margins. The futures exchanges have such deposits ranging from 3% to 15% of the actual cash value of the contracts. In the case of stock indices, approximately $15,000 will control about $150,000 worth of stocks.

In the stock area, as prices increase, margins decrease in relative terms, thereby fueling price volatility. (With increased volatility, price movements are rapid.) Contrary to the stock side, within the nature of the futures business, futures margins have often increased with increasing volatility, pointing to the desire on the part of futures authorities to dampen price volatility within their own markets. But if one moves from futures to stocks via stock indices, the reader easily sees that margin is in a continually decreasing trend as prices of the actual stocks or their derivatives actually increase, thereby accelerating price volatility.

The change actually occurred years earlier (from the Dow Jones Industrial low in 1984 to current highs in 1992), as prices of stocks climbed to higher levels. In the futures markets, it occurred as early as the 1970s. During this decade traders saw prices for commodities that had never been seen before.

Figures 3.1 through 3.6 will illustrate how the price patterns bounded by defined highs and lows gave way to price patterns that became more unbounded. Soybean prices traded to the record $12.90 per bushel in the middle of 1973. As late as 1972, soybeans traded between $3 and $4.20 per bushel (Figure 3.1). Sugar in 1973 traded at around 12 cents per pound and in 1974 had catapulted to over 65 cents per pound (Figure 3.2). Spot tin prices went from $1.80 per pound in 1970 to over $4.00 per pound in 1975 (Figure 3.3). Wheat moved from $1.50 per bushel in 1970 to $6.50 per bushel in 1974 (Figure 3.4). Pork bellies went from 20 cents per pound in 1971 to well over 80 cents per pound in 1973 (Figure 3.5). Cottonseed meal went from a low of $70 per ton in 1970 to well over $200 per ton in 1973; four decades earlier, cottonseed meal traded to a low of $11 per ton (Figure 3.6). As a purely defen-

Figure 3.1
Weekly soybean futures, 1964–1975. (Reprinted with permission, © 1992 Knight-Ridder Financial Publishing, 30 South Wacker Drive, Suite 1820, Chicago, Illinois 60606.)

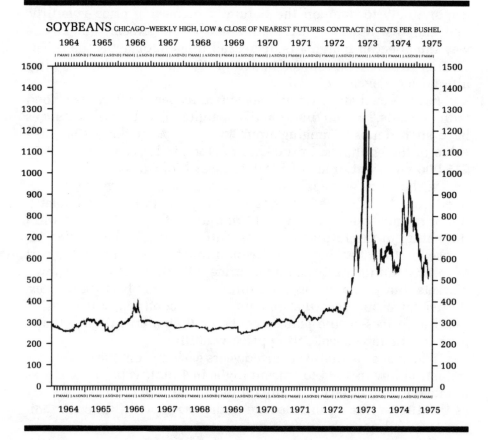

sive measure, commodities traders applied technical analysis techniques when there were merely price-sensitive indicators to help them trade successfully.

Prices may move from a low of $3.50 per bushel in beans to a high of $12.90 a year later, but there is no fundamental technique to forecast such moves. Even applying fundamental analysis validly to overvalued situations is impossible. Yes, the fundamental techniques would have shown that soybeans at $5 were undervalued. At $6 also. Even as high as $10. But to expect fundamental analysis techniques to show that at $12.90 per bushel soybeans were *overvalued* would have been trying to get David to slay not only Goliath, but also a second giant with only one stone. (I have been known to take longshots at the racetrack, but my money would have been on the second giant for a successful outcome!)

With the earlier stellar price move reflected in the commodities markets, it was only natural that technical analysis would take hold there first. Most of the current technical analysis techniques were developed first in the commodities markets.

Figure 3.2
Spot sugar prices, 1840–1975. (Reprinted with permission, © 1992 Knight-Ridder Financial Publishing, 30 South Wacker Drive, Suite 1820, Chicago, Illinois 60606.)

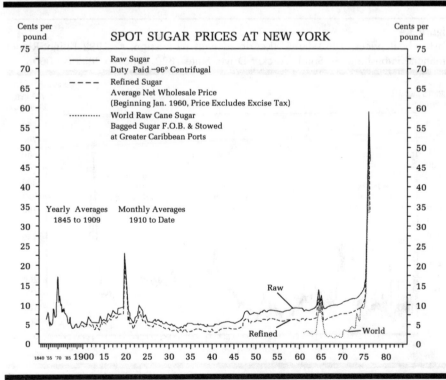

Figure 3.3

Spot tin prices, 1840–1975. (Reprinted with permission, © 1992 Knight-Ridder Financial Publishing, 30 South Wacker Drive, Suite 1820, Chicago, Illinois 60606.)

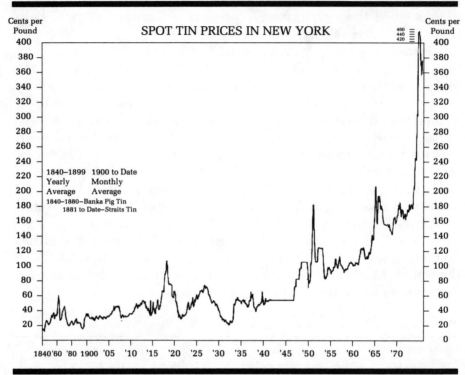

Figure 3.4

Cash wheat prices, 1860–1975. (Reprinted with permission, © 1992 Knight-Ridder Financial Publishing, 30 South Wacker Drive, Suite 1820, Chicago, Illinois 60606.)

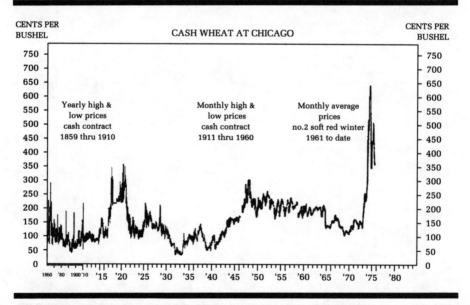

Figure 3.5
Cash pork bellies, 1949–1975. (Reprinted with permission, © 1992 Knight-Ridder Financial Publishing, 30 South Wacker Drive, Suite 1820, Chicago, Illinois 60606.)

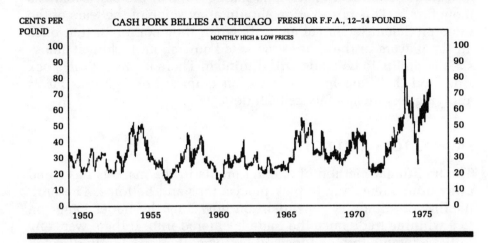

Figure 3.6
Spot cottonseed meal prices, 1910–1975. (Reprinted with permission, © 1992 Knight-Ridder Financial Publishing, 30 South Wacker Drive, Suite 1820, Chicago, Illinois 60606.)

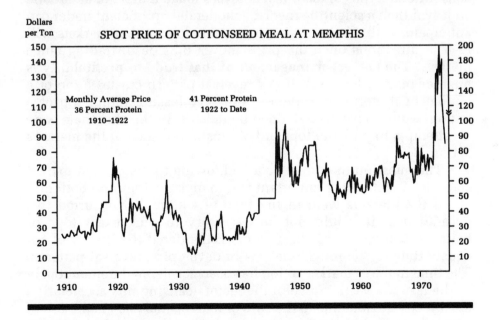

The stock markets are now becoming more volatile, primarily because of the relatively higher prices from a decade earlier and the onset of stock index trading on the futures exchanges; as a result, technical analysis is taking hold in the stock markets more firmly. This observation should allay some of the fears of the more proficient technical analysts when they complain that once all the players in the futures markets know about technical analysis, the profits to be made will diminish. There is always the stock side, and that field has not yet been tapped thoroughly as far as applying technical analysis techniques!

PICKING TOPS AND BOTTOMS

The traditional method of making profits in the markets has shied away from attempting to pick precise tops and bottoms. The profitability of a trade is dependent on how long the trader hangs on to a winning trade once the trade is entered into. If there were any initial attempts to pick tops and bottoms, they were only directed to the task of finding general reversal areas where prices traded in a tight range. The profits to be garnered were generated from the market movements as prices retraced back to supports or prices rallied to resistances.

With the advent of market volatility, it is now more important than ever before to be able to pick tops and bottoms. Though the conventional types of technical analyses make it more of an artistic endeavor than a scientific theory, a moderately proficient trader can anticipate, with a better than 50 percent chance, that markets will reverse directions once the price moves outside of trading range markets. **The correct management of that trade to profitability is another matter, however.** If any reversal pattern creates a top or a bottom in its formation, then at the very least, a minor top or a bottom would have been defined by default. In the past there were no attempts to pick the tops or bottoms in advance of the market's action.

The question that must be asked, owing to the current market stage, is "Exactly how important is it to pick the tops and bottom?"

If the markets were in the type of action that occurred two decades ago, it would not be necessary to pick exact tops or bottoms. Lethargic and sluggish markets offered the luxury of adequate time for thorough analysis of developing reversal patterns. The time frame of market action has been accelerated tremendously in the last few years. Some of the factors causing this acceleration are directly attributable to the ease of market analysis via the use of personal computers and telecommunication lines with databases.

The ease of raw data manipulation, which has shortened the time required for the thorough market analysis needed in decision making, has made it easier for the masses to trade the markets. In the process of doing this, the overall bar chart *patterns* that once were commonly defined as approximate reversal areas (not price or time points) have given way to singular reversal patterns: key-day reversals (one spike day in the direction of the general market, which is often correlated with high volume and significant new highs or new lows for the move), island reversals (one or two days of price action, again in the general direction of the market, set off by no price activity either going into or coming out of that time frame), and others.

Market action that once took days or weeks to occur now occurs with greater frequency on an intraday basis. This observation is valid regardless of techniques used to observe price actions.

It is then necessary for the trader to observe and analyze market action in shorter time frames, moving from the daily analysis area to that of market action within a day's time. If an uninformed reader says that it is not necessary to shorten the time frame for better trading, the realization that prices of stocks, indices, and futures can move dramatically in a few hours will bring home the point more effectively.

So the answer to the question of whether or not it is important to pick precise reversal points, that is, tops or bottoms, is "yes," not because it is a luxury item but because it is a necessity for market survival in our current trading environment.

Risk and Various Market Instruments

The various intricacies of making the markets available for other types and grades of traders and investors make the markets risk-laden. The use of margins, the markets' derivative instruments such as options and cash forwards, and the ease of shorting markets makes the markets themselves available to more participants. The availability of markets to the common man comes at a great cost.

With the use of margins, participants don't have to come up with 100 percent of the required capital to actually own the particular positions. Yet the fact that the participant can play the market with a fraction of the amount normally required puts the participants at risk for the balance of the investment. This is so despite the fact that the risk to all participants is no more than the actual value of the particular market. The market does not know whether one trader has the full amount in reserves to honor any additional capital losses or whether the trader is capable of meeting any and all margin requests. To this extent the markets are very fair; but if one were to bring in the real conditions of each participant, the matter is very different.

In the case of allowing participants to go short markets through the use of margin accounts, as well as to go long, bad market judgement exposes the player to additional chances to lose money. Going short at the top is the ideal situation, but bad traders can also go short at the bottom, or at the very least, *not* go long at the top. How is the market going to be fairer than this? Anyone, regardless of race, creed, or religion, can go short at anytime. Going short at the bottom of markets is potentially more damaging and also extremely volatility fueling at the opposite end of the volatility spectrum (remember that at high prices also, the industries' mechanics make for increased volatility).

Options, marketed as risk-limiting derivative instruments, can, on the other side of the risk coin, be inadvertently used for increasing risks. The players cannot only buy the options, they can sell the options naked; that is, they can sell the options without owning the underlying futures or stocks. Short option positions will generate premium erosion on a constant basis; the few times that premiums do not erode, they explode with a vengeance. (The saying in the trading business goes as follows: Eat like a bird, excrete like an elephant. The words have been modified somewhat for the international reader.)

The multiplicity of problems inherent in the markets would be diminished greatly if one could only go long and invest only with cash positions. The use of margin accounts, which bring in less capitalized investors and traders, allows the short sales. The argument given by the advocates of short sales, that such sales will eventually have to be covered, thereby giving potential market support to any selloffs, is valid—at certain stages of the market cycle. If short sales are enacted in time for a tremendous runup to the upside, the informed short sellers would be scratching their trades at small losses. In the case of naive short-sellers, shorts created before the runup would push the move higher.

The argument given by the distributor of stocks, that making stock ownership more readily available to more players by allowing purchases and sales of stocks through the use of margins, is valid, again at certain stages of the market cycle: The distribution of stocks has to be done at the best advantage to the previous owners—prices have to be high before distribution is beneficial, because it would be foolish to distribute stocks at the lowest prices. If prices must be high for distribution to be effective, where will prices be after the distribution?

THE TRADE DECISION

There are three parts to a trade: trade decision, trade execution, and trade management. Only one part makes the money, the other two parts increase a trader's chance of entering trades correctly.*

Trade decision is the part of the trade where the trader studies the fundamental and technical approaches to markets. Once the trader understands the objectives of these approaches, then he or she must decide on the following choices: buy, sell, or stay out of the market. (I also make the distinction in decision making in terms of market entries and market exits. The majority of technical analysis studies center on market entry and not on market exit, despite the fact that most practitioners of technical analysis treat all the studies as equally applicable to entry **as well** as exit tools. Therefore, it is incorrect to assume that both market entry and market exit decision making are given equal weight. Nothing could be further from the truth.)

Market entry decisions require more analysis because there are a myriad of reasons why anyone would want to enter the markets. One may want to be long a particular stock, option, or future owing to fundamental reasons, technical analysis, or a combination of both.

Market exit decisions, however, require hardly any analysis because the only reason that a trader must exit existing positions is for the reason of losses: If the position is losing money, regardless of what technical analytical techniques the trader has used— regardless of what justifications—the position must be eliminated. If the trade shows a profit from entry price levels, traders must maintain that position on the books. The application of fundamental analysis to market exits is acceptable only if the trader is ready to accept the fact that the price at which the trades are closed out has no relevance to value.

If the day trader has such a trade on his books, he can make a decision to carry the winning trade to the next trading session, in which case he moves from the realm of day trading to that of position trading. But he is not faulted if he closes out his winning trades on the same day they were initiated. Most experienced traders, however, will recognize that if the trade shows a profit, the chances are greater that it will continue in that direction. So, from a mere probability approach, keeping a winner begets more winners!

*This section is partially excerpted from William F. Eng, *Trading Rules: Strategies for Success* (Chicago, Dearborn Financial Publishing, 1990).

There is often a great amount of misunderstanding on the part of the traders when they expect that the amount of time they have spent studying the many techniques of decision-making will somehow actually make profits. The more time they spend, the more money they should make. The decision-making part does not make the money; it only serves to help the trader to get on the right side of the markets!

This point cannot be emphasized enough: decision-making does not make the money. This is true despite the fact that most of us would want to have one encompassing action in trading: one action that would make the decision, the execution, and the management. As a simple case in point, consider marriage. In our day and age, anyone can get married: We make the decision to marry, not marry, or stay engaged. This, however, does not guarantee the success of the marriage. As far as the act of getting married is concerned, it's a *fait accompli* once the bride and groom walk out of the church. The success in the marriage, however, is found in the correct management of all the aspects of the marriage while the marriage is in existence. Is it any wonder that there are so many failed marriages? There is no attention given to the management of the marriage.

Of the three parts of a trade, trade execution is the simplest to learn and also to implement. The trader merely needs to execute the decision by using some form of market orders or limit orders. The trader can buy or sell at the market or with limit orders. No more need be said about this; simplicity is the driving force behind success in most areas of market trading, as well as in most areas of life.

The final part of the trade, correct management, is where all the money is made. It is therefore not surprising that the mismanagement of the trade is also where the losses occur. Most traders excel at the mismanagement of trades. Again, no more need be said about this final part of a trade either. But because this part summarizes all the endless time and attention riveted to the total trade, I believe you would feel cheated if I wrote less than a chapter on this part (see Part Three of this book).

If the trade, once properly decided upon and properly executed, shows a profit, let it stay on the books. If it shows a loss, get rid of it.

The second part of the book, The Science of Day Trading, is dedicated to the decision-making part of the trade. Using the detailed tools of technical analysis, you will find excellent techniques to help you decide on whether to buy, sell, or stay out of the markets. Concentration on this part, the actual mechanics of day trading, will help you get on the right side of the markets, but it won't make any money for you.

The third part of the book, The Art of Day Trading, is a series of day trading examples. The correct management of the trade is here (even a professional like myself has forgotten about more mismanaged trades than remembered the ones that were perfectly managed to maximum profits). The essence of the book is here and a careful study of this portion of the book will help you improve your techniques for correctly managing the initiated trades.

4

Chaos Theory
and the Day Trader

Is it valid to apply the body of technical analysis techniques from daily bar charts to those of shorter time frames? Most people have an inherent faith that what happens in a large scale is also duplicated in a smaller scale. Events that occur in a smaller scale can be expected to occur also in a larger scale. This faith has always been part of our thinking. However, is there any scientific validation for such "inherent faith"?

To understand this section there is a need for a basic understanding of the concepts of chaos, fractal bifurcation, and the reductionist philosophy suggested by Newtonian physics.

The concept of chaos was popularized by Benoit R. Mandelbrot, an IBM fellow at the Thomas J. Watson Research Center. Mandelbrot created the concept of a fractal, which is defined as follows: "a way of describing, calculating, and thinking about shapes that are irregular and fragmented, jagged and broken-up—shapes from the crystalline curves of snowflakes to the discontinuous dusts of galaxies." *

Mandelbrot broke new ground in his work, not in discovering information that had not yet been known, but by taking what was already observed by physical scientists and reorganizing those observations into similar, and therefore repeatable, patterns. Mandelbrot started with what most people would call randomness and organized this "randomness" into repeatable observations! In one brilliant stroke, Mandelbrot created order out of disorder by merely redefining observational points and opened the world to a new vision of nature.

*James Gleick, *Chaos: Making a New Science,* New York: Viking Press, Inc., 1987. Mandelbrot authored the seminal work on fractals, *The Fractal Geometry of Nature* (New York: W.H. Freeman & Company Publishers, 1977.)

What Mandelbrot did is similar to what traders must do constantly: make order out of disorder. In analyzing price charts, traders see random patterns, most of which can be categorized once repeatable patterns have been drawn out of them.

Instead of looking at patterns as merely being whole-numbered dimensions—1 dimension, 2 dimensions, 3 dimensions, or 4 dimensions—Mandelbrot was able to discern patterns as being fractions of dimensions! That is, some Mandelbrot observations were classified with dimensions between 1 and 2 dimensions, such as 1.524, 1.328, or 1.975 dimensions.

In a very similar fashion, all traders are constantly looking at the same charts with the same obvious patterns, yet each and every trader has an entirely different viewpoint. The one trader who is able to classify her observations into sets of patterns is at an advantage because she can then compare one set to another set. Please note that I haven't even allowed that these repeatable patterns may be correctly analyzed. The traders who see nothing but random patterns cannot apply what can be learned from one "haphazardly" revealed pattern to the next. The conclusions that can be drawn from the same starting charts are therefore infinite. (Most conclusions drawn from the same set of charts must be, on average, incorrect; infrequently are the same conclusions drawn.)

Traders can take what seems to be supposedly random price patterns and view them from different perspectives, from different scales, and extract order from disorder, thus finding patterns in chaos. The successful categorization of short-term trading patterns accounts for the popularity of Candlestick charting. Candlestick charting, developed by Japanese traders, is a form of pattern recognition that is more holistic in its approach than current bar pattern analysis.

FROM NEWTON TO MANDELBROT

To obtain an understanding of chaos theory as it is applied to markets, you must know some background of where and how our current view of nature and natural patterns evolved. We can observe nature's models of behavior and apply this knowledge to market analysis. We therefore can create guides for our trading strategies.

Since the time of Isaac Newton and René Descartes, scientists have held a firm belief, either implicitly or explicitly, that all of nature can be reduced to discrete, analyzable actions. Following that logic, then, all actions can be considered to be smaller components of larger-scaled actions.

In scientific circles, Newton developed the laws of celestial mechanics from which the majority of our current beliefs about mechanical physics are derived. These ideas held sway until the turn of the nineteenth century, when quantum mechanics entered into the analytical picture and threw the belief system into a tailspin. Newton asserted that all reactions in the universe were forecastable given the existence of certain actions. All actions and reactions were therefore reducible to finite actions and reactions, depending on how deeply one wanted to delve. These actions could then be described by mathematical models or in mechanical terms. His peers and those who came after him believed that nature could be reduced to smaller and smaller component vectors, a strict application of the cause-and-effect deterministic philosophy. Conversely, all smaller causes eventually resulted in larger-bodied determined actions.

The day trader's action is directly related to how much credence he gives to the Newtonian deterministic model. If the day trader embraces the logic of Newtonian physics, he can take trading techniques that have been designed for long-term trading and reapply them in more discrete time intervals, following the "if-this-occurs-then-this will-happen" approach to forecasting. A simplistic example is the high reliability of conventional head-and-shoulder daily bar chart patterns implying a price reversal. If the day trader embraces the Newtonian model, then he would believe that a Head-and-Shoulder reversal pattern in a 15-minute bar chart would herald a high probability price reversal in the 15-minute bar chart.

On the other hand, if the Newtonian model has no application to life in general, or trading in specific, then the day trader would not be able to conclude with any degree of probability whether or not any pattern that formed on daily bar charts could be applied to shorter-time-frame charts. Here we are broaching the subject of seriality and sychronicity. If supposed reactions are independent of preceding actions, then it is useless to attempt to forecast because nothing would be dependent on what preceded.

This Newtonian model belief system served physicists well for centuries. In the process of accepting the basic premise that nature is reducible to basic formulas, Western science continued onward in its quest to find smaller and smaller building blocks of nature. When supposed observed actions did not create the forecasted, and necessary, reactions, such Newtonian scientists dismissed these cases as mere exceptions to their rules.

The Universe in the Newtonian Model

To understand Newtonian logic, think of the motion of the earth around the sun and the moon around the earth. With the use of Newton's formulas, the location of the earth and the moon can be found exactly for the present, the future, and the past. (There are slight perturbations in planetary cycles which cannot be accounted for by Newtonian physics. This is the area where quantum physics has come into play.) As Newtonian physicists later discovered, the problem of finding the exact location of these celestial bodies is made difficult when a third planetary body is factored into the movement of the earth relative to the moon, that is, when the physicist attempts to factor in the effects of the sun on the motion of the earth and the moon. The formulas developed by Newton could be solved easily as long as they were single- or dual-variable equations. If the number of variables increased beyond two variables (e.g., if we added several more planets), Newton's equations became unsolvable. As unsolvable as they eventually are, the concept of reductionism was carried forward, accompanied by the belief that the complexity of these multi-variable functions merely made them harder to solve at the time, but that they would eventually be solved in the future.

In a sense, what the Netwonian physicists practiced is what traders practice also. The fact that they couldn't figure how the pattern looks didn't mean that they couldn't use them functionally. As the Newtonians did not allow the lack of formulaic precision to prevent them from applying the model in real-world experiences, neither do traders allow the lack of absolute certainty to prevent them from using these implicitly derived techniques.

In a simple, mechanistic world, solutions could be derived from such formulas because the formulas were themselves very simple. As the number of variables increased, as the solutions themselves became dependent on more variables, the solutions were more difficult to find. Newton himself tried to resolve this dilemma: He developed an approach to approximate answers through his discovery of calculus. He assumed that his single- and dual-variable formulas could be approximated. However, he also assumed that the multi-variable formulas were linear! If they were not linear, his calculus could not be used.

All simple formulas, as functions, were found to have slopes, approximations of an answer. Newton's calculus was a method to determine the slope of the linear function. It was assumed that all such functions were linear; that is, their slope could be plotted on a simple X-Y coordinate graph of two dimensions. Once so plotted, another requirement was that if a line were drawn vertically to parallel the Y-axis, the drawn line would intersect with the plotted formula's answer at no more than one point: The function could not go back on itself (in chaotic terms, the function could not "fold" back on itself).

The World is Non-Linear

As long as the real world could be plotted in such simplistic terms, Newtonian mechanics was useful. However, every so often a function was found that produced a plotted curve (not quite a curve now, because it convoluted every which way) that could fold onto itself! In 1834, Bernhard Bolzano discovered the first function that was continuous but was nowhere differentiable. However, Karl Weierstrass, a mathematician who in 1872 discovered another such curve, is widely credited for the discovery. The curve, the "function," actually folded into itself. Calculus could not be used to differentiate this curve and thus approximate an answer. (Toward the end of the nineteenth century, Debois Reymond presented Weierstrass's equations.) More and more curves that could not be formulated using the old mathematics and perspectives were discovered. In the words of Carl B. Boyer, "[there] was the recognition that there are pathological functions that do not behave as mathematicians had always expected them to behave." *

In 1890, Giuseppe Peano discovered the "space-filling curve," a curve that twisted every which way such that it actually filled a whole flat plane of the paper on which it was drawn: No point on the plane existed that could not be intersected by the "Peano curve." This was practical heresy as far as the application of calculus to nominally accepted Newtonian maximum-two-variable formulas was concerned, and thus these curves were initially dismissed by mathematicians as oddities in an otherwise sane, mechanistic world. The curves existed, and yet no one could explain why they existed. No one had come along to change the perspective of observation.

The eventual acceptance of these recursive curves opened the way to the study of other curves and shapes and eventually led to a more detailed study of the real world. Scientists originally studied Newtonian mechanics, which involved descriptions of larger subsets of natural laws to impose on the real world; now their perspective was challenged with the acceptance of these newly

---

*Carl B. Boyer, *A History of Mathematics* (New York: John Wiley & Sons, 1968).

discovered curves. Benoit Mandelbrot looked at these "newly" discovered curves and, by viewing them from different scales or dimensions, saw that these apparent "exceptions to the theoretically
mechanical world" actually exemplified the general rules of the
world. Mandelbrot discovered a way to measure and categorize the
"irregularity" of the real, real world.

MARKETS ARE NONLINEAR

This is similar to the categorization of irregular market waves
through Elliott Wave theory filtering. What market analysts once
saw as irregular patterns of congestions and impulse waves were
now collected and categorized into a holistic analysis derived
from Elliott waves perspectives. When a trader plotted daily bar
charts of various markets, the seeming randomness with which
impulse waves and corrective waves occurred and disappeared
defied the attempts by scientists to actually force these patterns
into simplistic formulas. Now natural scientists, in their search to
understand the workings of nature, are pursuing an approach that
can summarize "irregular" plots neatly with simple formulas.

Can the study of chaos and fractionation now be applied to the
study of "irregular" curves of market patterns? In order to answer
this, let's look at some of the ideas following the conclusion that,
in the real world, nonlinearity was more the rule than linearity.

CHALLENGES TO THE NEWTONIAN MODEL

The first mathematician to question the Newtonian orderliness of
the universe was Henri Poincaré, the French mathematician, physicist, and philosopher. Poincaré argued that perhaps the validity of
reductionism was merely an illusion! In reality, it wasn't true, but
it merely served to reflect our own inability to measure certain
observations. It was definitely the first indication that what was
accepted to be truth was beginning to be questioned.

Once the Newtonian model was challenged, other derivations
from its axiomatic foundation were challenged as well. The greatest
derivation challenged was the belief that time was reversible. How
was this view of time developed?

Implied in the Newtonian model was the belief that the future
location of any planet can be determined through the application
of Newton's laws, and that the planet's past location could also be
calculated. The formulas used to forecast future locations could
also be used to determine where these planets were in the past!
Thus, in a purely mechanical world, time is reversible. If market

price action is derived from the passage of time, then what happened in the past could be reconstructed if a formula could be created. Implied in this reasoning was that what happened in the past with market action caused what was to happen to the market in the future.

Even though it was Poincaré who noted the possibility that what was accepted as real wasn't really so, it was the German scientist Rudolph Clausis who really threw the wrench into classical Newtonian physics and its view of the reversibility of time. He formulated the laws of thermodynamics. The relevant one here is the Second Law of Thermodynamics, which states: In a closed system, entropy never decreases. Entropy is defined as a measure of time potency of heat energy; states of matter move from low entropy to high entropy. This process is irreversible.

I've prepared an example of the states of entropy. I have a bottle of red-colored, hot water. I dribble the hot water into a bottle containing clear, cold water. As I empty the hot water into the clear water, the two different waters mix. After all the hot water is put into the bottle containing the cold water, it will eventually achieve two observable equilibrium states: The two differently colored waters will mix to form an evenly pinkish solution and the waters of different temperatures will mix to form a solution with a combined temperature that is bounded by the upper temperature of the hot water and the lower temperature range of the cold water. What is amazing to Newtonian physicists is the fact that no matter how long we allow the combined solution to stand by itself, we won't see the two solutions separate back into their two respectively different colorings or their two separate temperatures. The two waters have mixed and cannot now be unmixed. The action is totally irreversible.

If the reversibility of the laws of Newtonian physics were to hold for bodily motions, why don't they hold for the mixing of the two differently colored and heated waters?

In the 1870s, the Viennese physicist Ludwig Boltzmann sought to accommodate both the Newtonian physicists' time reversibility and thermodynamics' time irreversibility: He merely stated that thermodynamics was a subset of Newtonian mechanics. He tried to show that Newtonian mechanics was still universally true on the basic level of atoms and molecules, but in complicated systems where trillions of atoms and molecules are colliding with each other, it becomes less and less likely that they'll stay in an ordered relationship and thus they approach a state of high entropy.

In uniform matter, there is order. When it is confronted with another piece of matter that differs from it in temperature or heat energy, melding the two units together creates chaotic conditions. Take the example of mixing the heated water and the cooler water. When an equilibrium is established, what was once uniformity of order in the separate hot and cool waters is now chaotic. Boltzmann demonstrated that the degree of chance of either condition existing, that of two separate waters or that of the combined waters, was more important.

From an orderly existence to a disorderly one, there is a greater chance for a disorderly one to occur: It hardly works the other way, where disorder engenders order. The orderly existence of certain states of molecular behavior occurs only rarely; disorder is more of an accepted fact of existence. The degree of disorderliness corresponded exactly to the maximum state of thermodynamic equilibrium, that is, maximum entropy.

In a similar sense, a trading market can be considered disorderly and chaotic and a trending market can be likened to a less frequently occurring orderliness. How can this classification be so? Why can't a trending market be chaotic and a trading market be orderly? The clue rests in the time spent in each condition. There is more time spent in chaotic conditions and less in orderly conditions. Trading markets occur most of the time (about 60% to 70%) and trending markets less frequently. We are now talking about the time factor.

EXTERNAL INFLUENCES TO DESTABILIZE THE EQUILIBRIUM

Scientists have discovered that time is reversible in one sense (the implied Newtonian mechanics model: To forecast the future validly, one can and must induce the past) and irreversible in another (the Clausius model: Once matter moves from one energy state to another through entropy, there is no going back).

Boltzmann attempted to bridge the two apparently contradictory models by viewing them in different scales: At subatomic levels, Newtonian modeling is valid, but in a macroscopic universe, it becomes more and more difficult to apply Newtonian cause-and-effect relationships.

If we were to think of both the Newtonian model and the Clausius model not as separate viewpoints of real-world events, but rather as a series of stages in a linear progression, with one model at one end of the scale and the other model at the other end of the scale, we find that we are missing a dynamic that can bridge the two models.

What causes the shift of validity from the Newtonian model to the Clausius model, and vice versa? In market parlance, what causes the shift of market action from trading market to trending market or from trending market to trading market? Any trader, especially the day trader, would find it extremely profitable to know exactly when the shifts of market stages begin or end.

One of the unresolved enigmas of quantum physics is exemplified by the fact that light behaves both as waves of energy and as particles of matter. In one regard light can shoot through space at its own speed, and at other times, light has particular properties of matter. What causes the transformation of light from matter to energy? The answer probably rests with the acceptance of the fact that matter can be understood from a material-world perspective, and that energy can only be understood from an energy-world view.

THE ANSWER: PASSAGE OF TIME

A Nobel laureate in chemistry, Ilya Prigogine, contends that time is the "linchpin of creation."* Prigogine hypothesizes that chaos exists in a linear fashion: from one end, called "equilibrium thermal chaos," to the other end, called "far-from-equilibrium turbulent chaos."

It is at the "far-from-equilibrium turbulent chaos" end that systems not only break apart, but that new systems emerge! In a sense, a trading market, given enough time, will break apart, and a new order will be created: the trending market.

In my own work I've discovered that the passage of time is a critical factor in markets changing stages from trading to trending and from trending to trading. At certain times, forecasting accurately is possible, and at other times, forecasting accurately is impossible. It is as if there is a time window to accurately use time to forecast, so to speak.

Here is an example from *Turbulent Mirror:*

> If a pan of liquid is heated so that the lower surface becomes hotter than the upper surface, heat at first travels from lower to upper by conduction. The flow in the liquid is regular and smooth. This is a near-equilibrium situation. However, as the heating continues, the difference in temperature between the two layers grows, a far-from-equilibrium state is reached, and gravity begins to pull more strongly on the upper layer, which is cooler and therefore more dense. Whorls

*John Briggs and F. David Peat, *Turbulent Mirror: An Illustrated Guide to Chaos Theory and the Science of Wholeness* (New York: Harper & Row Publishers, 1989).

and eddies appear throughout the liquid, becoming increasingly turbulent until the system verges on complete disorder. The critical bifurcation point is reached when the heat can't disperse fast enough
without the aid of large-scale convection currents. At this point the
system shifts out of its chaotic state, and the previously disordered
whorls transform into a lattice of hexagonal currents, the Bernard
cells.

Turn up the heat further and the Bernard cells dissolve into chaos.
(p. 137)

The important point to note from the quoted paragraphs is that an
external energy source is applied to the boiling liquid. The boiling liquid is not in a closed system; the heat applied to it can be
varied, and in this case, it is increased continuously. The increasing temperature forces the liquid to go through several stages of
behavior: from chaotic to ordered and then to chaotic. Comparing
the two stages of chaos and ordered-state, the greatest amount of
time is spent in chaotic states. The ordered state, that of a lattice
of hexagonal currents called the Bernard cells, exists at a certain
level of heat, and that heat level must be kept relatively constant.

What is interesting to observe is that there is a sequential ordering in the process of moving from chaos to an ordered state,
and vice versa: The heat is increased in an orderly fashion. The
chaos preceded by the Bernard cell structure cannot be achieved
by skipping the conditions that caused the Bernard cell lattice to
be created. In other words, heat first had to be applied so that chaos
was created, then the Bernard cell lattice structure showed itself,
and then the final chaotic state appeared.

In market action, a trading market eventually engenders a
trending market. What causes the bifurcation of its stages? What
causes the "branching out," so to speak, of its market action to
another level?

I don't know what causes bifurcations of functions, except that
in "closed" systems something eventually will force them to "break
out." At times I have been able to forecast the exact breakout points,
and at other times, my forecasts were useless.

It is as if all matter and energy "pulsates" to a universal heart-
beat, even markets. The points in time in which markets shift correlate with other universal phenomena.* The weight of the evidence
points to a synchronizing of actions and behaviors to some order.
This order has yet to be discovered.

---

*A lucid analysis of time can be found in G.J. Whitman's book, *The Nature
of Time,* (London: Thames & Hudson, 1972.)

GANN ANALYSIS:
A SIMPLISTIC REVERSE PROGRESSION

Some types of esoteric market analysis are based on the assumption that any one point in price or time is a reflection of some important events that occurred in the past, and correspondingly, any action occurring in the present will foretell some future price actions.

A good example involves the application of William D. Gann lines. Gann lines are drawn with direct ratios from major market reversal points. The ratios vary as multiples of 1/8, such as 0.25, 0.50, and so on. The Gann lines are systematic ways of forcing randomly charted price actions into a predefined set of angular lines.

Figure 4.1 contains four Gann angled charts. Figure 4.1a shows the angled lines, which are correlated with planetary movements,

Figure 4.1
Gann angled lines of support and resistance in bull and bear markets. (Copyright© 1988 by William F. Eng.)

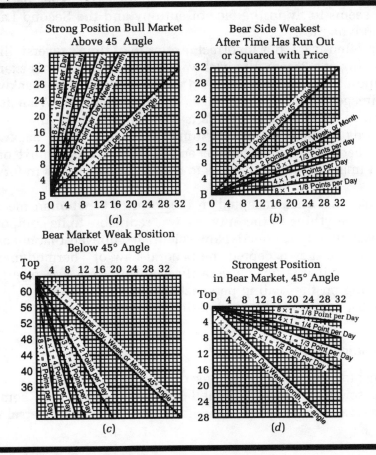

in up markets. Figure 4.1b shows angled lines once a critical juncture has been reached—in this case, where price has reached time—which will provide support to any selloffs.

Figures 4.1c and Figure 4.1d show the angled lines in bear markets which will provide resistance points in both time and price.

In bear markets, there are no supports, and in bull markets, there are no resistances. Conversely, what the Gann angled lines show is that in bull markets, there are support levels, and in bear markets, there are resistance levels.

The advanced Gann analyst draws Gann lines starting at the current price levels and moves them backwards in time. The assumption is that certain lines will intersect with certain past price points! It is a known fact that Gann systematically applied planetary motions to his price charts. For the reader who is well-versed in this area, the reverse Gann lines are a simplistic way to look at converse progressions. The forward lines are merely forward progressions.

This observation of the works of someone who tried to mechanically take time backwards and "reforecast" what had happened seems to fly in the face of entropy and the Second Law of Thermodynamics.

An often-used, but incorrect, example of time's reversibility is the playing of a 35mm film backwards. Proponents of this example have indicated that the mere act of playing the film backwards gives images of action sequences going backwards. What is not recognized by these proponents is that the act of playing the film backwards is done in forward time; playing the film backwards gives a backward movement of action within the context of the viewed images, but the film has to be played backwards in forward time!

What was once accepted in the form of Newtonian mechanics, that everything in the universe was reducible to its component parts, was now questioned. Now scientists believed that chaos existed because they accepted the Second Law of Thermodynamics and because it was not necessarily true that time was reversible. Depending on the scaling perspective, time may be reversible, in one sense, or irreversible, in totality.

Fractionation and Day Trading

An amazing set of observations came along in the early 1970s from a scientist named Mitchell Feigenbaum. He took some of the observations made by Mandelbrot and found a universal constant.

He took some other formulas and observations, reworked them, and again found the same constant. It was like discovering pi: Here was another number to be reckoned with. Feigenbaum discovered that in nonlinear problems there existed a universal constant that could always be derived upon continued manipulation of formulas.

An analogy that will help the reader understand this is the difference between induction and deduction in logic, or interpolation and extrapolation in mathematics. In the case of induction, the scientist takes observed phenomena and tries to figure out factual points bound within those observed phenomena. In the case of deduction, the scientist takes observed phenomena and tries to figure out factual points unbounded by these observed phenomena. In the case of interpolation the mathematician takes a set of numbers, for instance, 2 to 15, and interpolates points bounded within the range: interpolated whole numbers would be 3, 4, 5, ... 12, 13, 14; in extrapolation, the mathematician starts with the same range and then moves out of it; that is, extrapolated whole numbers would be less than 2 or greater than 15.

THE SCALPER AND THE TREND TRADER: NONLINEAR AND LINEAR TRADING

How, you may ask, will knowing this help me trade the markets successfully? In a sense, the scalper works within a nonlinear environment, whereas the trend trader works in a linear environment.

The scalper essentially sells against all trends: short-term, intermediate, or long-term. The reason why he sells against the trend is that he expects prices to gravitate back to some central point, this central point having been passed before.

The trend trader is working in a linear problem world. When the trend trader enters a long position, he expects prices to punch to not only highs, but new highs. And when he sells short, he expects prices to go to new lows. In each case, the prices that he expects to be reached by market action will be in new price territory.

In one type of market analysis, that of using Gann lines off major highs or up from major lows, the logic used is that of a nonlinear perspective. The range of prices of the high swing and the low swing is bracketed and then partitioned out into equal 1/8ths. The trader using this approach expects prices to reverse from some critical 1/8th, or multiple thereof, of the high-low range.

In another type of Gann analysis, the trader uses major lows and projects Gann lines from these lows into uncharted price territory. This is a linear problem world.

Both worlds are correct; both analyses are correct. The trader must know when the move away from bracketed high and low prices (a nonlinear problem world) will enter new price territory (a linear problem world). Trading approaches in each world are different.

The key to finding out what world one is entering rests on the fractal point when one scale is left behind and another one is entered. The use of day trading techniques, where essentially the trader can take smaller-scaled price patterns and discover similar patterns found in larger-scaled price patterns, can help in assessing *when* this point of fractionation is reached! It is beyond the scope of this chapter to detail how the point **in time** can be discovered.

PART TWO

THE SCIENCE OF
DAY TRADING

5

Tape-Reading Techniques

The mechanics of day trading can be approached in two basic ways. Each of these approaches has different features and weaknesses.

The first approach is to use techniques that have been created specifically for the purpose of day trading. Various attempts have been made, unsuccessfully, to extend these approaches to longer time frames (specifically, the Market Profile approach and Liquidity Data Bank). The approaches accurately forecast potentially profitable moves as long as the minor scale was maintained; however, any attempts to extend time frames using these techniques resulted in unsuccessful trading.

The second approach is to take intermediate to long-term trading techniques and reduce them down to one day. Certain basic assumptions have to be made before one can apply these reduced approaches, similar to the assumptions in Newton's reductionism. This matter was discussed at great length in Chapter 4.

A third approach, which is less significant, combines some of the longer-term-brought-to-shorter-term methods (daily bar charts and mathematically calculated indicators) and the shorter-term methods only (Market Profile, Liquidity Data Bank, tape-reading tactics, and so on).

The mechanics of the first approach, that of using methods specifically designed for day trading, will be discussed first. Within this approach are four specific methods for day trading.

The first method is reading the tape. In tape reading, certain assumptions about the stock markets are made. These assumptions, once valid in the past, are less valid now. Tape reading is real-time analysis of supply and demand. With the advent of fragmented executions from competing marketplaces, the tape reader is less apt to be able to judge real market supply and demand.

The second method is spread trade trading. This type of trading involves many types of markets, but the underlying thesis of spreading is to be balanced long and short, often varying the degree of the net positions.

The third method is the application of Market Profile and Liquidity Data Bank analysis of the conventional half-hour bar chart. This method is not without its weaknesses, and, as shall be seen later, some underlying assumptions of this method beg the question of when markets actually change in their underlying tone from trading to trending and from trending to trading.

The fourth and final method of day trading is a hybrid approach called the Sequential Patterning approach. It is a hybrid because the trade incepted on one day is a result of decision-making information derived from previous days.

Tape Reading

> A tape reader must keep a notebook. On even the dullest trading day, you might notice a dozen stocks that appear to be under accumulation. You can't buy every stock that looks good for 10 minutes. Tape watching merely alerts you to potential prospects for purchase. You have to carry the process further, either by looking for repeated instances of accumulation in the same stocks or by bringing fundamental and technical factors into play.*

Tape reading is a self-taught skill practiced by market professionals primarily in the stock markets. The creation of third markets (where stocks listed on the major stock exchanges are traded over the counter) and fourth markets (where institutions swap blocks of stocks without disclosing such transactions to the exchanges) for trading stocks has lessened the viability of tape reading as an accurate method for price forecasting in breakouts, breakdowns, topping-out, or bottoming-out actions. The advent of global trading, where blocks of stocks are sold to foreign companies and eventually find themselves back on the open market in foreign transactions, serves also to dampen the advantages of centralized exchange executions: centralized price and volume reporting.

The stock ticker tape has no counterpart in the futures markets, because the futures tape does not disclose trading volume per transaction. The need to know volume per transaction is critical for the trader's ability to read supply and demand factors in day trad-

*Jerry Helzner, "Every Symbol Tells a Story: Why It Pays to Watch the Tape," *Barron's*, March 21, 1988.

ing stocks. The futures tape only reports two items of information: the last sales price of the futures, and spread trades between two different expiration months of the same futures. The tape reader would be at a greater loss here because he would not have the most critical information in tape reading: volume per trades. The Chicago Board of Trade, the world's largest futures exchange, has created the Liquidity Data Bank component of the Market Profile analysis, and it is this type of data that comes closest to allowing the tape reader access to cumulative volume of trades per price, not volume per trade. The Liquidity Data Bank data has spawned its own sets of analytical tools and approaches. See the section on Market Profile as a specifically designed approach to day trading in Chapter 7.

The implicit assumption in tape reading is that large traders are better-informed traders. Small traders are less informed and as a result will trade in smaller numbers of shares. Large traders will therefore trade in large blocks of stocks, because these are more efficient to execute. Small traders will trade whatever number of shares their accounts allow. A proficient tape reader will note the amount of sympathetic buying from the small traders that goes on after a signal is read from the transactions.

The Ticker Tape

The ticker tape machine was developed by the Western Union Company, which was founded by Thomas Edison, the United States inventor. The machine was designed to distribute price and volume information of transactions executed on individual stocks on the stock exchanges.

The modern ticker tape is a product developed and sold by Trans-Lux™. In 1919 the founder, Percival Furber, replaced the paper tape from the ticker tape machine with a translucent plastic tape and shone a strong light through it to project images onto a blank wall. (Shortly after this, Trans-Lux developed the concept of rear-view projection.) The Trans-Lux jet has the capacity to display 900 characters a minute from right to left. Mechanically, the Trans-Lux jet could display more characters, but the human eye would not be able to read the information. With the development of the composite tape, the primary exchanges have attempted to continue the centralized function of exchanges: the distribution of prices and volumes per trade of transactions from one source, even though the actual trades may be executed on physically separated locations.

At the beginning, data came only from the primary exchanges. In the particular case of stocks, the transactions reported came only from the New York Stock Exchange or the American Stock Exchange, both located in New York's Wall Street district. The *Composite Tape* was developed as a viable response to display the increased trading activity on the regional exchanges and the third markets. As the efficiency of computers increased, the ease of creating transactions away from the primary markets also increased. This started when the primary exchanges decided to incorporate the information from the transactions of dually listed stocks (stocks that traded both at the primary market and the regionals, such as IBM and GM), which were also actively traded on the larger regional exchanges: the Pacific Coast Stock Exchange, Philadelphia Baltimore Stock Exchange (the most active of the regional stock exchanges for options) and the Midwest Stock Exchange (the most active of the regional stock exchanges for stocks).

In the past the only communication between the primary markets and the regional exchange on which the dually listed stock was traded was between the executing brokers representing the specialist on the primary market and the executing brokers representing the specialist on the regional exchange. There was no direct electronic hookup between the regional exchanges and the primary markets. The regional specialist would essentially work off the price of the next trade that the primary market's specialist would create; from that price the regional specialist would transact the trade in a block of IBM stock (a block meaning that the number of shares had to be a relatively large amount) or offer the IBM stock at the last sale plus a tick if the number of shares was relatively small (the tick representing the profit to the regional specialist) or bid a tick under if he was a buyer.

THE COMPOSITE TAPE AND THE SELECTIVE TICKER

The Securities Industry Automation Corporation (SIAC), a market information distribution group created in 1972 by merging the data-processing facilities of the New York Stock Exchange and the American Stock Exchange, now serves to supply transaction data for the Composite Tape. SIAC is also the data originator for the National Securities Clearing Corporation. In the early 1970s average daily volume amounted to about 11 million shares and the old hardware could handle the information. In October, 1987, the month of record volume, the SIAC systems handled the record volume well; on October 16, 1989, even though the total volume of 400 million shares traded was less than that of October 19, 1987, there were peak 5-minute blocks of record volume activity, which SIAC again handled well. As of 1990, in preparation for additional record volume days, SIAC can handle in excess of one-billion share days (as bullish as this may seem now, there will come a day when such volume activity is normal; perhaps not in our lifetimes but certainly one day).

The main problem with trying to glean information for an adequate interpretation of the price and volume activity based on the transactions reported on the composite tape centers on the inability of the tape to report sequential ordering of trades. Yes, the reporting of the trades to SIAC is in the order executed; however, the trades may or may not be reported immediately by the regional specialists. Trades may have been done earlier by two agreed parties, but the actual reporting of the trade may not have been made until later. If a client needs to have shares to trade on a regional exchange and if there is no prearranged price from the primary market to cross the trade, the specialist of the regional exchange will execute the pricing of the block of stock based on pricing created from the primary market. In other words, the regional specialist works off the buying and selling activity of the primary market.

The flow chart in Figure 5.1 is provided by the Securities Industry Automation Corporation. As the flow chart shows, the in-

Figure 5.1
Flow chart of market data to specialists' trading posts.

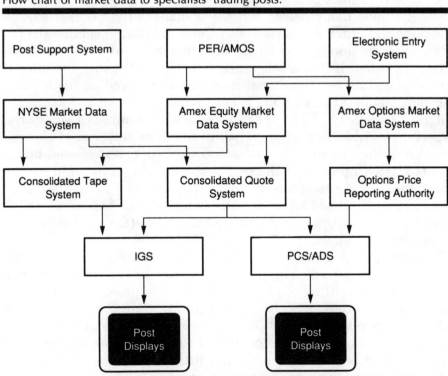

formation created from the three sources—Post Support System, PER/AMOS, and the Electronic Entry System—is put together and reaches the displays within the specialists' posts. From this point, the data is then distributed outwardly to the public.

One feature of the SIAC is the centralization of bid and ask markets for all stocks. This is known as the Consolidated Quote System (CQS). The Intermarket Trading System (ITS) corrals the best bid price and best asked price from specialists and brokers on trading floors of the New York Stock Exchange, the American Stock Exchange, and the regional exchanges for customer orders.

Suppose the last transaction on the primary market is 5,000 shares of IBM at 112⅜, with the primary market bid-ask spread at 10,000 shares bid for at 112¼ and 60,000 shares offered at 112½ (in the parlance of the business, the market is "¼-½, 100 × 600; ¼ representing the 112¼ bid, ½ representing the 112½ offer, 100 representing 100 round lots of 100 shares each, and 600 representing 600 round lots of 100 shares each). The experienced tape reader would know that the next transactions will most likely occur at either 112¼ or at 112½ but would not know the volume of the trade. If there are trades continuing to come across the ticker tape at 112⅜, with neither a bid nor an ask price of 112⅜ showing, then the tape reader can conclude that there is an order being worked at 112⅜ by a floor broker on the primary exchange.

The most likely reason for this is that the floor broker who is working the order doesn't want to show the IBM specialist the order. Once the floor broker enters the order with the IBM specialist, then the order, if it is a sell order at 112⅜, will cause the offered price to be lowered from what it originally showed on the bid-ask screen, 60,000 shares at 112½, to the then-revised bid-ask price of 10,000 shares bid at 112¼ and whatever number of shares the specialist wishes to post on behalf of the floor broker at 112⅜ (the market is then quoted at "¼-⅜, 100×99"; the "99" offered represents a large number of shares for sale). If the order held by the floor broker is instead a buy order at 112⅜, then the revised bid-ask market becomes whatever number of shares bid for at 112⅜ and the same 60,000 shares offered at 112½ (the market is then quoted at "⅜-½, 99×600").

There are delays in reporting the transactions created on the regional markets to the composite tape. This delay in accurate price and volume reporting of regional activity is a problem for conventional tape readers, but as you will find out later, it is a problem that can be resolved with additional sources of information. Despite the misread information tossed to the tape reader, there are always solutions. Even though the little toys get more complex, they all require the same batteries to run.

The amount of information that goes through a ticker tape is far greater than it was as recently as 20 years ago. Modern computers have made it easier to break down the amount of information and selectively cull out the markets the trader has interests in. The development of the *selective tape*, a generic concept, is a boon for the trader who is now overloaded with stock information.

On most specialists' desks are found computers that can be selectively programmed to display volume and price information of selected issues. Instead of tracking the trading information of all the issues of stocks that are displayed in the Composite Tape, the selective tape is preprogrammed by the specialist to extract only those trades of certain selected stocks. Within this section the volume and prices of each transaction can be displayed on this abbreviated information tape. The Composite Tape has all transactions data (name of market, price, and volume), and is therefore subject to increased activity problems, such as delayed price reporting.

One major problem is similar to trying to pour water into a funnel: The individual drops of water still have to wait their turn to pass through the funnel's opening at the bottom. With the Selective Tape, only those stocks that have been preselected show through. In effect, any and all transactions completed for the selective tape will be displayed, without delays.

With the selective tape, complete data is available instantaneously; also, the *sequencing* of the transactions is displayed. It is theoretically possible, however, to overload even the selective tape function by having a large amount of selected issues to monitor, in which case the effectiveness of the selective tape to instantaneously give the right markets and transactions is correspondingly diminished.

This quirk of information massaging and distribution creates a special problem. Outside the industry, the Composite Tape is available to display actual transactions. The information distributed, however, cannot be effectively used for tape reading by the public. On the other hand, the professional can use the *exact* trade data available to effectively read supply and demand interactions.

The only way to dissect the information that crosses the Composite Tape, without the use of the selective tape, and determine whether or not buys and sells are created is to check the actual markets both primary and regional, on each individual exchange. The investigative trader, after seeing a *significant* volume trade (one that is reported fully with volume) occur on the Composite Tape, can check each exchange to see if the volume of that one particular trade as reported on the Composite Tape matches a similar volume increase in any of the individual exchanges. By knowing where the actual trade occurred, whether on the buy or the sell side of the bid/ask market, the trader can determine the supply or demand pressure and hopefully can forecast some imminent upticks or downticks.

This approach is laborious and useless; if the inquiring trader has access to that much direct information from any of the exchanges, he certainly would have access to some form of selective tape with its bid/ask and size markets. In order to find the volume increase in the regional exchanges, the trader would already have had access to the regional markets.

A second problem due to the lack of useable information on the Composite Tape is attributable to the number of stocks so traded. Twenty years ago the professional tape reader was able to view the ticker tape and literally obtain a feel for the market. It was much easier to sense waves of buying and selling orders hitting the markets. When the technology stocks, for example, would move, the tape reader could see the lead stocks move, followed by the secondaries, and ending with the tertiary stocks in that industry. The tape reader could actually see individual sectors of the markets move, at first discordantly, and then finally in harmony. Now, once the high-speed Composite Tape hits its maximum-peak character distribution, the Trans-Lux emits a monotonous hum and certain detailed information is dropped (individual large volume transactions are retained, however) to speed the information distribution. The hum literally makes each trade appear similar to the other trades, which is not what the tape reader is looking for to make informed decisions. The abbreviated reports drop important details.

Traditional Tape Reading

In order to find out how trying to read the activity of supply and demand accurately is thwarted by the inadequacies of the Composite Tape, the effectiveness of reading the tape correctly must be understood.

In the early 1900s the primary stock markets (the New York Stock Exchange and the American Stock Exchange) controlled the creation of prices and volume activity through their monopoly of the source of that data: the interaction between the stock specialists and the brokers who represented the other side of the transactions. Of course, within this environment sharp market manipulators were able even to control the dissemination of such information by the specialists themselves: They manipulated the outside orders through their representing brokers.

Market manipulation could only be done on a small scale. However, if market manipulators were able to get a following of either buyers or sellers, then it was easier to move from the small scale to the larger scale. The bigger players in the early 1900s were highly skilled in giving out the right signals at the right times. The primary method through which market manipulators could give the intended messages to the other market players was through the signals they could generate from forcing the sequence and the size of trades disseminating through the ticker tape. This became known as "painting the tape."

Because the specialists on member exchanges had their own interests in mind, they were not easily controlled by outside speculators. However, control of individual brokers working independently of each other by the outside speculators was much easier and more easily executable. The speculators could instruct their representative brokers to buy or sell. The market manipulators painted the tape by creating fake signals.

The vigor with which new traders on the floor report buying and selling orders to their retail clients off the floor is only offset by the validity of their observations. The obvious is obviously wrong, if I may paraphrase Joe Granville, the market guru of on-balance-volume. The following is an example to illustrate the false impressions that reporting such transactions can give to the outside traders.

Several times in my trading career have I entered orders to buy stock when I actually wanted to sell my total positions. A second and third brokerage firm were allowed the discretion to buy blocks of offered stock—which I offered—from my offering agent. My actual block of stock was not offered with discretion but only at one fixed price. The volume of my offering varied depending on who was on the buy side, always less or more than my total block, but never the actual number of shares. In other words, not only did I offer my delicious bait but I also constantly jiggled it. I even "hired" the two fish to make my bait appealing. I found my two fish for the mere cost of paying commissions and instructed them to nibble at the bait. Every so often I even allowed the fish to take a bite of the bait. Of course, after every bite, my two fish would tell me in braggadocio fashion how tasty the bait was, not worrying that the other fish mingling around would hear.

In the process of telling these fish that there was bait ready to be had, these fish also brought in other fish. It was to these innocent fish that I needed to unload my stock. The sophistication level of the innocent fish was very low and it was easy for me to unload my block of stock.

All of these transactions were performed on a foreign exchange that did not have strict laws against this type of market activity. It is my opinion that market manipulation can serve a purpose; however, such actions must be conducted within current Securities and Exchange and Commodity Futures Trading Commissions regulations.

If the manipulator needed to unload a block of stock that he had accumulated at lower prices, he first had to make the stock activity on the tape appear bullish. A stock is most obviously bullish if there is continued buying activity. The degree of buying activity is important here. If a bona fide buyer wishes to accumulate stock, he does not make his bullish intention known; rather, he attempts to buy as much of the stock at low prices as he possibly can. He waits in the weeds, so to speak, ready to pounce on every sell order that enters his domain. When he has accumulated as much of the stock as possible—by buying what is offered at prices he wants to pay—he marks the stock up by actively making it known that buying by moneyed interests is apparent.

One way in which the attention of other tape readers throughout the country can be riveted to some buy or sell activity that can be displayed on the ticker tape is to create an **abnormal** event. During the course of the trading day, there is an average number of transactions that occur in any one particular stock. The speculator is keenly aware of the norm. Once that norm is altered by either increasing volume (not decreasing volume, which would only show a lack of interest by market participants) or increasing or decreasing prices, the speculator is only too ready to jump at the opportunity for profitable action. Once the normal equilibrium is disturbed, the inference is that there are now outside factors causing this disequilibrium.

Two obvious ways to flash signals are available to the market manipulator: change price and/or change volume dramatically. What other way is there to flash such interests? The only other way, that of suspending trading while waiting for news, is controlled by the specialists of the exchanges. Suspension of trading activity really does get the interest of the speculators, but without much possibility of accumulating positions for some gains.

Stock Ticker Data

In the normal pattern of information distribution, both old and new ticker tapes report three valuable pieces of data: the acronym for the stock in which the transactions are executed, the price of the stock transaction, and the number of shares traded at that price. Price is important here, but more valuable in the analysis of the price is the change in price from the previous transaction and, nowadays, the price of the next transaction. Volume is extremely important because it shows the strength of the buying and selling interests. More will be said later on this particular point.

The old tape and the Composite Tape show the same information. However, the way in which the information is collected for redistribution differs greatly. What could be read once in the past cannot be read using the tape nowadays: Is there buying or is there selling? Other methods of uncovering buying and selling power must be used.

The Speed of the Tape
and the Four Modes of Reading It

Basic tape reading involves the confirmation of price action by volume action. One condition of tape display, the "fast" market condition, shows abbreviated prices and volume data, thereby leaving the tape reader with less than enough information to make an informed evaluation of market conditions. This does not help the tape reader in using volume action as a confirmatory tool.

In normal markets, the original ticker taper displays the full amount of information. This "normal tape" mode (or mode 1) is shown in the following message display on the ticker tape: Ticker Mode Normal.

500 IBM	IBM	IBM	200 IBM
112 1/4	112 3/8	112 3/8	112 1/2

The above illustration of a normal mode tape indicates that 100 shares of IBM stock traded at a price of 112 3/8. The trade that followed was 200 shares at 112 1/2, an uptick from the previous sale.

There are three other modes of tape reading, each defined by what information is deleted in distribution and not by how late the tape is in reporting transactions. It might appear that the modes of information distribution would contribute to how late the tape is running, as the tape will also show how much the tape is behind the actual transactions. Conditions would warrant the change in information distribution, and as a result of such conditions, the tape would run 1 to 3 minutes late.

The second mode of information distribution is the *digits and volume deleted mode.* In this mode, the actual digits and volume are deleted, but the prices are retained:

IBM	IBM	IBM	IBM
12 1/4	12 3/8	12 3/8	12 1/2

As you can see, the above illustration shows only the name of the stock and the limited price of the transaction. The tape reader would be missing the full price of the trade, which can be induced, and the volume data, which cannot be determined easily.

The third mode of information distribution is the *repeat prices omitted mode.*

IBM	IBM	IBM
12 1/4	12 3/8	12 1/2

Note that the second trade of IBM at 112 3/8 is completely ignored in price reporting. In this case the second trade was 100 shares so the loss of that trade's data is not critical to reading the tape effectively. However, if in this mode, the *normal* transactions were this:

500 IBM	IBM	10000 IBM	200 IBM
112 1/4	112 3/8	112 3/8	112 1/2

the tape reader could easily see that the 10,000 shares traded at a price unchanged from the previous trade. The sharp trader who wants to hide her trade from the tape readers could trade the 10,000 shares after she creates a small trade at a previous price, followed by the block at the same price. In this case the smart trader might be taking out the offers of IBM stock. The market might be 112 1/4 bid for 1000 shares and 112 3/8 offered for 10,000 shares (1/4-3/8, 10×100) and the trader wants to cover her tracks by not showing that the 10,000 shares offered is bought on an uptick by preceding that takeout of the 10,000 shares by inserting a trade of 100 shares at the price that the 10,000 would show before the 10,000 shares is traded. In the above tape, the trader takes out 100 shares and then takes out the 10,000 shares. In this way, technical tools that monitor upticks and downticks, for example, would not be able to discern whether there was an aggressive buyer of the 10,000 shares.

Of course, if the tape is running in mode 3, where repeat prices are omitted, the second transaction at $\frac{3}{8}$ is totally omitted.

The fourth mode of information distribution is called the *minimum price changes omitted mode*. Here, the very sharp tape readers can cover their tracks even better. This mode was created in early 1984 to accommodate even faster abbreviated information distribution. In this mode, the tape dropped prices of trades that changed from the previous trade *more* than a tick. That is, if a first trade showed a price of 112$\frac{3}{8}$ followed by a trade of a price of 112$\frac{1}{2}$, the second trade would not be reported; a second trade would be reported only if the price changed more than $\frac{1}{8}$ point, or traded at or above 112$\frac{5}{8}$. So, in effect, from a first sale of 112$\frac{3}{8}$ all the way up to 112$\frac{1}{2}$, no trades need be reported in such mode. Many sales could be transacted on upticks without anyone other than the actual stock specialist knowing what was transpiring.

The fourth mode was modified after the October 1987 market crash because the mode was not able to contain all the information that was forced through it. Now the trades that can be deleted range up to any limit, as long as this fact was broadcast on the tape; the tape can drop trades that deviate from the previous trades a half point away. The message displayed now reads: *Minimum Price Changed Omitted Now X Etc*, where X can be $\frac{3}{8}$, ONE DLR, 1$\frac{1}{4}$, or whatever.

This tape:

500 IBM	IBM	IBM	200 IBM
112$\frac{1}{4}$	112$\frac{3}{8}$	112$\frac{3}{8}$	112$\frac{1}{2}$

would then be displayed as follows if the fourth mode's *Minimum Price Changed Omitted Now $\frac{1}{2}$ Etc* were displayed:

MIN PRICE CHGS OMITTED NOW $\frac{1}{2}$ ETC	IBM
	12$\frac{1}{4}$

Practically all useful information would be dropped.

As you can easily see, the more information that is forced through the system, the more difficult it is to read accurately. Market professionals basically close up shop when the tape is running 3 minutes or so behind because they don't know where the markets are trading.

The first table in Figure 5.2 details the modes of information displays. The second table shows the types of messages that will

---

Figure 5.2
Modes of information display and mode changes in ticker tape.

Mode		Message Text
Normal	1	Ticker Mode Normal
Digits & Volume Deleted	2	Now in Digits & Volume Deleted Mode
Repeat Prices Omitted	3	Now in Repeat Prices Omitted Mode
Minimum Price Changes Omitted	4	Min Price Chgs Omitted Now N etc.

In Mode	To Mode	Message
4	4 (Changing N)	4
4	3	3
4	2	2
4	1	1
3	4	4
3	2	2
3	1	1
2	4	4
2	3	3
2	1	1
1	4	4
1	3	3
1	2	2

be displayed on the ticker tape when there are shifts in modes of information distribution.

Of course as a regional stock specialist, the trader has access to the actual bid and ask of the particular stock with size shown. The regional specialist has no access to any orders away from the immediate markets. Until recently, information such as the number of shares bid for at the closest price to the last sale and the number of shares offered at the closest price to the last sale was not available to the public speculator. The availability of such information makes the task of reading supply and demand activity much easier.

SEAQ: An International Trend

From the international arena, a unique development in stock trading is evolving in London. This is the *Stock Exchange Automated Quotation System (SEAQ International)*, a computerized trading system that specializes only in large blocks of stocks.

There are about 50 large British, American, and Japanese securities firms that participate in crossing huge blocks of stocks of international companies. It is, in the words of the *Wall Street Journal*, "block-trading business gone electronic."

The success of SEAQ portends an ominous trend for the New York Stock Exchange. Since SEAQ was created in 1985, it now accounts for as much as 40 percent of the volume of many Euorpean stocks. In 1988 it traded $132.2 billion dollars of stocks, and in 1989 it went to $277.1 billion, a 100 percent increase. SEAQ is a two-tiered market in which block traders and institutions trade among themselves and avoid reporting price and volume data, which they would have to do if they traded on the trading floors.

The New York Stock Exchange, which is not a direct competitor, will nevertheless lose transactions to this overseas electronic exchange. SEAQ has one feature that block traders need: anonymity. The New York Stock Exchange, on the other hand, reports both volume and price per transaction under regular market conditions. In 1988 it traded $132.2 billion dollars of stocks, and in 1989 it went to $277.1 billion dollars, a 100 percent increase.

An investment manager gave the obvious reason why they use SEAQ: "It gives us more transparency in market prices." Additionally, the system does not report volume figures until the next day, and there is no last-sale trade reporting. It is important to know immediate volume with last sales data to read the transaction tapes accurately.

The Front-Running Issue in Global Markets

With the ease of access to real-time data created from the stock exchanges now, a problem unique to tape reading has developed. The institution that wants to take a position in a stock can be accused of the act of front-running. With the derivative products available on several different exchanges, the institution could go to the nonprimary markets to accumulate positions prior to the actual trade in the stock. The institution could go to the stock options exchanges and pick up the many options available for the stock that they wish to buy, or they can go the regional exchanges and pick up whatever stock is offered in the regional specialists' order books. After they have bought as much as they can, they can go to the primary markets to pick up the total block. This is a case of front-running. In brief, the front-running is created when the interested party picks up peripherally available stock and/or its derivatives before it goes directly to the main source. An inference from this type of activity is that the main markets may not eventually be the main markets. Perhaps the evolution of increased market activity is starting to spread to the regionals.

Several years ago when I traded options on one of the options exchanges in Chicago, a block trading institution exerted its weight in the front-running issue. The particular stock in this example was traded in the primary market, the New York Stock Exchange. It also had stock options traded both at the American Stock Options Exchange and the Chicago Board Options Exchange (CBOE). For several weeks the options market makers at the CBOE noticed that this particular institution came in and took out most of the offers in the board brokers' books and then made offers to buy more options from the market makers. Shortly afterward there would be a block of that particular stock cross at the primary market, the New York Stock Exchange. The block of stock always traded at several ticks higher than the last sale. The market makers at the CBOE who had sold the options short took losses. This continued for several weeks until the market makers figured that they were victims of an institution that was front-running orders.

The market makers in Chicago are brasher than their counterparts in New York. They told the floor brokers representing the institution that they were going to report this hanky-panky to the Securities Exchange Commission (SEC). And they did it. But before they did, the floor broker came into the crowd and told the market makers that if the SEC began an investigation, the order flow, not only in this one stock but also in others, would never get to the market makers again but would instead be rerouted to the American Stock Options Exchange. The market makers in Chicago figured that they had nothing to lose anyway, because any orders emanating from the institution always bagged them. The orders were eventually routed to the American Stock Exchange. The volume in the options traded in Chicago eventually decreased. To this date the volume activity has not recovered.

All institutions, in the short run, take advantage of the fact that they are capable of moving blocks of stocks in the primary market and can create short-term profits in picking off the peripheral market makers. This is not an easy issue to deal with, because there is the element of profit involved in this particular type of transaction. All financial centers operate on the thesis of maximizing profits. Whoever complains the loudest at getting taken are those who, unfortunately, get taken care of, either for good or for bad.

In day trading stocks, the issue of front-running is always possible. This is similar, but not identical, to arbitrage. In arbitrage, the trader buys in one market and sells a similar item in another market, locking in a very small profit. In front-running the trader buys in the peripheral market and then *buys* a similar item in the main market; the institutional trader accentuates the buying or selling process.

6

Spread Trading

Spreading is not a traditionally accepted way of day trading. It was originally conceived by market professionals as a method to reduce risk and to inventory large amounts of stocks, futures, or options for distribution to public participants, when and if the public came into the market.

The spread approach borders on a totally mechanical way of day trading. In this particular case, spreading requires no market judgment but relies more on primitive mathematical calculations and odds determinations.

The definition of spreading, according to the Chicago Board of Trade, is as follows: "the simultaneous buying and selling of two related markets in the expectation that a profit will be made when the position is offset. Examples include: buying one futures contract and selling another futures contract of the same commodity but different delivery month; buying and selling the same delivery month of the same commodity on different futures exchanges; buying a given delivery month of one futures market and selling the same delivery month of a different, but related, futures market."

The concept of spreading can be successfully applied not only to futures or commodities, but also to stocks and bonds.

SPREADING IN STOCKS

Stocks are spread from one company to another company in similar industries: buying Ford Motors and selling General Motors or buying IBM and selling Digital Equipment stock.

The spreading can continue not only within the same types of stocks, but also into the derivative products of such company stock: buying convertible stocks and selling the common stock. One can also spread against time: spreading a long instrument against a short-term instrument. With the development of long-term options (exchange-traded options on stocks that have initial maturity of two years, which effectively make them warrant-like) by the American Stock Exchange and the Long-term Equity AnticiPation Securities (LEAPS) at the Chicago Board Options Exchange, there should be substantial opportunities to spread short term against a long-term base. In the last example, the subject of *hedging* is considered: the practice of offsetting the price that is risk inherent in any cash market position by taking an equal but opposite position in the futures market. Hedgers use the futures markets to protect their business inventories and production from aderse price changes.

This case may appear to be extreme, but market professionals use these instruments and this approach to reduce market risk and also to leverage the positioning power of their trading capital.

SPREADING IN DEBT INSTRUMENTS

Spreading is also done in the debt instruments market: treasury bills, commercial paper, certificates of deposits, eurodollars, bonds, and notes. The yield curve is used here. Within the maturity spectrum, the wider apart the maturity between two instruments used in the spread, the greater is the market risk.

In bonds, the spreading is done from different delivery maturities, using the yield-to-maturity values as the basis of valuation of the two different-length bonds. A trader can buy the May 1995 8 $\frac{1}{8}$ percent coupon bonds and sell the June 1995 12 $\frac{1}{4}$ percent bonds; the total position is completely neutralized as far as market volatility is concerned. The case where availability of deliverable bonds in such spreads can cause the spread to widen or narrow beyond the carrying charges is rare, but it can happen and often happens when the cash bond trader is least likely to expect it.

A SPREADING IN OPTIONS AND CASH

With the use of options on futures, options on stocks, and options on currencies, the spreading can extend beyond spreading within markets to spreading within different instruments. The art of trading different expiration series and different strike prices is a recently developed strategy. Prior to the development of the *modern* put and call option (developed by the Chicago Board Options Exchange, which eventually superceded all puts and calls developed previously for the over-the-counter markets), no such sophisticated strategies existed.

Within the spreading of options against options, the calculated value used to determine net market risk is the hedge factor per option. The cumulative value of the hedge factors of individual options offers the spreader a starting point for evaluating market risk of his *total* position. This hedge factor is not to be construed as the spread in a cash basis hedge. In this situation, where there is a difference between the cash price and the futures price, the basis is part of a hedging program to limit potential losses. This spread factor, when applied toward the cash (the actual soybeans, if a soybean/future spread, or the actual stock, if a stock/option spread where the options are very deep in-the-money), is called a "basis."

INTERMARKET AND INTRAMARKET SPREADS

Now, we go to a different category of spreading: Spreading between markets that are not fungible. In the previous examples, I talked about spreading between stock options on the same stock, in various length debt instruments, between options and their underlying stocks or futures. All of these markets are related in some manner. In this section spreading between markets that are not related in any manner will be discussed.

Spreading can also occur between two different markets: spreading hogs versus cattle, oats versus wheat, corn versus soybeans, or S&P 500 versus NYFE (each stock index traded on a different exchange).

The advantage of spreading in this case is attributable directly to the markets being traded in the same exchange—this allows the same clearing firm to track the trades and thus charge less "margin" money for the maintenance of the hog/cattle position, otherwise it would be treated, for the sake of margins, as two separate trades, which would be more expensive to maintain. The margining of two such different positions, when initiated on two separate exchanges, can be decreased to reflect similarity of markets. The rules and regulations on such spreads are so varied and dependent on market situations that the trader must inquire to the exchanges directly.

The sophistication level of intermarket spreading is much higher than the knowledge required for intramarket spreading. This is because the spread traders in such markets rely more heavily on the need for fundamental market analysis. In the simplest case of spreading—spreading one month of December Wheat against the next month of wheat, March—there is no need to know about market analysis to determine the direction in which the wheat market will move. When one spreads hogs against cattle, there is a need to determine the trends of the respective markets because each market acts independently in fundamentals. Different supply and demand factors affect hogs and cattle.

Here it is necessary to explain the actual reason why any retail speculator should spread. Contrary to the explanations often given to such speculators, the retail clients must look at the two markets that will be spread—one market must be definitely bullish or definitely bearish. If *both* markets are bearish, or bullish, then the technique of spreading is not as profitable. The outside speculator must be long the bullish market, or short the bearish market. One mustn't allow the oscillation of the actual spreads to dictate the basic decision to enter the spread. (Professionals use spreads, where there are long and short different markets, as a method to minimize market risk. They leg in and out of their spreads with ease.)

What advantage is it, then, to spread two obviously different markets, markets that respond to different fundamental conditions? For the same reason one spreads December Wheat against March Wheat—to dampen market risk. Despite the fact that the hogs and cattle respond to different fundamentals, to the extent that they both are red meats, they are similar. The meat markets will respond to more generalized market fundamentals; if some unexpected news affects the generalized meat markets (an overall embargo on exports of meat products to overseas buyers, for example), both the hog and the meat markets will respond bearishly. In this way the intermarket spread trader will be insulated from dramatic market volatility due to political announcements. Spreads such as these are specifically implemented in foreign exchange markets because of the volatility of foreign government policies.

THE MECHANICS OF DAY TRADING SCALP SPREADS

This approach to day trading was developed, and is practiced daily, on the floors of the exchanges. This approach depends on two major assumptions, both of which are frequently accurate. The first assumption is that there is continuous fluctuation in prices of the markets traded. The second assumption is that the markets being spread are generally liquid. In cases involving less price fluctuation and liquidity decreases, the spread trader is at a disadvantage.

The Need for Price Fluctuation

In normal markets prices occur between the high price and the low price, the high and low prices having been defined by market forces early in the trading day. When the extreme prices are yet to be reached, the scalping spread trader encounters problems. Such markets are not normal markets and are classified as trending markets, the trends being of a minor scale. In *all* viable markets, there is a need for market movement. (Try to remember a case where a profitable market existed without any movement.) There are no profits to be made for any market participant if there are no movements. Different types of market movements, one directional movement or oscillating price movements bounded by a high and a low price range, benefit different types of traders. Trend traders make profits less frequently but in larger amounts. Trading market traders make profits consistently, but in smaller pieces.

In the case of the scalp spreader, the trading range has to be defined by a consistent high/low range. The ideal situation for maximizing profits for a scalp spreader is when prices during the course of the trading day oscillate between high and low five or six times. The continuous travel of prices over the period allows the spread scalper to initiate positions and trade against the minor trends, which is important to the profitability of the spread scalping method.

An added bonus to the price oscillation is the increased possibility that trades will be extracted from public participants. In a sense, the markets in their movements from low to high, to low again, to high again, *ad infinitum*, will extract more buyers and sellers into trading than if prices were to remain static. The added price probes will increase the volume of trade activity also.

Professional floor traders will often take it upon themselves to initiate price probes by bidding up or offering down the markets. In the futures pits, this occurs frequently; in the stock exchanges, the role of executing open orders and other types of trades is held by the stock specialists, and the price probes are more deliberate and calculated.

Certain markets are known in the trade as being "stop running markets." In these markets, the currency markets and the meat markets in particular, the pit traders deliberately probe for buy stop orders by bidding prices up and perform similar price probes on the downside by offering the markets down to stop sell order levels. New York futures markets have developed notorious reputations as stop running markets (I caution you to allow greater stop placements when placing protective limit orders in such markets). There is a profit incentive for both pit traders and stock specialists to probe for stops, push prices up and down, and trade against orders entered in response to these types of professionally initiated action/reaction chains.

Liquidity is critical to the scalp trader. Without liquidity, the spread scalper would find it difficult to lay off risks or take scalp profits when it would be necessary to spread off the positions.

The Key to Success: Averaging Correctly

A trader can average either in the direction of the main trend, or he can average against the trends: main, intermediate, or short-term.*

The spread scalper and the trend trader differ in how they trade the various trends: major trend, intermediate trend, and minor trend. The spread scalper will be a seller in all time spans of up markets, hoping to buy on any selloffs. The spread scalper looks to sell into new highs, fully expecting that prices will dip at least a tick for him to cover all his sales.

The trend trader, however, will selectively sell and buy. The trend trader will be a constant buyer in major uptrends. He will also buy into intermediate and minor uptrends. The distinction between the scalp spreader and the trend trader rests with what each does in intermediate downtrends. The short-term trader will sell into intermediate downtrends. The trend trader will, instead, look to buy into the intermediate downtrends, expecting prices to resume their major upward bias after the intermediate downtrend has ended.

The point to understand is that the trend trader trades with the trend. He assumes that prices will continue in one direction. The scalp spreader trades against the trend. The scalper assumes that even though prices will go in one direction, they will also weaken and back off enough for him to cover his positions.

Figure 6.1 shows the trading decisions of scalpers, intermediate trend traders and major trend traders in bull markets. Note the extremely long period of the market's move, in which the long-term uptrend traders will have open positions, and the shorter in-and-out trading that the short-term scalper partakes in.

Figure 6.2 shows, in converse fashion, the trading decisions of scalpers, intermediate trend traders and major trend traders in bear markets. Again note that the longest-term traders, the major trend traders, have decidedly longer periods to have open positions.

There are two ways to methodically average the total position; the viability of each depends on the purpose of trading for the

---

*For a thorough discussion of averaging techniques as related to pyramiding, see William Eng, *The Technical Analysis of Stocks, Options and Futures*, (Chicago: Probus Publishing, 1988).

Figure 6.1
Trading decisions of scalpers, intermediate-trend traders, and major-trend traders in bull markets.

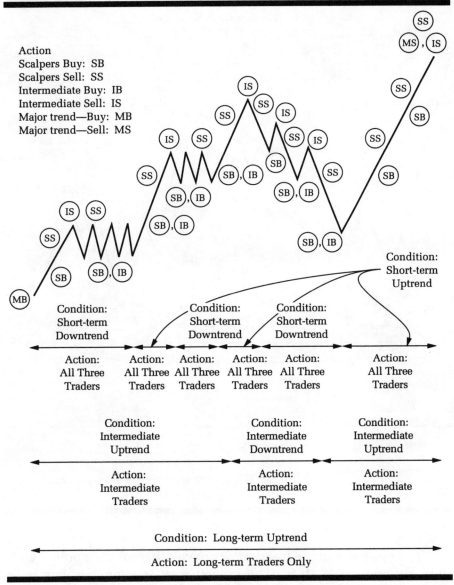

market players. The scalp trader can vary the number of contracts or shares of stocks to add to the total position and the price to add to the position. Unlike the long-term trend trader who adds positions in the direction of the trend by adding fewer and fewer positions as the price moves in the direction of the position, the scalp trader adds larger and larger positions as the price moves against the trader's positions.

Figure 6.2
Trading decisions of scalpers, intermediate-trend traders, and major-trend traders in bear markets.

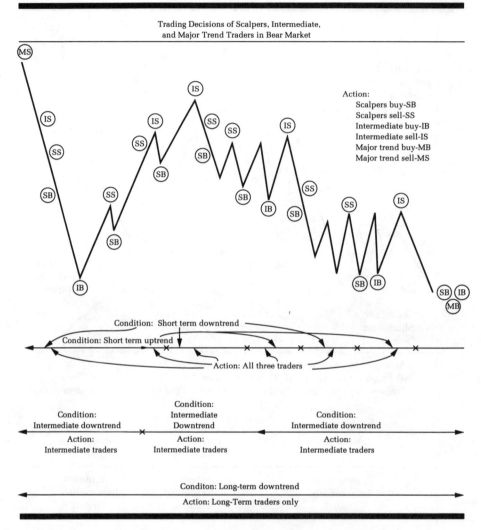

The scalper and the trend trader have different viewpoints and, thus, different objectives. The objective of the trend trader is to increase the total position and also at the same time to force the average price of the total position *further* away from the current market price. The objective of the spread scalper, however, is to increase the total position by adding to the total position in larger and larger positions against the trend, forcing the average price of the total position *closer* to the market price.

The scalp spreader adds positions in a mechanical way, always the initial position fewer in size than the last addition. The ideal sequencing of contract addition is: 1, 3, 6, 9, 18, and continually doubling the last number of contracts. The ideal price to add these increasing positions is in a predetermined price move, always based on the average daily price range. It is an arbitrary calculation to determine what the average price range should be for the averaging sequence to work. However, you should use a basic starting point by averaging the daily price ranges of the particular market traded over the course of 5 days; there shouldn't be much deviation from the average of 5 days from that of 15 days, 20 days, or an even greater number of days.

If the range of the wheat market is about 6 cents, then the 1-3-6-9-18 sequencing, which contains five additions, should be divided into the average price range of 6 cents, or a position is added at every $1\frac{1}{5}$ cents. For easier calculations, we round the addition of positions at every 1 $\frac{1}{4}$ cents decrease against a major uptrend, or every 1 $\frac{1}{4}$ cents increase against a major downtrend.

Table 6.1 illustrates the mechanics of spread scalping. As the price of the wheat futures drops from $3.00 per bushel to $2.96 $\frac{1}{4}$, the scalp spreader adds positions in increasing lots, if the price continues downward. If, for example, the spread scalper is down to the third addition, when she adds 6 more contracts for a total 10 contract position at an average price of $2.98 $\frac{1}{8}$, she continues to add 18 positions at $2.96 $\frac{1}{4}$. If the price hits the third addition and holds there, and then bounces up to $2.98 $\frac{1}{8}$, the trader is at a breakeven. The last lot of 6 contracts added at $2.97 $\frac{1}{2}$ is only $\frac{5}{8}$ of a cent from the total averaged position of 10 contracts.

How, then, is it possible for the scalp spreader to make money? Because the scalp spreader is on an exchange where he has access to the order flow coming in from the wirehouses, he sees what the orders are. If an order then comes in to buy wheat, with wheat at

Table 6.1
The Mechanics of Spread Scalping

Price of wheat	Add	Average price	Cumulative positions
3.00	1	3.00	1
2.98 $\frac{3}{4}$	3	2.990625	4
2.97 $\frac{1}{2}$	6	2.98 $\frac{1}{8}$	10
2.96 $\frac{1}{4}$	9	2.972368	19

Source: William F. Eng, *The Technical Analysis of Stocks, Options and Futures* (Chicago: Probus Publishing, 1988).

$2.97 $^1/_2$, the trader offers the wheat at a price at least one tick higher, or several ticks higher if he can get away with it. If he offers the wheat, size unannounced, he offers it at $2.97 $^1/_2$ plus an "edge," a term used in the business to refer to a "markup" on inventory. The edge is normally a tick better than the last trade, which would be $2.97 $^1/_2$ plus $^1/_4$ cents, or a price of $2.97 $^3/_4$. The average price of the scalp spreader's inventory is $2.98 $^1/_8$; and by offering the wheat at $2.97 $^3/_4$, and actually getting a last trade at that price, the traders on the floor are able to offer it at the last price plus the edge once again: $2.97 $^3/_4$ plus $^1/_4$, or $2.98. If there is enough demand for the wheat at the lower prices, traders can offer the wheat at two ticks higher or more, immediately to $2.98 from $2.97 $^1/_2$.

Floor brokers representing these orders for the outside speculators and hedgers have executed large orders at two different prices. As a matter of floor courtesy, the floor broker who needs to fill a large order to buy wheat executes the buy in the following manner: The floor broker announces that she is buying at a tick above the last sale, or $2.97 $^1/_2$ (the last sale price) plus a tick, for a total price of $2.97 $^3/_4$. If the trader was on the floor and was acting as a spread scalper, he would sell her a few contracts at $2.97 $^3/_4$ and retain the balance of his inventory for sale at higher prices—the broker is only representing part of a large buy order and it would be foolish for the scalper to sell his total inventory at low prices when he already knows there is a buy order for more. Because he was the first trader to fill the floor broker's initial contracts, the floor broker should go back to him and fill the balance of the order by bidding the balance of the order at a tick or several ticks higher from the now-current last sale of $2.97 $^3/_4$. This is an unwritten rule of conduct on the exchanges. The trader can then offer some of his positions at $2.97 $^3/_4$ plus a tick, for a total price of $2.98. If somewhere in between these executions, the order is still unfilled, he can then continue to offer the wheat at $2.98 $^1/_4$, $2.98 $^1/_2$, and so on.

Once the trader can offer the wheat at $2.98 $^1/_4$, he has a rough idea that his accumulated positions are showing a profit of about $^1/_8$ cents from his average price. From the last added position of $2.97 $^1/_2$ to the average price where he shows a slight profit, $2.98 $^1/_8$, there is about 2 $^1/_2$ ticks of $^1/_4$ cents per tick ($^1/_4$ cents multiplied by 2 $^1/_2$ equals $^5/_8$ cents): after 2 uptick trades (the first at $2.97 $^3/_4$ and the second at $2.98), he will be only $^1/_8$ cents away from breakeven in his total position.

This scalp spreading method is fine by itself, but there is a condition that exists in the futures markets, the option markets, and the debt markets that increases the chances of the spread scalper to lay off his total position or take scalp profits. The existence of *parallel* markets offers the spread scalper additional chances of getting rid of the risk of his outright positions. Parallel markets are those that match the price movement of the first market.

One way to evaluate how a particular issue behaves relative to another is to use the concept of *beta.* The conventional definition of beta is based on the measure of a stock's relative volatility with the Standard and Poor's 500 Stock Index having a beta coefficient of 1.00. Stock ABC could have a beta of 0.56 relative to the S&P 500. If stock XYZ also had a beta of 0.56, then a relatively risk-free spread could be considered between ABC and XYZ, with the beta coefficient as the common denominator. Unfortunately, the real world isn't as simple as this; the spreader would have to know dividend payout dates, ex-rights trading, and so on, in order to increase the chances that there is a correlation in price activity between ABC and XYZ stock. There are also other factors: Will the stocks act similarly to the upside or downside? How do other derivative markets affect the underlying? And so on.

Please note that the use of such parallel markets enables the trader to remove the risk of general market moves, not the outright positions. Removing the outright positions requires unwinding all positions.

HOW CARRYING CHARGE MARKETS BENEFIT THE SPREAD SCALPER

In the case of the wheat contract, the addition of the positions is done in the current front month. If the trader is trading in during the actual calendar month of November, then the December Wheat futures contract is the front month futures contract traded on the exchange. The deferred months are the next expirations. In the case of wheat, price differences between two different months are often based on the carrying costs of taking delivery in the front month, then paying for storing, insurance, ownership transfer costs, and the ubiquitous "fudge factor," for future delivery in the deferred month. This relationship is constant in carrying charge markets.

When there is a carrying charge market (where commodities taken in one month can be offset into another delivery month only), the trader can lay off market price risk to other tradeable months.

In the above example, if the price difference between one month of deliverable wheat to an adjoining month is, say, 5 cents, or if the December Wheat low is $2.97 $^{1}/_{2}$, then the next month,

March Wheat, should be priced 5 cents higher, or $3.02 $\frac{1}{2}$. If, instead of having a December Wheat order to buy after the trader has added his third addition in order to average out his price to $2.98 $\frac{1}{8}$, an order comes in to buy March Wheat instead, the trader can offer the March Wheat at $2.97 $\frac{1}{2}$ + 5 cents (which is the carrying charge), or $3.02 $\frac{1}{2}$ plus a tick (the spread scalper's profit), or $3.02 $\frac{3}{4}$ and effectively he would have sold a pseudo-December Wheat contract also. Because the mechanics of futures trading creates a premium for liquidity and a discount for illiquidity, the edge that can be extracted from deferred months contracts is often higher than in the front months. The trader can offer the deferred months at $\frac{1}{2}$ cents higher instead of only $\frac{1}{4}$ cents; for contracts in extremely deferred out months, the trader can even offer it at as much as $\frac{3}{4}$ cents higher. (Take into consideration that the normal carrying charges accumulate from month to month; the extra $\frac{3}{4}$ cents is added to the accumulated carrying charges; does not replace the charges.)

A similar situation exists with the valuation of options on stocks. Options premiums are calculated to reflect the cost of borrowing money to hold the stocks for the selected length of time, dividends paid out during the holding period, and a risk premium. In the cash debt market, similar situations exist and are commonly referred to as a positive or negative cost of carry type of markets. In all situations, there is a direct element of fungibility, in which one instrument can somehow be used to replace another instrument.

Once the spread scalper is able to lay off the net long position in the front month by selling a deferred month for several ticks better, he has insulated himself against basic market risk. He has, in effect, protected his equity from the effects of market volatilities while locking in ticks of profits.

The total position of spread scalper now is as follows: He is long X amount of the front-end commodity contracts and short a Y amount of commodity contracts in the deferred month. Or the situation can be the other way around: He is short the X amount of the front end and long the Y amount of the deferred month. With this position, the trader is vulnerable to bull market moves. When there are bull market conditions, the front end can move beyond the carrying charges and can go to a premium condition to the back end. As a general rule, these bullish conditions do not occur overnight, so the spread scalper who finds himself in such bearish spreads has ample time to unwind the positions. If the general complex goes up in price, both his long and short positions will go up in similar price movements. If the general complex goes down in price, then both his long and short positions will go down in similar price movements.

It must also be considered that the spread difference between two different futures months is affected by the actual underlying prices themselves. There is a greater cost to borrow money if the price of a commodity is at $10, for example, than it is at $5; it is exactly double the cost. For example, if the spread of two commodities is 5 cents with the front-end commodity priced at $12.00, the spread will be less than 5 cents when the front-end commodity drops down to $6 (not decreases by $6) because of the difference in the cost of carry: Half the interest paid is required at $6 compared to $12. It is possible for a commodity to drop from $12 to $6, but it is not probable, and the average spread scalper does not need to neutralize against such improbable price movements.

However, if the spread positions taken are large (instead of 5 spreads, the scalp spread takes on 5,000 spreads), then even a minor price move will be magnified many times as the actual value of the spread will only change fractionally. In cases where the spread positions are large, the scalp spreader will create a "tail," which will effectively be used to neutralize this price effect. The spread could be as simple as long 5,000 front-end commodity and short *5,002* back-end commodity with the 2 extra short positions placed specifically for the purpose of neutralizing the magnified price volatility.*

The scalp spreader then moves to unload the total positions. Because the scalp spreader's position is completely neutralized, he does not have to worry about his total position. He can then take off his total position if there is a basic bid for his total spread from the spread brokers or he can try to leg off the positions. As a spread scalper in the exchanges, he has access to the bulk of the incoming buy and sell orders.

DIFFERENT PERSPECTIVES FOR DIFFERENT STRATEGIES

All trading techniques can be applied successfully in certain market situations. This particular strategy is no different. The correct application of the right strategy to the right market situation is what makes the strategies successful. As is the case with all trading techniques, this one has flaws. The inherent flaw with this approach,

---

*For the actual calculations, see the Chicago Board of Trade documentation on spreads; also, Jack Schwager's *A Complete Guide to the Futures Markets* (New York: John Wiley & Sons, 1984) pp. 545–549 shows how to calculate the tail of a spread.

from the viewpoint of a longer-term trend trader, is that price could continue onwards in a one-directional move and the scalp spreader would never have any opportunities to cover his position.

This approach is directly contrary to what the trend trader is expecting: a long, continued, one-directional move that will make the positions profitable for the much larger positions.

The scalp spreading method is similar to a Martingale betting system. This betting system was developed to play in games of chance that had even odds of winning. The bettor makes a single bet. If he wins, he continues to bet in single units. If he encounters a losing bet, then on the next bet he doubles up on the bet. If he encounters a losing streak, he continues to double from the previous bet until he wins again. Then he is back to betting in single units. The doubling of the bet allows the bettor to double his profits when he wins, enough to offset the loss from the previous bet(s) and give the bettor a breakeven return plus a small winning.

In the area of spread scalping the bet is not over, in effect, until the trade(s) are closed out, but the spread scalper acts as if the last position added signals the actual loss of the previous bet in a game of chance. The scalp spreader esssentially adds to his total losing position mechanically, always maintaining an average price as close as possible to the then-current market price. The fact that the scalper is adding in approximate doubling numbers forces the average value of his total position to be closer to the then-current market price. If the spread scalper were to add to his total position in any other ordering, the average price would not effectively be closer to the current market price.

WEAKNESSES OF SPREAD SCALPING

The critics of spread scalping point out that the trader increases his positions to fortify one losing position. The scalper takes on bigger positions trying to break even on the losing trades. The other point raised is that the markets can go straight down when the spread scalper is adding to his losing positions, or straight up when the spread scalper is selling into strong rallies.

The first point is valid and must be addressed. The counter to this is that for a greater portion of a trader's positioning, the trader makes money, and when he loses, he loses very, very big. When the trader wins, he wins in fractions of ticks, but when he loses, he loses in multiples of ticks in geometrically increased positions. There are several ways to mitigate this potential problem. One way to offset this is to keep an eye on the main trend of the market traded and create the averaging in a minor selloff to a major trend, thereby adding another dimension of analysis to the spread scalper's toolkit.

If the spread scalper can determine the trend, he has the potential to make at least multiple tick profits, if not whole points of profits. Instead of making a few ticks on a huge position, he makes several points on a huge position. In this sense, the strict Martingale betting system, as applied to games of pure chance, has no benefits; in trading, a game where skill in *management of profits and losses* is an essential element to profitability, the trader can control his profit potential by allowing his profits to run, which increases his profits to offset against potentially large losses. In applying the Martingale system to *games of pure chance*, the bettor has no control over the maximum payout to his bet because the maximum payout to his bet is determined in advance.

Certain games that involve the element of chance are biased for the survival of the players. In the one extreme, there is racetrack betting; in the other extreme, futures trading. Racetrack betting is designed for the survivability of the small gambler. Why is this so? Because the track controls each risk, not the payout. In reality, the bettor cannot lose more than his minimal $2 bet. The bettor can lose more only if he bets more, and in order to bet more he has to have the money in his hands first. There is no credit given at the racetrack (however, there is one recent innovation I have observed: the installation of cash money machines at the off-track betting parlors in the state of Illinois). The track controls the bettors' losses on each bad bet.

The house does not control the losses with futures trading. The brokerage firms do not limit the amount of bets the players put in: The trade, if it turns bad, can be stopped out at the $2 window, so to speak, if the trader himself limits the loss to such a price. Or the trader can lose more by allowing the trade to go against him more. This is one game where the *player* can predetermine the size of his bets. Even in stock trading with margin accounts, the player has no predetermined loss amount, unlike the race track, where the bettor loses a maximum of $2 on each $2 wagered.

On the other side of the coin, the profit side, the race track bettor has a more or less predetermined profit on each bet; there are variables that account for larger or smaller payoffs based on the actual cumulative amount wagered on the horse entry, but for all practical purposes, the payoff is set. In trading, the player can vary the amount of profits he desires in a winning trade. He can cut his profits off at the $2 window, or he can let his profits run up to the payout from a $100 window, if the markets are so primed. Of course, the problem here is that the trader is never really sure of whether or not his profits will run up to the payment from a $100 window. Suffice it to say that if the trader ends his profitable trade at the $2 window, it is a fact that the trader will not be able to go for the $100 window payoff.

What happens, then, if the markets drop like a lead balloon and the scalp spreader is adding at lower and lower prices (or in raging bull markets if the scalp spreader is selling into rallies)? The only way to guard against this potential, and financially debilitating, disaster is to limit the numbers of positions added and to unload the total position once a maximum loss is reached. Setting an arbitrary cutoff point for numbers of positions to add will save the scalp spreader from disastrous losses. I have stopped adding positions after the fourth opportunity to add positions transpired. At that point, if the price does not move to above the fourth, and hopefully, above the third and second add-on point, I unload all my positions after the fifth add-on point is reached instead of adding more positions at the fifth add-on point. In this manner I rid myself of large positions at huge losses and relegate myself to making back the losses over a span of several trading sessions. It is rare that this situation occurs and often there are rallies that will take me out of my total position at substantial profits. But if it doesn't occur, I am ready to bite the bullet, so to speak.

SPREADING OPTIONS*

There are many, many ways to spread options because there are so many different options strike prices and series. Spreading in options is made possible by the development of a value, theoretical though it might be, called the *delta* value of call and put options. In a sense, the value of an option is based on several values, one of which is the underlying cash product from which the price of the option is derived.

As in the case of the spread scalper, spreading options versus options and spreading options versus the underlying are mechani-

---

*For further information on spreading, please consult the following references: Claud Cleeton, *Strategies for the Options Trader* (John Wiley & Sons, New York: 1979); Lin Tso, *How to Make Money Trading Listed Puts* (New York: Frederick Fell Publishers, 1978) Lawrence McMillan, *Options as a Strategic Investment* (New York: Institute of Finance, 1986); and Gary Gastineau, *The Stock Options Manual* (New York: McGraw-Hill, 1988).

cally done in the same fashion—averaging the position and then hitting or taking out the other side when the bid or offer is available. The following are the general classifications of spreads and how they are created, in a nutshell.

The Volatility Spreads

Volatility spreads are spreads derived mainly from the cumulative delta values of the options.

1. *Backspread.* A spread derived from more long positions than short positions. All positions must expire at the same time.

2. *Ratio vertical spread.* A spread derived from more short positions than long positions. All positions must expire at the same time.

3. *Straddle.* A spread position consisting of either (1) a long call or a long put; or (2) short call and a short put. Both options in each situation must expire at the same time and have the same exercise price.

4. *Strangle.* A spread position consisting of either (1) a long call and a long put; or (2) a short call and a short put. Both options in each situation must expire at the same time and have different exercise prices.

5. *Butterfly.* A spread position consisting of three consecutive exercise prices, all of the same type (all calls or all puts) and all expiring at the same time. If the trader is "long" the butterfly, she is long the two extreme exercise prices and short the middle exercise price. If she is "short" the butterfly, she is short the two extreme exercise price and long the middle exercise price.

6. *Time spread* (also known as calendar spread or horizontal spread). A spread with two different expiration dates, but with the same exercise price and which can be done with either calls only or puts only.

7. *Diagonal spread.* Spreads constructed with options that expire in different months and also have different exercise prices.

Bull/Bear Spreads

1. *Bull/bear spreads.* A spread created in calls only or puts only where there is a short call at a lower price and a long call with a higher strike price. This spread is designed to take advantage of

market movements. Delta ratio spreaders can neutralize these positions by increasing or decreasing the positions to net a zero delta.

2. *Bull/bear butterflies*. Essentially a butterfly spread, but with exercise prices higher than the current market value of the underlying if bullish, or exercise prices lower than current market value of the underlying if bearish.

3. *Bull/bear time spreads*. Essentially time spreads but with the added dimension of market forecasting. If the trader is bullish on the underlying he can create a time spread with exercise prices higher than the current underlying market price; conversely if bearish.

4. *Vertical spreads*. Long an option at a different exercise price than the one that is short.

5. *Buy/sell writes*. Buying the underlying and selling the call options against it or selling the underlying and selling puts against it.

Arbitrage Strategies

1. *Synthetic positions*. Synthetic positions are created from call options or put options, which can only become the actual underlying positions after expiration. The spreader is long the call and short the put, same strike, same expiration, or short the call and long the put, same strike, same expiration. In this strategy the spreader has two options positions to play and one potential underlying position to play (which then turns into a conversion or a reversal).

2. *Conversions and reversals*. A synthetic position that is offset by a position in the underlying. A conversion is represented by the following: Synthetic short underlying plus long underlying is the equivalent of short the call derivative option plus long the put derivative option plus long the underlying. The reversal is the opposite of the conversion: Synthetic long underlying plus short the derivative is the equivalent of long a call derivative option plus short the put derivative option plus short the underlying.

   a. *Boxes*. Essentially when a conversion and a reversal are created in the same expiration month but at different exercise prices. The spreader can either be long the box or short the box.

b.   *Jelly Rolls.* Essentially the long synthetic position is created in a different delivery month from the short synthetic position.

The scalper must lock himself into each of these categorized option spreads. The mechanics of averaging his positions out in one series and then laying off the total risk in one or several different series is a day trading tool. This approach is exactly the same as the spread scalper's approach, except that the actual trading products used are call and put options.

The major problem in spreading options is the lack of liquidity in the deferred months and in the out-of-the-money options or deep-in-the-money options. It is seldom that the call or put options trade more volume than the underlying contracts or instruments; it is possible that the summation of all the options traded in one underlying can surpass the actual underlying volume. Once the price of the underlying extends beyond the strike prices, the liquidity in these options decreases and the spread scalper in these markets cannot unload his position at a moment's notice. Instead, he is forced into the role of waiting for incoming orders from the public to take him out of his positions. The final solution to the lack of liquidity in deep-in-the-money options is to merely exercise the option.

7

Trading Market Profile

This approach was explained in *The Technical Analysis of Stocks, Options and Futures.* However, I wish to discuss some important points of the approach concerning the actual use of the Market Profile and Liquidity Data Bank in day trading.

The Market Profile concept was developed by Peter Steidl-mayer, a veteran trader at the Chicago Board of Trade. The Liquidity Data Bank was also his brainchild, but it required the cooperation of the Chicago Board of Trade for its implementation.

This concept of market analysis was specifically designed for day trading purposes. The principles upon which the approach is based are intuitively sound. In the real world an infinite number of events occur all the time. Yet they occur with frequencies that have high statistical probabilities. If we were to give a test to a randomly selected sample population of students, and a range of test scores and the number of students having such scores could be plotted graphically, the graph would have a shape common to other such events with similar variables. This shape is universally known as the *bell-shaped curve* of frequency distribution. Statistically, the bell-shaped curve appears about 70 percent of the time. The other 30 percent of the time, the shape created is not so easily defined.

The bell-shape distribution in Figure 7.1 shows the shape of a normal population of data when plotted against a frequency distribution. Statistical analysis indicates that the bell-shaped curve will encompass 70 percent of all the data within one standard deviation from the norm.

From bell-shaped curve statistics we can forecast that given a large enough number of occurrences, bell-shaped graphs will be

Figure 7.1
The normal distribution, or "bell-shaped," curve.

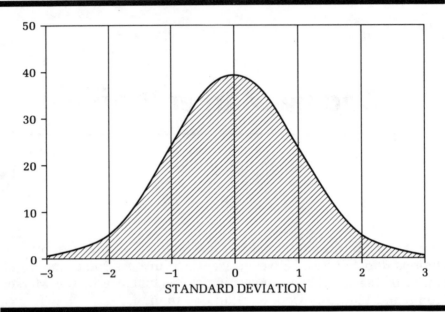

created about 70 percent of the time. This forecastability is extremely powerful. All Peter Steidlmayer had to do was to take market price data and create a way to plot those price occurrences onto
some two-variable matrix. If the frequency of real-world events fit
into two-variable bell-shaped matrices 70 percent of the time, why
can't market price data also, if so plotted?

The original premise on which the Market Profile concept
depended was intuitively acceptable, but it was not very rigor-
ously defined. What exactly are "large" occurrences? In statistics,
given a large enough sample to work with, bell-shaped distributions would pop up all over the place. If the sample population
was too small to derive any interesting or statistically significant
graphic plots, then the sample itself could be modified to force
its curve into the bell-shape! Statistically, there are ways to correct for small numbers of occurrences in the population. But the
use of these statistics assumes that the bell shapes created from a
large universe of data will apply even to small data sample popu-
lations, such as one day of price data. This is self-evident in the
light of the concept of fractals and chaos presented in the previous
chapter.

Constructing the Profile

The developer of the concept took the *range* of prices for a fixed half-hour time period and mapped them onto other ranges of prices. This is not unlike a plot of frequency distribution for every price during the course of the trading day. Taking every trade in a particular market and overlaying it onto an X-Y coordinate graph created the closest bell-shaped curves that could be found. This approach to market analysis was originally developed for the commodities markets by Steidlmayer, so the raw data used was only the price of the commodity. There just wasn't anything else to analyze. The frequency of occurrence of these prices was the other variable.

The three profiles in Figures 7.2, 7.3, and 7.4 encompass all the patterns that the Market Profile analysis will create: the normal profile, the nontrend profile, and the trend day profile. With this universe of three profiles the profile trader can trade successfully.

Plotting every price that shows up on the ticker tape can be taxing and displays too much useless information. The developer took the half-hour range to be more practical.

Many stock traders have asked whether or not they could use this approach to tracking stocks. My response is this: why would a stock trader want to use this approach? This approach was developed for a market that did not display volume per transaction. The only piece of information that was offered to traders who tried to read the commodities ticker tape was price, and thus the

---

Figure 7.2
Normal day profile. (Copyright© Chicago Board of Trade.)

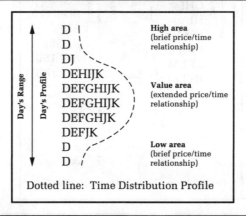

Figure 7.3
Nontrend day profile. (Copyright© Chicago Board of Trade.)

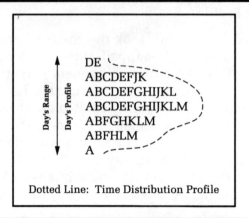

Figure 7.4
Strong trend day profile. (Copyright© Chicago Board of Trade.)

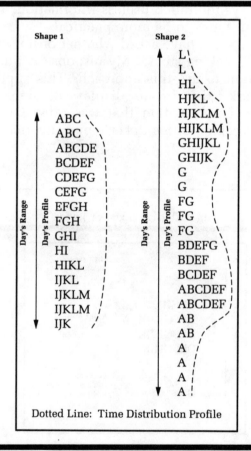

approach plots prices only. In the area of stock trading, volume and the bid/ask market are provided by the many data resellers. This approach can be applied to stocks, but not as a primary source of day trading information. The only use of plotting profiles with stock data is to determine where the stock is generally going to find support or resistance in the form of price congestions. However, in the "Market Profile and the Nonstandard Distribution" section of this book I provide a reason to plot a volume profile for stocks also. There are other techniques in day trading that can utilize the greater amounts of information for stock traders.

TRADING WITH THE PROFILE APPROACH

Once the market prices could be depicted visually in terms of frequency of occurrences, the developer of the profile created a set of trading instructions. The most basic of all instructions concerned the actual formation of the shape of prices during the trading day.

If the prices reported on the commodity ticker were arbitrarily plotted on a fixed time interval, bell-shaped distributions would appear 70 percent of the time and would be absent 30 percent of the time. Regardless of whether or not the trader is looking at data in 30-minute blocks for one complete trading day, 60-minute blocks for one trading week, or 15-minute blocks for 87 days, *ad absurdum,* bell shapes would always appear with that frequency within the confines of those time limits. The ramifications are now crystal clear.

Whatever time interval the day trader is using, he can expect the 70/30 split. The beauty of this conclusion is that within the sampling of fixed time intervals, the yet-to-be-formed bell shape is evolving. Seventy percent of the time it evolves into a bell shape and 30 percent of the time it doesn't; of course, the shape is not known until the actual number of sampling periods is completed. What pre-indications can be found that would lead to above average conclusions?

If the trader goes on the assumption that there is a 70 percent probability that a bell shape will occur after a specified time, he would not be far wrong in concluding that prior to the end of that specified time period, certain developing formations will lead to the eventual bell shape. If the trader breaks the trading day in half, and he concludes that the evolving shape will turn into a bell, then he could reasonably infer that half of the bell had formed after half of the day's trades were in, and that the other half of the bell would be formed before the end of the day!

We now have a powerful conclusion.

Figure 7.5
A hypothetical first half of a trading day.

```
262 1/8
262        X
261 7/8    XXX
261 3/4    XXXX
261 5/8    XXXXXX
261 1/2    XXXXXXXX
261 3/8
261 1/4
261 1/8
261
260 7/8
```

If the shape on the right side of Figure 7.5 forms during the first half of the trading day, the implication is that a normal price distribution with a 70 percent probability of occurrence will be completed, creating a perfect bell-shaped distribution pattern Figure 7.6.

Of course, a distribution of data rarely creates a perfectly shaped half-bell exactly at the halfway mark of the data distribution chain. However, this is the theoretical framework into which real-time data can be fit. In actual trading the bell is never formed with such harsh demarcation of prices, but more with gentle shading, and overlapping that begins progressively and moves toward full violation of the theoretical borders.

Figure 7.6
A normal price distribution.

```
262 1/8
262        X
261 7/8    XXX
261 3/4    XXXX
261 5/8    XXXXXX
261 1/2    XXXXXXXX
261 3/8    OOOOOO
261 1/4    OOOO
261 1/8    OOO
261        O
260 7/8
```

Figure 7.7
Progressive development of the normal market profile pattern.

#1 Profile		#2 Profile	
TYM	$9621\frac{}{32}$	USM	$9401\frac{}{32}$
B		BDE	
B	$9619\frac{}{32}$	BDE	$9331\frac{}{32}$
B		BDE	
BD*	$9617\frac{}{32}$	BCDE	$9329\frac{}{32}$
BD*	←	BCDEG*	
BCDEH*	$9615\frac{}{32}$	BCDEFGH*	$9327\frac{}{32}$
BCDEFGH		BCDEFGH*	
BCDEFGH	$9613\frac{}{32}$	BCDEFGH* ←	$9325\frac{}{32}$
BCDEFGH		ABCEFGH	
ABCEF	$9611\frac{}{32}$	ABCEFG	$9323\frac{}{32}$
ABEF		ABCEF	
AB →	$9609\frac{}{32}$	ABCEF	$9321\frac{}{32}$
A		ABC	
A	$9607\frac{}{32}$	AB	$9319\frac{}{32}$
A		AB →	
A	$9605\frac{}{32}$	A	$9317\frac{}{32}$
A		A	
A	$9603\frac{}{32}$	A	$9315\frac{}{32}$
A		A	
A	$9601\frac{}{32}$	A	$9313\frac{}{32}$
A		A	
A	$9531\frac{}{32}$	A	$9311\frac{}{32}$
A		A	
	$9529\frac{}{32}$	A	$9309\frac{}{32}$
		A	
		A	$9307\frac{}{32}$
		A	
		A	$9305\frac{}{32}$
			$9304\frac{}{32}$

As Figure 7.7 shows, the normal profile is seldom initiated in such a perfectly formed fashion as the previous two profiles showed. Instead the profiles will start with one period, followed by many overlapping periods, which then eventually form a normal bell shape.

Applying the above observation of the developing profile allows the trader to take positions fully expecting that prices will move to form the other half of the yet-unformed bell before the full set of trading data is created. This, then, is the forecasting strength of the approach!

There are several strategies for trading the developing profile. The primary strategies are based on the 70 percent probability that, after all the data is plotted, a normal bell-shaped curve will be formed and that price will settle in the middle of the distribution. Two strategies present themselves here: Sell the upper end and buy the lower end. If the plotted data does not maintain a bell shape (a 30 percent probability), it will indicate either a trending day or a nontrend day. If it is a trending day, then the price will more often than not settle towards the breakout to either new highs or new lows. If it is a nontrend day, then the range will be relatively small and there will be no profitable trading signals, because the countermove will be limited.

FLAW OF THE MARKET PROFILE AND THE VOLUME-DERIVED SOLUTION

In the process of developing this masterful approach to viewing price data only, something was overlooked: volume data. The availability of volume data forced the next stage of Market Profile development and analysis—adding volume data as another dimension of analysis. As will be seen later, this was a red herring leading away from the real analysis; the move to expand the profile approach begged an obvious question: At what critical point does the profile shift? (This question is similar to the question found in chaos analysis: At what point does the physical behavior break into another fractal layer?) Again, the issue of necessarily knowing volume for transactions, even in this analysis, forced the developer to go back to this tried-and-true variable. Please recall that in reading stock ticker transactions, the interaction of volume as a confirming indicator of buy or sell orders was critical to correct analysis and interpretations. The irony of this situation is that there really is no satisfactory way to analyze volume.

If the plain Market Profile was able to serve its masters so well, why then was it necessary for the developer of the approach to view volume data? If you can recall the sequence of development, you can read between the lines and conclude something of great importance. The Market Profile approach—without volume breakdowns—was conceived by Peter Steidlmayer and he used it successfully to trade the futures markets. The volume data was not important for the effective execution of the profile approach. Then, several years ago, the developer obtained permission from the Chicago Board of Trade to take the data stream and display the cumulative volume of each price. Why?

The reason is apparent if you apply the 70 percent occurrence of bell-shapes in the frequency of real-world events to a larger or smaller framework. Within the conditions that Steidlmayer created to apply the observation of data occurrences, he encountered the 30 percent of non-bell-shapes in the 1970s. That is, when the markets moved on an intraday basis, instead of forming a bell-shape, the prices would go and punch through new highs for the day before the day was over, or prices would go to new lows. In the framework of statistics, this type of price behavior was accounted for by the profile approach. Unfortunately, it just so happened that the 30 percent of the time that bell-shapes do not occur started to occur with greater than 30 percent frequency! In a sense the markets moved to a higher fractal (degree of difference unknown) in order to accommodate this frequency of observations.

Suddenly the changing market conditions turned what was once a low frequency of pattern occurrence into a high frequency of pattern occurrence. For the stipulated time periods, what once was appearing with a frequency of 30 percent was now appearing with greater frequency. Of course, what was once occurring 70 percent of the time appeared less frequently; it was still there, but on a smaller scale.

From the early 1970s to the mid-1980s market volatility in the futures complex went through the roof; extending even to the stock and bond area, the increased volatilities created the profit opportunities in the derivative options (if you believe otherwise, observe the decrease in option trading once the markets decrease in price activity). What the profile trader saw was a continuous oscillation between a spectrum of fractals. One day, the profile pattern created with one set of parameters, say, a half-hour bar chart of a full day of trading, showed the bell shape. The next day such a chart did not show a bell shape but the shape did appear if the trader filtered the data through a 15-minute bar chart of a half-day of trading. It was this oscillation that caused havoc to the simplistic profile approach: What caused the increasing occurrence of the shift?

But before we attempt to answer the immediate question we should consider the following: How was the newly revised Market Profile, that is, with the addition of the dimension of volume to the analysis, going to help the trader in her analysis? From the earlier section on tape reading, you discovered how critical it was to know what volume was associated with what trade. The volume of the trade shows to the tape reader how important the price associated with that trade was to the parties involved in the trades. The inference is that increased volume reveals where most investors or speculators had interests. If price was not hooked up with an increased volume, then the inference is that no interests are there for that pricing.

The Liquidity Data Bank started as an end-of-the-day report because the hardware and software created by the Chicago Board of Trade could not cumulate the volume per price on a real-time basis. With the volume available per price, there were now in effect two profiles to compare: the first and original profile of price distribution and the second profile of volume distribution. Some real-time analysis software creates a tick-volume chart that can be reassembled into a volume profile distribution. This software shows the *actual frequency change in prices* during the course of the real-time trading, not the actual volume of contracts traded per price. From my observations, there is about a 60 percent to 70 percent correlation between the pattern developed from such a tick-volume distribution and the actual Liquidity Data Bank profile.

What type of analysis can be applied to this distribution of the volume data? Why, the statistical distribution of the bell-shaped curve, of course. If volume were distributed across time parameters, there would be a 70 percent occurrence of bell shapes. The ideal analytical situation then would be to have a bell-shaped distribution of price *and* a bell-shaped distribution of volume for one market.

Now, insight into any observed behavior is generally not gleaned by simply observing the normal behavior; rather, it is the comparison of abnormal behaviors against a backdrop of normal behavior that offers the most insight. In this particular case, both distribution patterns for price and volume should be the same shape 70 percent of the time. When the distribution pattern for price is bell shaped and the distribution pattern for volume is *not* bell shaped, the recognition that one of the two patterns, or both patterns, are not synchronized provides another level of understanding of the dynamics of the markets. In this case, the profiles offered the trader correct data, but inconclusive decisions.

Where there is correlation of patterns, the strategy is to sell the upper range and buy the lower range with impunity. Where there is no confirmation of the bell-shape, with both volume pattern and price pattern differing, selling the high and buying the low is not warranted; other actions are not warranted either, whatever they may be.

I am not indifferent to the issues of correct applications of the Market Profile or the Liquidity Data Bank. (In an academic fashion, the questions raised must be answered; in practical matters, the academics really beg the question: How does one make money?)

Because volume is important to value analysis, and price is only as valuable as the markets make it, it appears that the Liquidity Data Bank can be more accurately used to forecast *imminent* volume movement, with its corresponding price move. Remember that trading the expected formation of the volume pattern doesn't make the profits, but rather the eventual price of the positions. There is no corresponding action of price to volume; hopefully, there is enough time available to the profile trader, both the price profile and the volume profile analyst, that would allow him or her valuable time to discard positions that do not perform to expectations.

MARKET PROFILE
AND THE NONSTANDARD DISTRIBUTION

The original development of the Market Profile centered on the premise that real-world events occur in bell-shaped distributions. Implicit in this observation was the fact that price then could be forecast with a greater-than-even probability. But for all practical purposes the markets evolved so that the patterning of the price data flipped continually from one scale to another.

What was a valid strategy one day, that of selling the high and buying the low, was invalid the next day, when selling high or buying the low turned into buying the shorts in at higher prices or selling out longs at even lower prices. The patterning for the second day was valid, except that the observational scale changed, and in order for the trader to justify selling in the second day, he had to view the price action of the second day as part of a two-part composite pattern; for instance, if the trader took the second day's price action and plotted it with the third day, he could have seen that the high shown on the second day really wasn't the high of the two-day move, but rather the middle of the move.

The question that should have been answered was the following: How does the market shift from one patterning scale to the next? Unfortunately, the answer to that question will not be found in even more precise applications of the profile approach. This subject was broached slightly in the first chapter in the section on fractionation and will be the subject of future books.

In the evolution of this technique, the primary purpose was to make do with the only dimension of technical analysis then available to the commodity trader: price, made available during the course of a trading day. It is still the only available data for analysis. The genius of Peter Steidlmayer rests in the fact that he took statistical probability and forced the price distributions into

Figure 7.8
Procedure for market analysis and trading decisions using the CBOT Liquidity Data Bank and Market Profile. (Courtesy CISCO.)

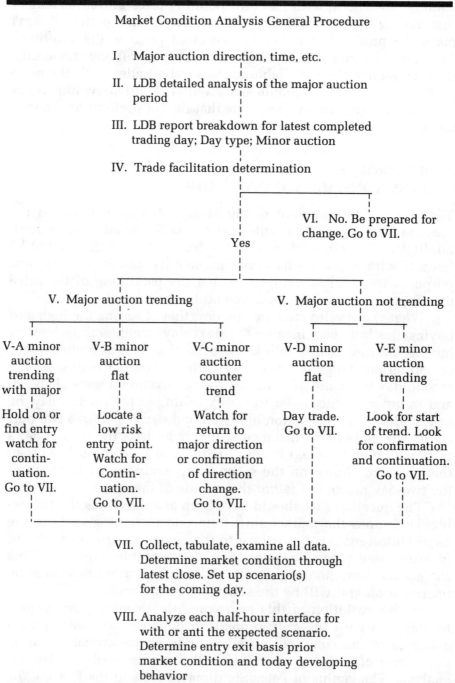

Market Condition Analysis General Procedure

I. Major auction direction, time, etc.

II. LDB detailed analysis of the major auction period

III. LDB report breakdown for latest completed trading day; Day type; Minor auction

IV. Trade facilitation determination

VI. No. Be prepared for change. Go to VII.

Yes

V. Major auction trending

V. Major auction not trending

V-A minor auction trending with major	V-B minor auction flat	V-C minor auction counter trend	V-D minor auction flat	V-E minor auction trending
Hold on or find entry watch for continuation. Go to VII.	Locate a low risk entry point. Watch for Continuation. Go to VII.	Watch for return to major direction or confirmation of direction change. Go to VII.	Day trade. Go to VII.	Look for start of trend. Look for confirmation and continuation. Go to VII.

VII. Collect, tabulate, examine all data. Determine market condition through latest close. Set up scenario(s) for the coming day.

VIII. Analyze each half-hour interface for with or anti the expected scenario. Determine entry exit basis prior market condition and today developing behavior shapes of frequency occurrences. In this manner he took a presumed and reliable shape and compared it to the prices forming the shape. If prices, as so distributed, took on the shape of a normal bell, then he played the market accordingly. If not, then he did not move into the markets.

Most of the time this approach did show what was expected in the developing bell shape. However, it also gave the impression that it could forecast all movements. Not so. The approach could forecast movements only if the shape developing looked like a normal bell; when the shape suddenly appeared to be moving into another pattern—nontrending or trending—the forecasting strength of the approach went by the wayside.

There have been minor attempts to forecast the development of the trending day. Trending days have prices that will be dramatically higher or lower than prices from the earlier part of the trading time period. One weak attempt to forecast the imminent development of a trending day rests on the observation that prices move dramatically in the first two time blocks; the direction of the move in the first two time blocks will show the general direction of the trend. Please note that the trending day's first two time periods are important in determining its formation, whereas the normal day requires about half the time period to be collected before a better estimate can be made. For most markets there are 12 half-hour time periods in a normal day, so the correctness of a prognostication of the possible formation of the normal day cannot be determined until at least 6 half-hour time periods have been observed. (See Figure 7.8 for the analysis.*)

*The flow chart in Figure 7.8 is reprinted courtesy CISCO from their book *Applications of the Market Profile: A Trader's Guide to Auction Markets* (Chicago: Commodity Information Services Co., 1988). For more details on terminology please refer to this work.

8

Using Chart Patterns

Applying long-term techniques to short time frames is a reduction-ist approach that works best when there is a major trend for traders to follow such techniques: It is a sort of self-fulfilling prophecy. In effect, each trader who gives credence to the microcosmic aspect of this approach adds to the validity of the forecastability of the techniques themselves.

There are three methods of technical analysis that can be re-duced to shorter time frames. The first one is the tried-and-true method that combines bar chart analysis, related point and fig-ure chart analyses, and arithmetic studies. The second method is pattern recognition on an interday basis, which extends to some degree from two consecutive day's patterning. The final method is the application of the Elliott wave theory on shorter time frames.

CHART PATTERNS

Chart patterns were popularized by Robert D. Edwards and John Magee with their seminal book *Technical Analysis of Stock Trends* (Springfield: John Magee Publisher, first published in 1948.) Ed-wards and Magee confined their work to the area of daily bar charts; however, current day traders have fractaled the charts out to cover shorter durations. In attempts to find these patterns in shorter du-ration charts, a certain amount of success has been ascribed to the correct reading of chart patterns.

Chart patterns are classified into three types: reversal patterns; congestion patterns; and the connective patterns between the re-versal and congestion patterns, which are called *trending patterns*.

The following section is illustrated with shorter-than-daily bar charts. The text is abbreviated by design because the method of daily bar charts analysis is applicable to shorter-term bar charts. It is therefore not necessary to rewrite this section specifically for 5-minute, 15-minute, or 30-minute bar charts.

Figure 8.1
Head-and-shoulder top.

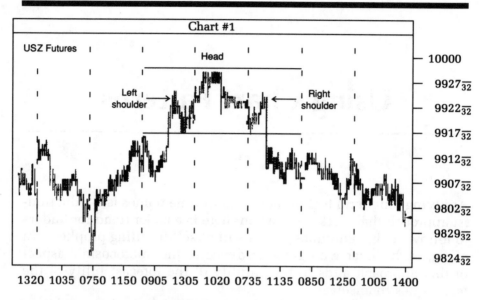

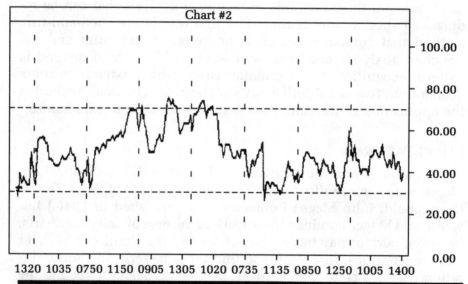

Reversal Patterns

The following are the reversal patterns that are found on interday
bar charts:

1. Head-and-shoulder tops and bottoms
2. Rounded bottoms or tops
3. Double bottoms or tops (multiple bottoms or tops)

Figure 8.2
Head-and-shoulder bottom.

4. Diamonds as reversals
5. Wedge tops

The head-and-shoulder top in Figure 8.1 was made with a 15-minute bar chart of the December U.S. bond futures contract. Note the left shoulder topped out at around the 99 26/32 level. The head was made with a high of 99 29/32. The formation took about two days to be completed and finished at a current level of 99 2/32.

The head-and-shoulder bottom in Figure 8.2 was made in the Dow Jones Industrials with a 5-minute bar chart. There is something very unique about this bottom: There is a double-bottom head. The first low head was made around the 2643.70 level and

Figure 8.3
Rounded top.

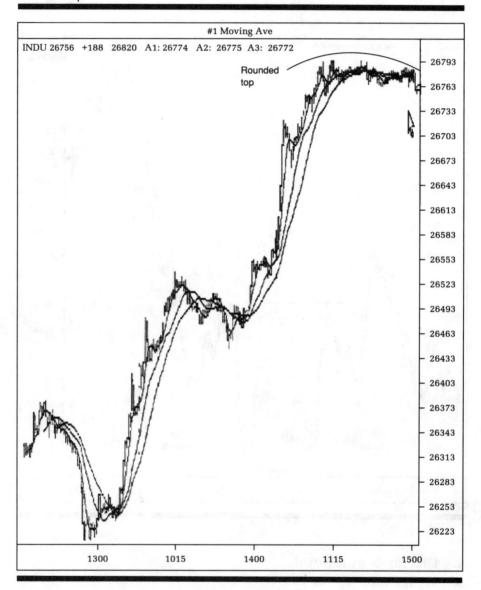

was followed by a move to the upside that was stopped at the 2654.00 level. A retest of the previous low dropped below the first support by a slight amount. The left shoulder was then evenly balanced by a right shoulder formation. Once price went above the right shoulder around 2661.20 level, the formation was complete and prices went to the upside.

Rounded bottoms or tops are rare in intraday charts, just as they are also very hard to find in daily bar charts. The one example

Figure 8.4
Triple-top formations.

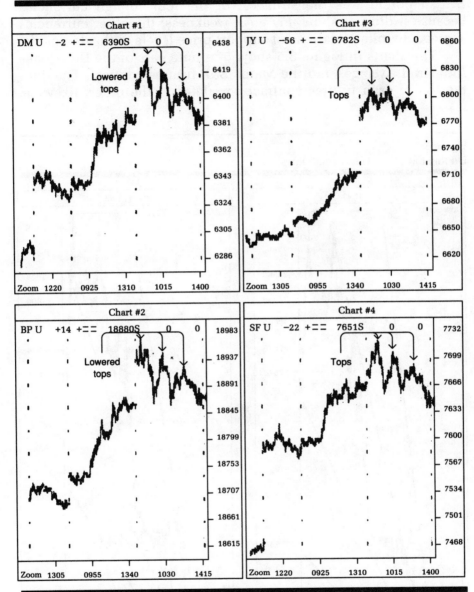

shown in Figure 8.3 is a rounded top of the Dow Jones Industrial Averages that took about 3/4 of a trading day to complete. The chart also shows moving averages of the 5-minute bars. The moving averages helped in determining when the topping formation was completed: It was completed when prices broke to the downside, away from the moving averages.

Figure 8.4 shows 5-minute charts of the September Deutschemark, the September Japanese yen, the September British pound, and the September Swiss franc. The topping-out action shows triple-top formations in all of the contracts. In relative terms, the British pound was the strongest of the four foreign currencies because it did not show any great weakness; the other currencies showed definite violations of support price levels to the downside.

The charts in Figure 8.5 show 5-minute bars of the Dow Jones Industrial Averages and the March S&P futures contract. The double top in each futures contract correlates to the other; likewise,

Figure 8.5
Double tops, with Gann angle lines.

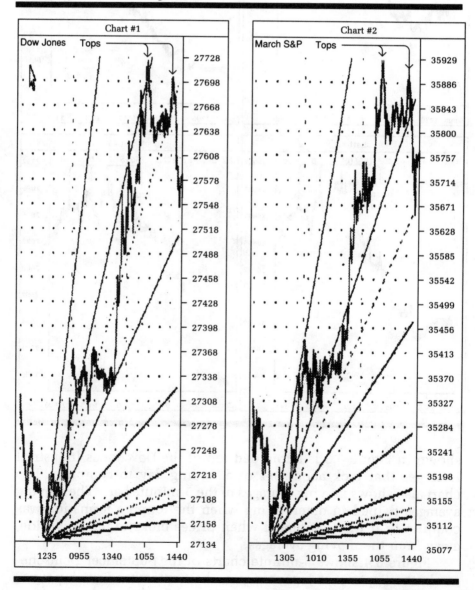

the validity of each reversal formations is confirmed by the other. The Gann angles that I have entered on the charts give the trader a series of reference lines to gauge market action. If you inspect the chart, you will observe that the Dow Jones Industrial Averages is the stronger of the two because it held above the 2751.80 level, which was a strong support line; the S&P futures touched the Gann line at 356.71 which was also a strong support line.

The charts in Figure 8.6 show the Dow Jones Industrials and

Figure 8.6
Double bottom in the Dow Jones Industrial Average, unconfirmed by the S&P futures contract.

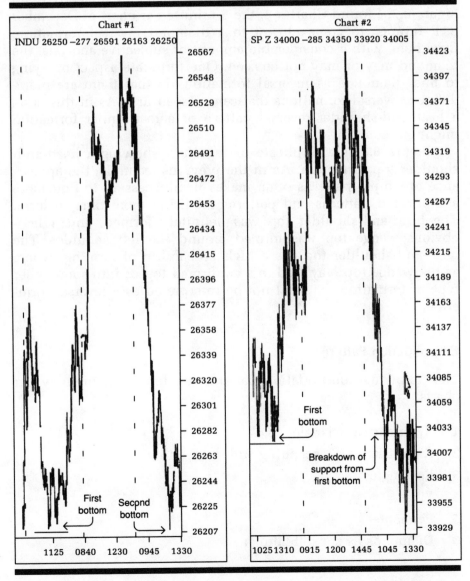

the December S&P futures contract. It is interesting that the double-bottom formation developed from the Industrials was not confirmed by any double-bottom formation in the S&P futures contract. In fact, the selloff of the S&P futures went considerably below the first support level around the 340.33 level. In this particular case, one of two situations is possible: the Industrials may cause the S&P futures to rally, or the S&P futures may drag the Industrials through the support levels. This type of price action serves to warn the trader not to go long or short, but to stop and observe.

Like rounded tops and bottoms, diamonds as reversals are very hard to discover. When you are trying to find a diamond formation, your viewpoint has a greater degree of subjectivity. In Figure 8.7, I found Chart #2, the 5-minute bar chart of December S&P futures, to come closest to a diamond reversal formation. Even here, with a considerable amount of subjective analysis, the diamond may or may not be seen. One fortunate aspect of trying to find diamonds as reversal formations is that there are more-defined reversal formations that can be seen first. As in this case, a head-and-shoulder reversal pattern or a rectangular formation might be seen.

Figure 8.8 is a duplicate of the chart showing a head-and-shoulder top formation. As in the previous example, the appearance of simple patterns often makes it unnecessary to find more complicated patterns and patterns requiring more time to form. The head-and-shoulder top was definitely formed, and a less-obvious wedge top was formed around the left shoulder. The head-and-shoulder top has a high probability of forming, where as the wedge top may lead to a confirmed top or into some other type of formation that will not be interpreted as a reversal formation.

Consolidation Patterns

The following consolidation patterns are found on interday bar charts:

1. Symmetrical triangles
2. Right triangles, ascending and descending
3. Rectangles
4. Flags
5. Pennants
6. Diamonds as consolidations

Figure 8.7
Possible diamond reversal formation.

Chart #1

INDU 26280 −247 26591 26203 26280

	26567
	26526
	26485
	26444
	26403
	26362
	26321
	26280
	26239

1425 1040 1325 0945 1230 0845 1130

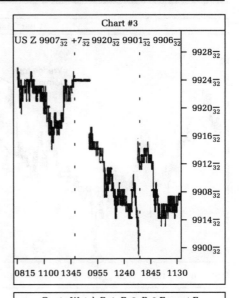

Chart #3

US Z $9907\frac{}{32}$ $+7\frac{}{32}$ $9920\frac{}{32}$ $9901\frac{}{32}$ $9906\frac{}{32}$

	$9928\frac{}{32}$
	$9924\frac{}{32}$
	$9920\frac{}{32}$
	$9916\frac{}{32}$
	$9912\frac{}{32}$
	$9908\frac{}{32}$
	$9914\frac{}{32}$
	$9900\frac{}{32}$

0815 1100 1345 0955 1240 1845 1130

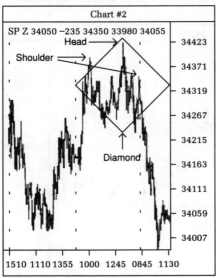

Chart #2

SP Z 34050 −235 34350 33980 34055

Head

Shoulder

Diamond

	34423
	34371
	34319
	34267
	34215
	34163
	34111
	34059
	34007

1510 1110 1355 1000 1245 0845 1130

Quote Watch Pg1, Pg2, Pg3 Format F

SYMBL	LAST	NET	SYMBL	LAST	NET	SYMBL		Pg
INDU	26280	−247	CT Z	7175	−56	W	N	1
TRAN	11764	−148	BO Z	1957	−17	W	U	2
UTIL	21969	−139	C H	242	$-1\frac{3}{4}$	W	Z	3
COMP	998	−9	C K	$246\frac{1}{4}$	$-1\frac{1}{4}$	S	F	4
XMI	52301	−379	C N	$250\frac{1}{4}$	$-\frac{1}{4}$	S	H	5
QEX	31671	−271	C U	$244\frac{1}{4}$	−1	S	K	6
SPX	33912	−249	C Z	$237\frac{1}{4}$	$-2\frac{1}{4}$	S	N	7
SP Z	34050	−235	O H	$158\frac{1}{4}$	$-1\frac{1}{4}$	S	Q	8
US Z	$9907\frac{}{32}$	$+7\frac{}{32}$	O K	$163\frac{1}{4}$	−2	S	U	9
SI Z	5720	+35	O N	$169\frac{1}{4}$	$-1\frac{1}{2}$	S	X	10
GC Z	3968	+10	O U	$173\frac{1}{4}$	−1	S		11
PA Z	14675	+115	O Z	146	$-1\frac{1}{2}$	BO	F	12
CP Z	10710	−170	W H	412	$-\frac{1}{4}$	BO	H	13
SM F	1853	−18	W K	$392\frac{1}{4}$	0	BO	K	14
						BO	N	15

Figure 8.8
Head-and-shoulder top.

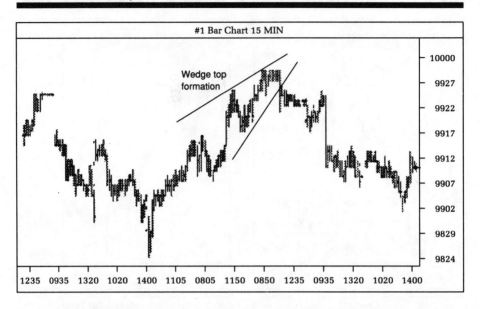

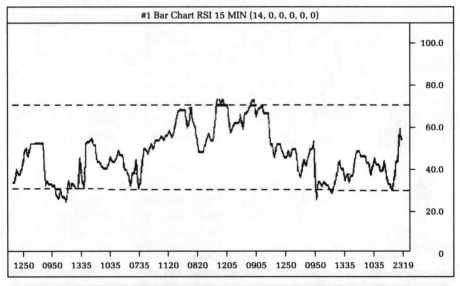

Symmetrical triangles can be found in almost any chart. These formations show an initial imbalance between supply and demand; as the formation develops further, though, supply and demand become more balanced and the market makes a move out of the pattern. In Figure 8.9, a 5-minute line chart of the Dow Jones Industrials, you can see that the symmetrical triangle eventually leads to higher prices.

Figure 8.9
Symmetrical triangle.

Figure 8.10
Symmetrical triangle.

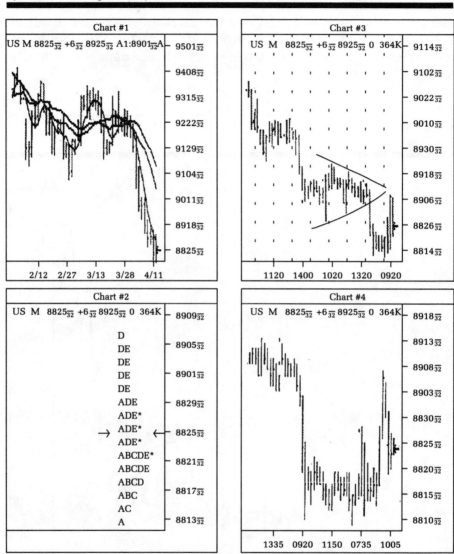

The symmetrical triangle in Figure 8.10 is found in a 60-minute bar chart of the June U.S. Treasury bond futures contract. As prices narrowed, the forces built for a continuation of prices from which the pattern evolved, which resulted in lower prices.

The right triangle in Figure 8.11 is of the ascending right variety. A 5-minute bar chart of the June S&P futures contract is marked with an ascending right triangle. Once prices took out 355.40 to the upside, the market moved considerably higher.

Figure 8.11
Ascending right triangle.

The 15-minute bar chart of the December U.S. bond futures in Figure 8.12 shows a descending right triangle that formed around 99 5/32. At the beginning of the chart, prices had just broken any supports around 99 2/32.

Rectangles are seldom found in intraday charts. The primary reason is that, in order for rectangles to form, balance between buy and sell orders must be established over a longer time period—

Figure 8.12
Descending right triangle.

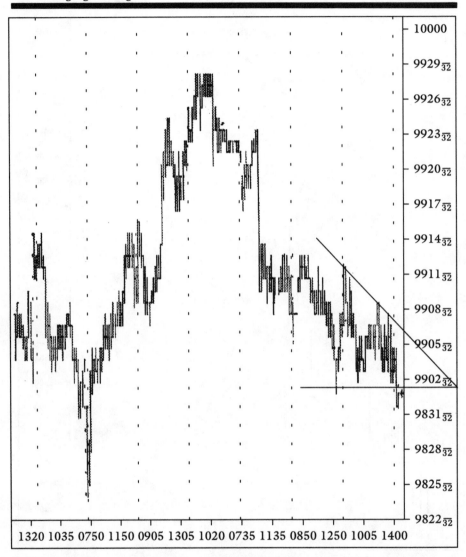

several days or even weeks. In intraday trading, analysis is given in 5-minute intervals—much too short a period for any solid balance between buy and sell orders. The example of a rectangle consolidation pattern in Figure 8.13 is actually closer to a symmetrical triangle formation. This is, however, the closest instance I found to illustrating a rectangle consolidation pattern.

Figure 8.13
Rectangle consolidation pattern.

Flags as consolidation patterns can likewise be discerned in intraday charts. In Figure 8.14, a 15-minute bar chart of the December U.S. bonds, one noticeable flag formation is marked. The problem with trying to find flag formations in intraday charts is that they are so fleeting, compared to larger formations such as the head-and-shoulders reversal pattern. When seen in intraday charts,

Figure 8.14
Flag formation.

flags happen so momentarily that they can easily be mistaken for other formations. In this example the flag could have been mistaken for a left shoulder of a head-and-shoulder bottom formation (if a right shoulder had formed after the lowest head).

This attempt at finding the more esoteric patterns in intraday charts is merely an exercise. In practical terms, there are other formations with more valid implications that can form.

Figure 8.15
Pennant consolidation pattern.

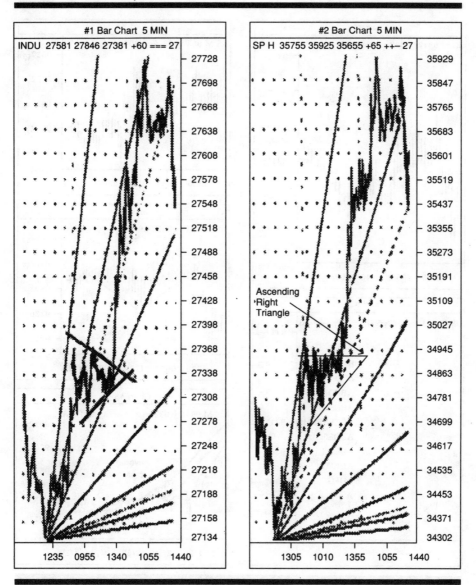

In my opinion, looking for pennant formations is pushing the aspect of pattern formation trading to an extreme. In Figure 8.15, a 5-minute bar chart of the Dow Jones Industrials, a small pennant consolidation is marked off as shown. Before discerning a pennant, however, you would have seen this as a simple ascending right triangle formation.

Diamonds are difficult to find, but there is something resembling a diamond consolidation pattern in #4 Chart of the June

Figure 8.16
Diamond consolidation pattern.

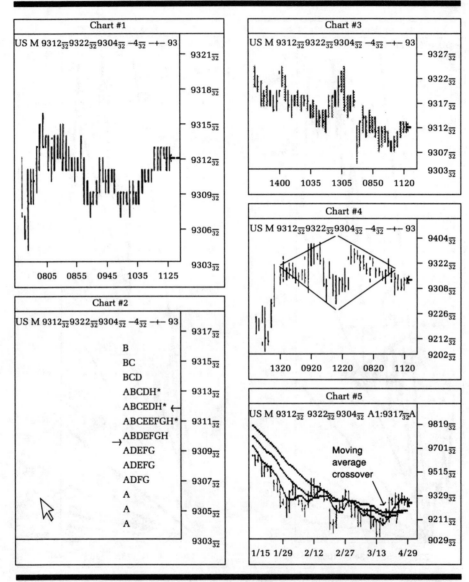

U.S. bond futures (Figure 8.16). The follow-through to the upside once the pattern was broken to the upside was weak; this can be interpreted by the analyst as a possible double top because prices traded across instead of upwards. But, upon inspecting the daily bar chart, one would find that a bottoming action had formed several weeks earlier. When one also learns that the moving averages crossed to the upside, it becomes apparent that this is, as predicted, a diamond consolidation extending to a wider congestion area.

Trending Patterns

The following are the *trending patterns,* or those that connect the consolidation patterns with the reversal patterns.

1. Fan lines
2. Gaps
3. Trendlines and channels

Fan lines are basic trending patterns. In Figure 8.17, a 5-minute bar chart of the June U.S. bond futures, I have constructed several

Figure 8.17
Fan lines.

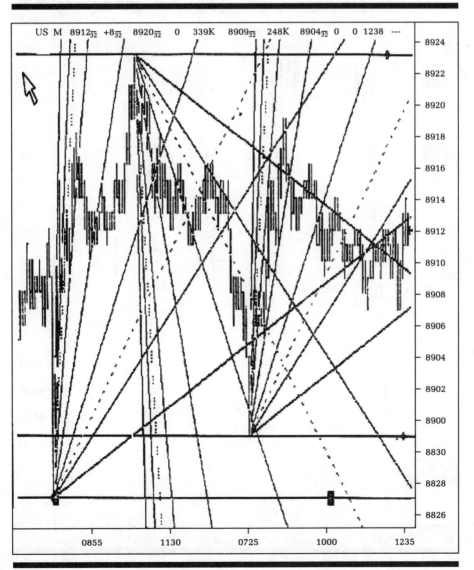

sets of Gann angle lines, which are more precise fan lines constructed around numerical ratios instead of empirically constructed trend lines. Note that, whenever prices broke through one supportive line to the downside, prices eventually went lower to another line. Conversely, note that, when prices broke a Gann line constructed from a high swing price point (that is, prices moved up), prices eventually tested other resistive Gann lines.

There are several varieties of gaps. In this blatant example of gaps (Figure 8.18), a 5-minute bar chart of November lumber fu-

Figure 8.18
Obvious gaps.

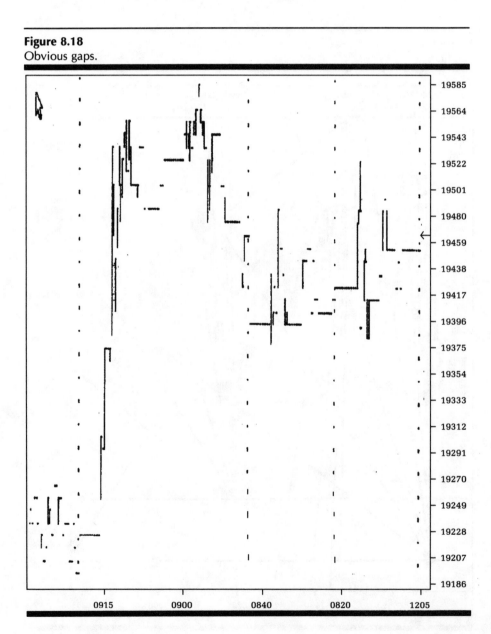

Figure 8.19
Smaller (but significant) gaps.

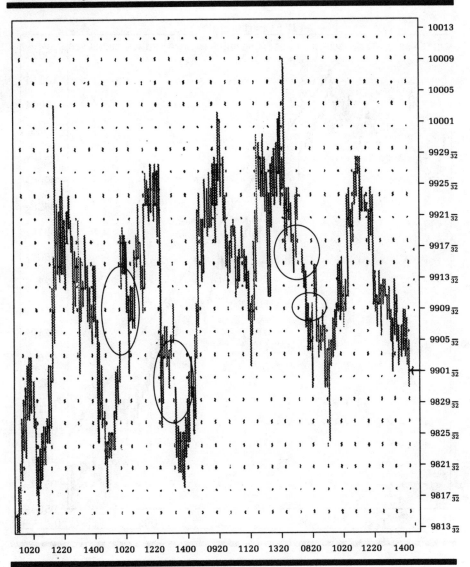

tures, you can easily see many gaps. These gaps all signify that
there is no interest in trading this futures contract. In this case
the fact that there are gaps, should negate any reasons an intraday
trader might have to consider trading this lumber contract.

In this example of gaps, a 60-minute bar chart (Figure 8.19),
you can see that this June bond futures contract trades with a great
amount of liquidity. Gaps that are found in this chart are of significance and deserve thorough analysis.

Figure 8.20
Downtrending trend line.

#4 Bar Chart 60 MIN

US H 9520$\frac{32}{32}$ 9521$\frac{32}{32}$ 9508$\frac{32}{32}$ 0 −+− 9521$\frac{32}{32}$ 9520$\frac{32}{32}$ 9521$\frac{32}{32}$ 9526$\frac{32}{32}$ 0 1315 202K −208

Figure 8.20, a, 60-minute bar chart of the March U.S. bond futures, illustrates well the downtrending trend line. Please note that prices could not move above this line. The question you should ask is, "How can one trade against this trend line?" The two times that the price touched the trend line could have been used as sell points, but where could other trades have been initiated? See Figure 8.21.

In Figure 8.21, the set of uptrending trend lines, one supportive (the lower one) and one parallel to the supportive, provides a channel in which prices will oscillate while trending upwards. By drawing a third trend line between the two existing trend lines, you can create a buying area. This buying area exists when prices reach the lower half of the area set off by the three trend lines. See Figure 8.22 to see an actual set of lines so drawn.

Please note that the 60-minute bar chart in Figure 8.22 has three parallel lines. The intraday trader would sell longs out in the area bounded by the upper two parallel trend lines and buy when prices dropped between the lower two parallel trend lines. Drawing the third trend line increases the range of prices where the intraday trader can enter positions. Just following one supportive trend line would only give a few buy points—at only those points where prices drifted to the trendline. In fact, it can be dangerous to buy at these price points because there is an uncertain situation that occurs when prices can get back to testing supports or resistance marked off by the trend lines: The supports may hold, or they might not.

POINT-AND-FIGURE CHARTING

Intraday analysis of point-and-figure charts is classified in the same manner as classical daily bar chart analysis. Such analysis is feasible only to the extent that the daily point-and-figure charts work.

The essential purpose of using point-and-figure charts is to determine where price activity is consolidating. Once a consolidation area is observed, then—depending on where price had been before the development of the consolidation area—a valid forecast can be made of future price activity. The consolidation area is defined by a range of price movements. That is, the greater the frequency of price movements, the less the price congestion; the more compact the price movements, the greater the congestion area. Once price moves away from the congestion area—depending on where it came from and how it came into the congestion area—prices will either reverse or continue. This approach is not

Figure 8.21
Uptrending trend lines.

#1 Bar Chart 5 MIN

INDU 27259 27295 27140 −153 = − = 27259 27261 28370   0 0907 24

Figure 8.22
Trend lines.

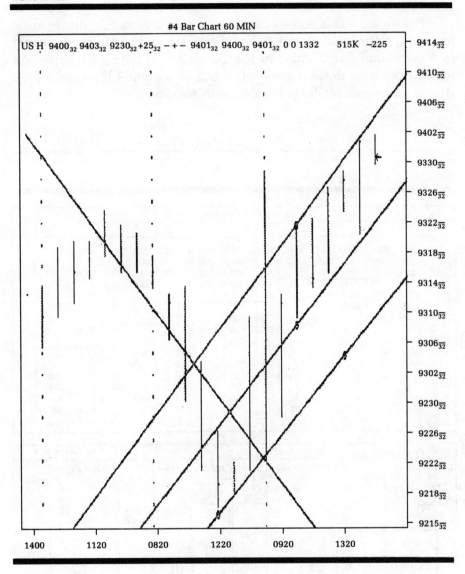

too dissimilar to the classification of price bar charts into the following three categories: price reversal, price continuation, or price resting.

Figure 8.23 is a screen capture of one screen the author uses to analyze the markets on an intraday basis. The rightmost chart is a point-and-figure chart of the December U.S. bond futures. As an adjunct technique it is helpful, but as a stand-alone technique it is rather weak for intraday decision making.

Figure 8.23
Point-and-figure chart.

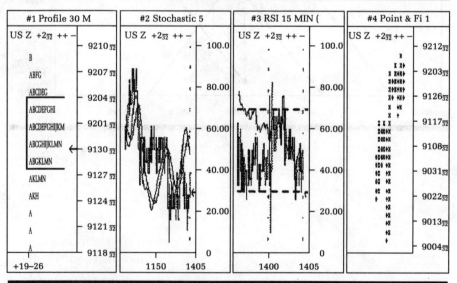

Figure 8.24
Daily bar chart.

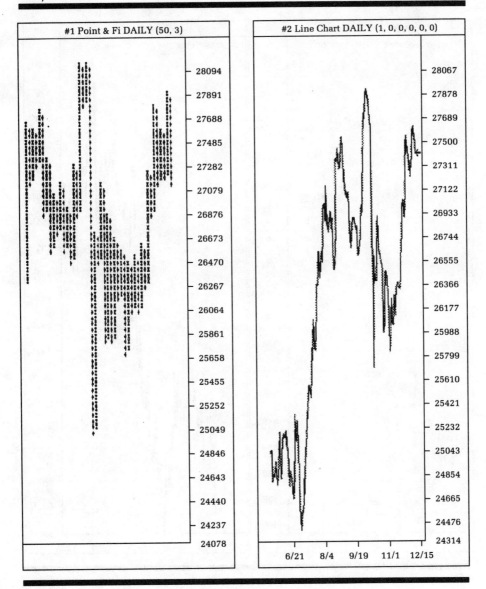

Figure 8.24 is of a daily bar chart of the Dow Jones Industrials. The author used this chart as a starting point of analysis for another scaled analysis. Note that waves and congestions are easily discerned with point-and-figure charts, unlike in the line chart, which has a bit of noise.

Figure 8.25
Point-and-figure chart.

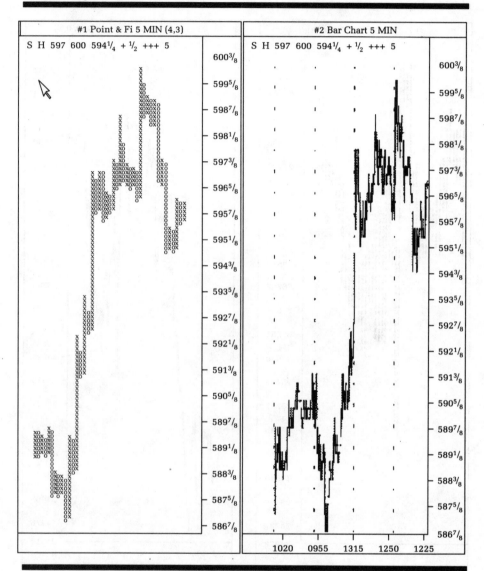

Figure 8.25, a point-and-figure chart of 5-minute bars of the March soybean contract, shows the waves forming with greater clarity. The congestions are also displayed with greater accuracy. Note that some of the jiggles and congestions in the bar chart never show up on the point-and-figure chart, which would facilitate Elliott wave counting.

9

Mathematical Approaches to Day Trading

The mathematical approaches are relatively new in the area of technical analysis. As daily bar charts and daily data point and figure charts were refined to be used in intraday trading, so also mathematical approaches were developed using daily bar chart data such as open, high, low, and close prices.

The following are typical mathematical approaches that have been developed for daily bar chart data and have now been refined for use in shorter time bars:*

1. Moving Averages
2. Commodity Channel Index
3. Parabolic
4. Oscillators
5. Relative Strength
6. Spreads
7. Stochastics

MOVING AVERAGES

There are several variant forms of moving averages, including simple moving averages, exponentially smoothed moving averages, smoothed moving averages, and weighted moving averages. Within the context of moving averages, the actual set of data can be offset forward or backward, depending on what the trader wishes to do with the data. (It is my opinion that offsets don't do much of anything in forecasting price movements.) The averages can be used on any of the prices found in the short bar and a series of envelopes

*The formulas for calculating these indicators manually are not listed in this book. Most formulas may be found in *The Technical Analysis of Stocks, Options and Futures* or in Jack D. Schwager, *A Complete Guide to the Futures Markets* (New York: John Wiley & Sons, 1984).

can be developed to encompass price action. Again, I have not found much use for enveloping price action, because prices will not necessarily be contained within a price envelope that the user predefines! There is a case where using a standard deviation to increase or decrease the envelope is helpful (they were created by John Bollinger; they are called Bollinger Bands).

The author uses moving averages on a large-scale analysis. A daily bar chart analysis is the starting point of using other tech-

Figure 9.1
Moving average charts for various financial futures contracts.

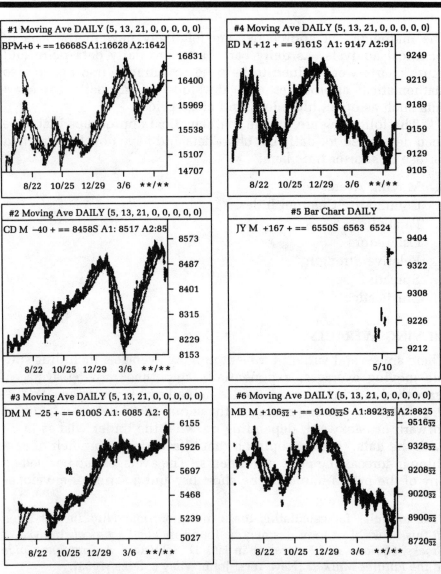

niques. Figure 9.1 is a series of charts of the foreign currencies and some interest rate contracts.

The moving averages are constructed to give me a general idea of the market strength or weakness.

Even though there are other moving averages—exponential, smoothed, and weighted averages—I seldom use them because they are redundant; I have seldom found them useful.

Figure 9.2 is a screen that I use to take the general perspective of moving averages into consideration. Note that from the moving

Figure 9.2
Screen showing moving average, bar charts, and Market Profile.

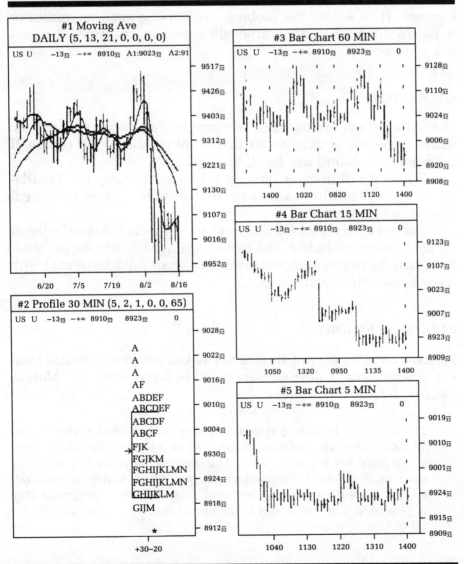

averages I also look at the simple 60-minute and 15-minute chart. The Market Profile chart is analyzed to see where possible signals could be generated.

THE COMMODITY CHANNEL INDEX AND DIRECTIONAL MOVEMENT

Neither the Commodity Channel Index nor the Directional Movement has done anything for me, and I see no reason why they would do anything for you. However, I welcome comments in this area.

Although I haven't found a good use for the Commodity Channel Index, I include a chart here (Figure 9.3) for your enjoyment. Here again, the problem with using such an indicator is determining when an overbought signal or an oversold signal is a valid one.

OSCILLATORS

Oscillators allow the trader to compare at least two sets of values. I have never found any use for this set of indicators. Of course, if the reader has found use for it, then use it.

Figure 9.4 illustrates, among other techniques, the Oscillator analysis. The time parameter of 5-minute bars is consistent throughout the analysis.

The #4 Chart is an Oscillator chart, a specific class of a larger set of momentum studies. The caveat, again, with momentum studies is that the overbought and oversold signals must be treated with more incisive interpretations.

PARABOLIC STUDIES

Parabolic studies are not studies per se but rather a technical trading system. The following paragraph is taken from the *Master-Chartist Instruction Manual*:

> The Parabolic technical system is a stop and reversal system based on both time and relative prices. When charted, the stops form a parabola or French curve. The system calculates a stop for each interval based on previous prices. When a stop is penetrated the current position is reversed and another appropriate stop is generated. Each indicator is therefore known as a Stop and Reversal (SAR).

Figure 9.3
Commodity Channel Index.

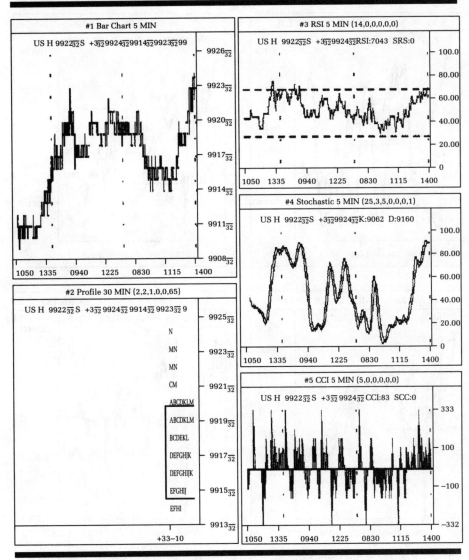

Figure 9.4
Oscillator analysis.

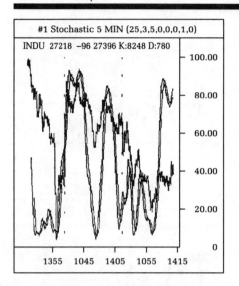

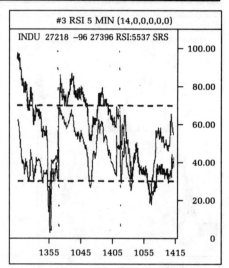

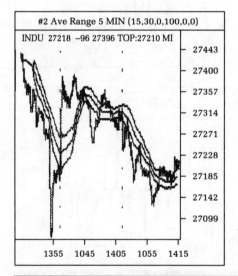

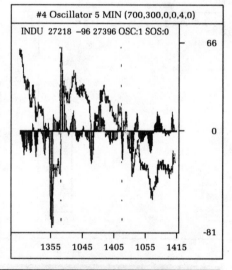

The Parabolic study found in Chart #5 of Figure 9.5 is constructed from 5-minute bar data of the March U.S. bond futures. Parabolic studies are not signal generators for the purpose of entering trades but rather are used to exit trades. They can be used to enter trades by merely treating exit signals as entry signals; however, this reinterpretation of signals creates the following situation.

Figure 9.5
Parabolic study.

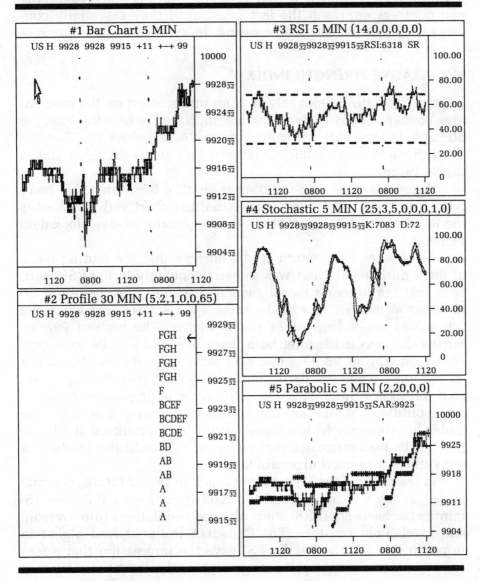

If used for exit signals, the trades would have had a chance to show profits prior to the exit so any loss of profits would not accrue to be a net loss of trading equity. If used as entry signals, the trades would not necessarily have shown profits, but they could definitely show large losses, which would be reflected in actual drawdowns of trading equity if the next signal showed exiting trades before any profits could have accrued.

The Parabolic study essentially generates exit signals for established positions. They work best in market stages that move from trading ranges to runaway markets. The signal numbers generated perform as lagging signals; that is, as the trending market ages, the exit numbers approach the last sales, until they essentially converge with the market price, meeting the generated signal price.

THE RELATIVE STRENGTH INDEX

Relative Strength Index analysis is an index based on the momentum concept. Tops or bottoms are indicated when the Relative Strength Index (RSI) penetrates above 70 or below 30. The RSI chart displays a thick horizontal grid line at the 70 value and at the 30 value.

Figure 9.6 shows a 5-minute bar chart of the March U.S. bond futures contract. #1 Chart is the actual bar chart and #2 Chart is the Relative Strength (RSI) study created from a 14-day block data segment.

As another momentum study, observe that the trading range of the 5-minute bar chart was shown adequately in the RSI chart. Note that the oversold signal generated when the price of the future was at 98 $^{19}/_{32}$ was in the same approximate area when the future was at 99 $^{11}/_{32}$, or 24 points higher. The high of 99 $^{18}/_{32}$ for the day was made after both these oversold signals were generated. Buying at 98 $^{19}/_{32}$ made 31 ticks of profit and buying at 99 $^{11}/_{32}$ only made 7 ticks of profit. Yet both signals to buy generated from the RSI study showed the same approximate degree of "oversoldness." While the signals were developing, how could the trader have known which signal would have produced the larger profit? The reader can see that using the RSI indicator by itself is not sufficient to maximize profits.

In the chart of the September Canadian Dollar futures contract traded at the Chicago Mercantile Exchange (Figure 9.7), the 15-minute bar basis chart RSI study showed oscillations into oversold and overbought territory. The Canadian Dollar moved higher in price. In this bull move, the RSI gave the impression that prices were trading in a tight price range. Again, the caveat to readers is to use momentum studies as an adjunct to other techniques.

Figure 9.6
Relative Strength Index (RSI).

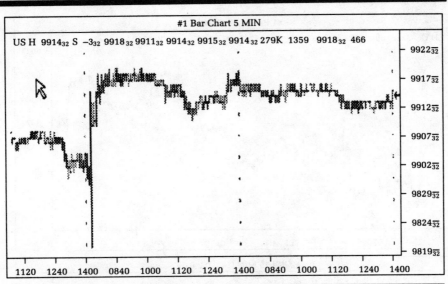

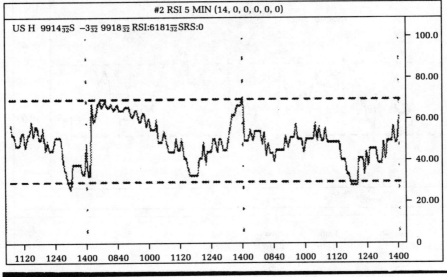

Figure 9.7
Relative Strength Index (RSI).

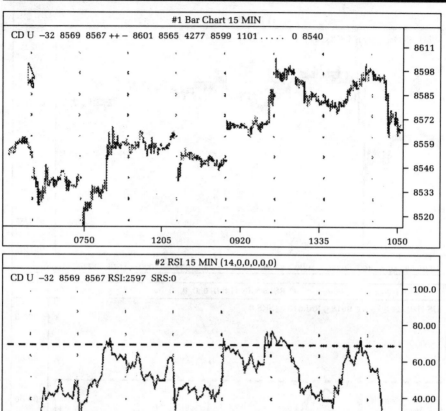

#	Time	High	Low	Last
223	1020	8578	8576	8576
>224	1035	8575	8572	8575
225	1050	8579	8573	8574

SPREAD CHARTING

Spread charts allow the trader to plot the absolute or relative difference between the last prices of one market and the last prices of another market.

The six charts in Figure 9.8 illustrate an overview of the underlying futures contracts and the spread relationship between such futures contracts. Note that the raw data for the charts is based on daily bar data.

Figure 9.8
Spread charts.

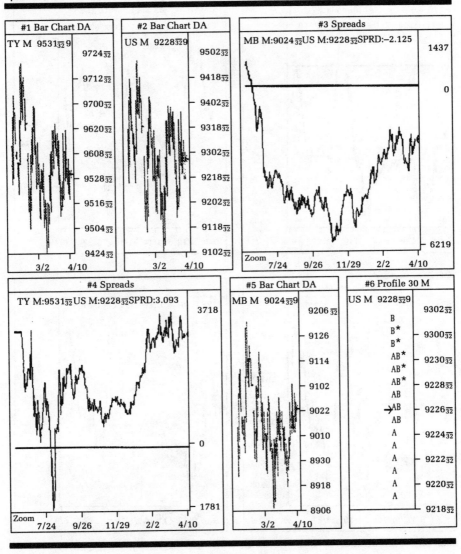

In each of the spread charts, line charts of the difference between the two separate closes of each underlying future are constructed. The line charts are created around a central zero point,
at which the two underlying futures of comparison are equal in
price. As you can see, there are many discernible chart trading patterns.

Figure 9.9 requires some explanation of background before I
can point out some interesting observations.

Figure 9.9
Spread charts.

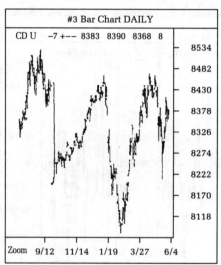

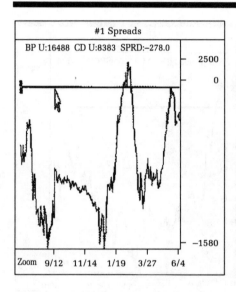

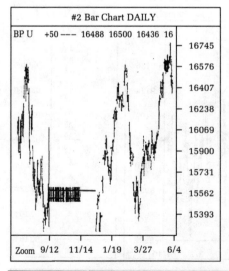

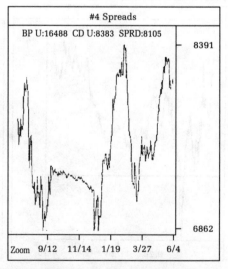

In #1 Chart, the difference between the September British Pound future (last sale of 164.88) and the September Canadian Dollar future (last sale of 83.83) is based on a difference between two times the number of Canadian Dollar contracts and one contract of British Pounds: [164.88 − (2 × 83.83)] = −2.78. The #4 Chart is a spread chart between one contract of September British Pound future and one contract of Canadian Dollar future: 164.88 − 83.83 = 81.05.

#2 Chart is a daily bar chart of the September British Pound contract. Note the period between 9–12 and 11–14 shows bad data, but the bad data will not affect the explanation. #3 Chart is a daily bar chart of the September Canadian Dollar contract.

Study the pattern of all four charts and note which ones are similar to each other: #1 Chart and #4 Chart. Recall that calculations for the two charts are somewhat different: #1 Chart has two times the weighing of the Canadian Dollar contract.

Interestingly enough, #2 Chart appears to be somewhat similar in appearance to #1 and #4 Charts. And lastly, #3 Chart is least similar to any of the other three charts.

What is the significance of this to spreading? In the language of spreading, the Canadian Dollar contract is the "dead leg" portion of the spread. This is so because the price movement of the Canadian Dollar doesn't affect the movement of the spread. The spread movement charts (regardless of the weighing of the Canadian Dollar value) resemble the outright British Pound contract chart, and not the Canadian Dollar chart.

For spread traders, then, trading the British Pound contract outright is just as good as spreading. In fact, spreading with these two markets doesn't dampen the volatility that would be inherent in trading the outright contracts themselves.

So why spread? The message here is that you shouldn't spread any market if you are not first willing to take outright long positions in bull markets or outright short positions in bear markets in any one particular market.

STOCHASTICS

Stochastics is a hybrid quantitative study of several different types of moving averages.

The charts in Figure 9.10 show 5-minute bar charts of November Soybeans and two separate studies: the Relative Strength Index and stochastics. They are presented here for inspection purposes. The formulas for their calculations can be found in my previous works.

Figure 9.10
Relative Strength Index (RSI) and stochastics.

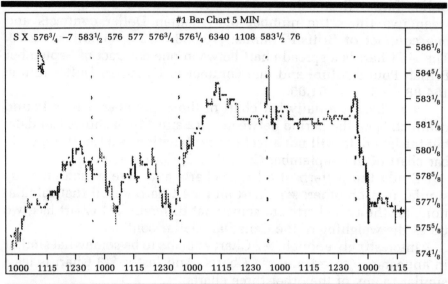

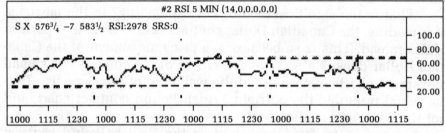

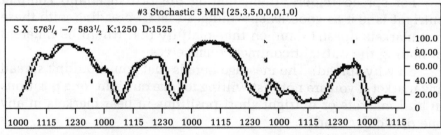

The set of four charts in Figure 9.11 shows how the stochastics differ when the lengths of the analyses are varied. All four charts are derived from the 5-minute bar chart data of the Dow Jones Industrial Averages, and the stochastic studies compare the 3-day moving average to the 5-day moving average. #1 Chart is derived from 25 bar blocks of data; #2 Chart is derived from 10 bar blocks;

Figure 9.11
Stochastics.

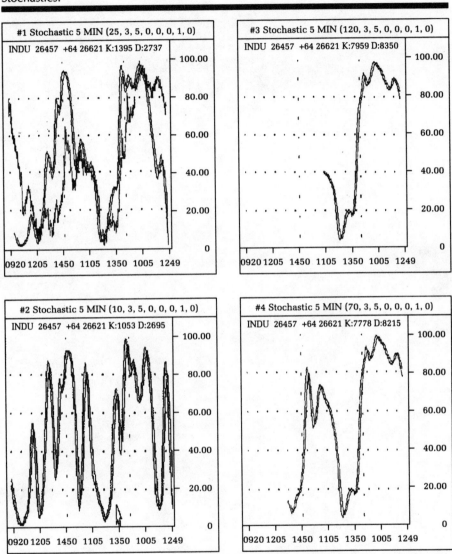

#3 Chart is derived from 120 bar blocks of data; and #4 Chart is derived from 70 bar blocks of data.

Compare the indicators shown in #2 Chart and #4 Chart. In #2 Chart, the stochastic indicator is approaching an oversold condition. Using the same raw data, but stretching the number of blocks from 10 to 70, #4 Chart just shows that the stochastic indicator is still above 80, or still in *overbought* territory!

10

Sequential Patterns
in Day Trading

Sequential patterning is a unique category in market analysis. In this particular approach the technical analyst records the up and down movements of the particular market studied in an attempt to find repeating patterns. From these repeating patterns, the analyst empirically forecasts the most likely next set of price movements.

Sequential pattern analysis is particularly well suited for day trading because an expected ending scenario is implied in the pattern approach. The time period of data collection may extend beyond the regular trading day to several days' market action. However, the time from the inception of the trade to the closing out of the trade is seldom more than one day.

There are five bodies of work that pertain to sequential pattern analysis. Early work and research was of limited use; however, it provides us with a backdrop for further analysis. The most recent work is the best among the five groups but is still of limited use. This is because the work does not study the sequential patterns across broadly defined variables, but rather, on selected variables.

FIRST PATTERNS

In 1921 a writer and market trader named William C. Moore wrote a book titled *Wall Street, Its Mysteries Revealed: Its Secrets Exposed.*[*] It was a thin volume amounting to less than 144 pages, but in its pages were the first reports on sequential patterns.

---

*William C. Moore, *Wall Street, Its Mysteries Revealed: Its Secrets Exposed* (Wells, VT: Fraser Publishing, 1921).

Moore proposed ten rules based on his observations of market price patterns. Not all of the rules pertained to sequential patterns and individual stocks, futures, and options; some of the rules applied to groups of stocks, futures, and options.

The warning to day traders is that these observations were made in 1909—the markets were then in different stages of market action. Some rules may be applied in our current market, but others should not be. The day trader must implement those observations that are still useful into a total trading strategy.

Rule One: Close-to-Open Market Action

Moore's first rule related to how stocks should be traded on the second day's opening prices with regard to how the stocks closed the day before. This was the first documented close-to-open pattern analysis. Moore indicated that stocks should, in general, be sold on the second day's opening if the previous closing prices of most of the stocks traded had been at their high prices of the day. The manner in which the first day's closing prices were recorded had a telltale effect on the next day's opening of prices: If the previous day's closing prices were mixed and irregular, then a similar opening action would warrant a sale.

The first rule was also applicable to the price action of a generally low and weak market close. If prices closed on the lows of the day, then a generally unchanged to slightly higher opening the next day would warrant a purchase. Moore viewed the weakness on high-price close (for sale on next day's opening) or the strength on low-price close (for purchase during next day's opening) of between one-half to two-thirds of the stocks observed to be a valid condition for executing his actions.

Rule Two: Buy on Three-Point Reaction

This rule pertains to individual issues and futures. If, in a sustained bull move, the stock takes out a former high by even a fraction and immediately reacts three points, it is then considered a purchase for at least a one-point upmove. The eventual expectation is that prices will take out the old highs (or at least a three-point upmove). If the price takes out a former high and retraces less than three points before it continues to new highs, then it is not considered to be a purchase. Why is this so? What Moore was looking for was basically a reaction in a bull market. Retracements of less than 3 points are not considered to be reactions, but merely to be interday price jiggles.

This rule was considered applicable only when the futures behaved in a conservative fashion. Moore stated that the rule was not to be applied to wheat, corn, and cotton because these markets were very erratic. The time frame in which this three-point reaction could occur ranged from one day to several days.

I believe that Moore's second rule is still valid in a few instances. There are two reasons why Moore's original observations have probable success. First, if the stock has enough strength to take out the old highs by a fraction of a point, there will be eventual buying to test the market's strength. Second, if the reaction immediately after the test is made is less than three points, then it is a high-probability prediction that the test of the previous high will be approximately three points or better. The point at which the high was made on the test is around the midpoint of a three-point sell-off and a three-point rally. That is, the old high will be right in the middle of the next swing up.

Rule Three: Taking Out Old Highs Warrants Purchases

This rule proposes that stock prices move in waves. If a stock makes a new high and, in a subsequent move to the upside, takes out the old highs by a half point, then, on any retracement, it is a purchase for an eventual move above the first high by at least two points. If the second move to new highs takes out the first high by a half point, then it is likely that a third move up will take it a full two points higher than the first high. Moore observed that prices in falling markets behaved with a sped-up time frame: The secondary move into new lows would oftentimes occur in the same day; in upmoves, the secondary move into new highs could occur as much as one to two months later.

Rule Four: When Rule Three Doesn't Hold

Moore developed this rule to accommodate the possibility where the reaction in the third rule doesn't hold and the trader is stuck with longs in a down market. If, after the purchase, the trader is long in a down market, the sell-off continues to between $2\frac{1}{2}$ and 3 points from the high (which then falls under the second rule if the sell-off is less than $2\frac{1}{2}$ points). At more than one point from the new high, the trader must unload his longs at losses somewhere in this area where prices are bouncing back and forth. The trader must also go short the same amount that he had been long in order to recoup his losses when prices resume their downward motion.

This approach to limiting losses if the market fails to show strength amounts to common sense. The trader sells short the same amount that he had been long prior to liquidating his long because the weakness of the market—as evidenced by the price action—should continue. The trader is thus able to make back his losses on the shorts.

I've always had a problem in doubling up—reversing my original position by selling twice what I was long to take advantage of a down market or buying twice what I was short to take advantage of an up market. I think a bit slowly, so when I close out on a bad position I have to reorganize my thinking to take advantage of the newly developed trend.

Rule Five: Halfway from Critical Support or Reversal Points

This rule was not developed for day trading, but its inherent logic for determining rule-of-thumb forecasts is indeed applicable for day trading. Moore observed in price action that—if a market moves from a low point to a high point, then reacts from where the move is halted, and an upmove then ensues—the forecasted high-price objective will be half of the first move from the low price to the first high price. This is similar to Elliott wave theory's A-B-C correction wave where the A wave is equal to the C wave in length.

Rule Six: Failure to Take Out Old Highs

If price runs up to new highs, reacts, and, in the secondary rally to new highs, fails to take out the old highs (shows a double top); then it is a sale if the price drops below the low of the first reaction. Price moves from 80 to 90, reacts back to 86, then charges up to 90. If the market fails to take out 90 1/8, then the trader should sell when the price falls through 86 to the downside.

Rule Seven: Larger Scope in Smaller Scale

I would now like to quote the following passage from Moore's works (p. 87): "In an advancing market as in a declining one, when movements are orderly, rallies and reactions in the minor movements are practically and proportionately the same as in the major ones, i.e., the law works the same in both movements."* There is an implied reductionism in the markets based on Moore's observations.

---

*William C. Moore, *Wall Street*, page 87.

Rule Eight: Two Days' Higher Openings
Forecast Highest Close

This is the first attempt by Moore to forecast price movements on an intraday basis using data from two previous days' opening price action. There are three days of observed price actions. The first day's opening price is lower than the previous day's opening price (that is, the first day minus one day). The second day's opening price is higher than the first day's opening price. Now, if the third day's opening price is higher than the first day's and the second day's, it is probable that the third day's *closing* prices will be toward the top of the day's range for the third day.

Again, applying a bit of common sense we see that there was a probability that the two higher opens showed some type of bottoming action. Opening prices had not been previously discerned by other bottoming types of chart patterns. Previously documented analysis showed the viability of two higher lows pointing in the direction of a higher close.

Rule Nine: High Close Forecasts Continuation
Into Next Day

Moore made this observation years ago and it is still applicable today. If the price of a future or stock punches through to new highs toward the close, then it is likely that the next day's *opening* will be strong and prices will resume upward (try this in a down market also). If the price on the opening of the second day does not follow through to the upside, then all longs must be unloaded and short sales must be made.

A caution must be given to readers at this point. This approach is entirely different for the options markets. Years ago, as a member of the Chicago Board of Trade, I traded stock options at the Chicago Board options exchange.

In the first week of my membership I learned something about derivative products. I stood in the Freeport Mineral crowd that first week, tracking its stock. The Friday of my first week in the crowd, Freeport Mineral seemed very strong. Toward the end of the day it got stronger and stronger. On the close the stock punched through all-time highs.

Having trained myself as a futures trader, I felt instinctively that I had to buy everything I could. I took out all the offers in the next strike price calls. I bid up for the next series and loaded up on an inventory I knew would be much higher in price.

On the opening of the next day, the stock opened unchanged and traded large numbers. I was long a bunch of options, and the opening rotation started. The offers for the options came rolling in—mostly at lower prices than the previous day's closes. The calls were being freely sold at ¼ to ½ point below the previous day's close.

As a futures trader trained to take quick losses, I immediately unloaded all of my calls, taking ½ point losses on over 200 calls. Meanwhile, the stock itself was trading at unchanged prices. This was a hard lesson learned: Stocks, options, and futures might trade similarly in the grand scope of things, but the professional trader must know the nuances and quirks of each market in order to be successful.

BURTON PUGH'S SCIENCE OF TRADING

A second body of work that is relevant to sequential patterning was written by Burton Pugh. Around the same time that William Moore was doing his work in sequential price patterning, Pugh was developing the methodology for his patterning approach.

In his *Trader's Instruction Book*, first published in 1929, Pugh developed several rules from his own observations. One observation was similar to Moore's sixth rule, which states that failure to take out old highs warrants short sales. Pugh described the phenomenon in this manner: "After a strongly advancing market, in each case the price halted and a moderate decline followed. Then a second decline set in which passed the point 'A,' the bottom of the first short decline. This low point of the first decline indicated by 'A' is the critical place. When price passes this point for a quarter or half, the decline may be expected to continue much farther, probably almost to where the swing started."* Whereas Moore specialized in stocks, Pugh applied this technique strictly to commodities.

One of Pugh's more remarkable observations concerns the price action of markets on the first day of trading of the week. If, after a sustained upward move, the markets close on the highs for the week, the news will affect market participants over the weekend (when there is no market trading) and the players will be interested in topping out the market on the following Monday.

As a day trader, one could sell into a strong Monday upmove expecting prices to back off for a retracement, covering the shorts either later in the day or on the next day, at lower prices. A similar situation occurs in downward markets. A low for the sell-off occurs on a Monday.

Pugh further observed that, in uptrending markets, a sign of a top occurs when the uptrend fails to continue and is followed

*Burton Pugh, *Trader's Instruction Book* (Miami, FL: Lambert-Garn Publishing Co., Inc., 1929), p. 88.

by a substantially lower close. I have observed that this is also the case in 5-minute bar charts. After an intermediate move has been made in 5-minute bar charts, the last bar shows substantially lower prices and the price resumes downwardly. Pugh did not consider going short the market; rather, he advocated merely getting rid of long positions. In downwardly trending markets, a higher close in the final bar shows the need to liquidate shorts, not necessarily to go long for an impending upmove.

A final strategy that Pugh used (one, however, that I question) involves the action and expected retracement after a market has made new highs or lows. Pugh wrote that a market moving into new highs can be sold short, expecting a quick scalp as the market retraces to the approximate area of the previous high price. If corn's previous high were $2.50, and it went to a new high of $2.55, Pugh would sell short—fully expecting the price to retrace to the $2.50 area for a quick 5-cent profit. From my observations, the market will indeed retrace to the $2.50 area, but not with great certainty as to when. It may retrace in a week's time, a month's time, or maybe not until the bull market has ended. Selling into such a move is a sure formula for disaster.

CONGESTION PHASES

A third approach to sequential patterns was proposed by Eugene Nofri. In 1975, as a member of the Chicago Board of Trade, Nofri wrote about his sequential patterning approach to trading futures, which concerned congestion phases.

Instead of tracking breakouts and breakdowns from congestion areas, Nofri used "short-term buying and selling, based on patterns formed by only a few days' prices."* He successfully categorized up-changes and downchanges over the course of several days' actions and forecasted the impending direction of the next day's activity.

From my observations, our current markets are markedly different from the markets in which Nofri learned how to trade. In the early 1960s and early 1970s markets had a tendency to gravitate back toward a mean. In Nofri's time, if prices were trading in a narrow range and broke to the upside, the markets would have a tendency within three periods (in Nofri's consideration, of daily price activity from close to close) to sell back to the trading range.

In current markets, if prices break away from a trading range, they have a tendency to move even further away. Eventually, today's market tendencies will pass away, and Nofri's observations may once again herald the trading day. In the meanwhile, the day

---

*Eugene Nofri, *Success in Commodities . . . The Congestion Phase System* (New York: Pageant-Poseidon Press, Ltd., 1975), p. viii.

trader is cautioned against relying too heavily on any particular set of observations, regardless of the success of the discourser.

Nofri classified 32 phases of patterns that occur within 75 percent of the market's congestion. Once a market was found to be bound within an upper range and a lower range, there were 32 observed patterns that had a 75 percent probability forecast rate.

Closing prices formed the most critical yardstick to measure his approach (he ignored the high and low daily prices). The success of his approach depended on the correct recognition that a market was in a congestion area. If the market was incorrectly diagnosed as being either in a congestion area or in a "straight-away" market, then the trader applying this approach would suffer a monetary loss.

Nofri's simplistic definition of a congestion was: "When a high and low price in your chart is not broken through by subsequent

---

Figure 10.1
Congestion phases #1 through #8: downtrend.

For an existing SHORT position: Take profit or cover position by *buying* at the bottom of the phase (circled).

To scalp: Buy at the bottom of the phase (circled); then *sell* on the close of the first day up from a previous day's close.

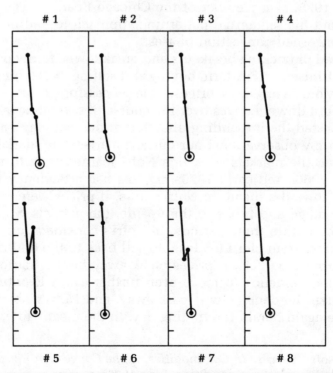

Figure 10.2
Congestion phases #9 through #16: uptrend.

For an existing LONG position: Take profit or cover position by *selling* at the top of the phase.

To scalp: Sell at the top of the phase; then *buy* on the close of the first day down from a previous day's close.

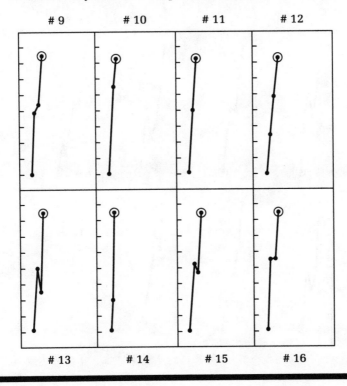

closing prices, and are both immediately followed by two consecutive closing prices in the opposite direction, the commodity can be said to be in a period of congestion" (p. viii).* When the market was so defined, he applied his pattern recognition approach. As you will see later in the chapter, this premise is similar to most successful methods of market trading.

Figures 10.1 through 10.4 illustrate the 32 phases that Nofri discerned.

The graphs in Figure 10.1 show the closing price action and the expected price action behavior after a downtrending action.

The graphs in Figure 10.2 show the closing price action and the expected price action behavior after an uptrending action.

*Eugene Nofri, *Success in Commodities*, p. viii.

Figure 10.3
Double congestion phases #17 through #24: downtrend.

For an existing SHORT position: Take profit or cover position by *buying* at the bottom of the phase.

To scalp: Buy at the bottom of the phase; then *sell* on the close of a second consecutive day up.

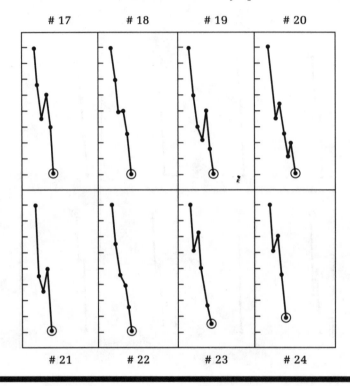

The graphs in Figure 10.3 show closing price action and the expected price action behavior after an extended downtrending action.

The graphs in Figure 10.4 show closing price action and the expected price action behavior after an extended uptrending action.

For the inexperienced trader, it may be somewhat difficult to grasp the importance of Nofri's work in applying pattern recognition to market analysis. In order for his pattern recognition approach to work successfully, Nofri defined the conditions under which it could validly forecast imminent price moves: He predefined what made up a congestion phase. Once the markets were so defined and categorized, he then applied conclusions of price behaviors from his empirical observations. To some extent, Nofri was guaranteeing his success by only looking for situations in

Figure 10.4
Double congestion phases #25 through #32: uptrend.

For an existing LONG position: Take profit or cover position by *selling* at the top of the phase.

To scalp: Sell at the bottom of the phase; then *buy* on the close of a second consecutive day down.

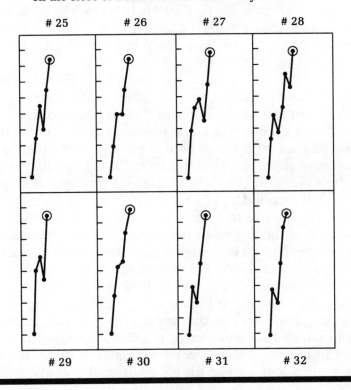

which his pattern recognition would function well. Like a good salesman who qualifies his leads, Nofri qualified the market conditions.

Nofri's approach was actually quite an accomplishment. Most pattern recognition approaches—and even some traders—fail to predetermine the markets under which they will work.

The importance of Nofri's work was driven home to me many years ago. I was taking a marketing course from a university professor who told our class that he often took on consulting jobs for Fortune 500 companies. In his negotiations for consultation, he always had a clause in the contract that stipulated that he had absolute control over projects. In this manner he was able to guarantee his consultancy's success. He told us that he dropped more jobs than he took when prospective bosses could not agree to his absolute control of projects. However, he succeeded more often than he failed. This is what successful trading is all about: pre-qualifying the market conditions under which one trades.

OPENING PRICE STATISTICS

The fourth methodology proposed was also the first systematized study of how opening price patterns forecast imminent moves. This research was presented by R. Earl Hadady in his book *Opening Price Statistical Data on the Futures Markets.** As a pioneer in applying computing power to price pattern analysis, Hadady led the way for further work in this area.

The most obvious conclusions drawn from Hadady's study of 154 pages of table patterns were presented in the book's first three pages. The book essentially showed that, if prices opened higher, they would back off down to a price level 80 percent of the time. To the trader, this meant that—depending on the particular market—one's market position could be protected from liquidation 80 percent of the time with the right placement of stops. If stops were placed correctly using the 154 tables of data, the trader would be in the right position in that particular market. Hadady did not attempt to forecast the degree of the move. He only stated that if an opening occurred at X cents higher than the previous close, there was an 80 percent probability it would not retrace back by much.

A second approach used was to forecast whether the opening price would be toward the higher end of the day's current range or toward the lower end of the day's current range. Such a forecast would depend on whether or not the price after the opening continued in the same direction by a variable amount. If, after the opening, corn prices moved up an additional 3 cents, instead of $2\frac{1}{2}$ cents, then it was 90 percent certain that the opening price would be at the lower half of the day's range. This suggests that the day trader would have had a 90 percent probability of making profits had he bought on the opening range.

Enclosed are sample charts from 154 pages of data. The raw data was collected over a span of one year—from April 1, 1983, to March 31, 1984. The reader is advised that the span of days studied was limited; because the data has not been tested, it is not known whether the current markets would reveal the same probabilities.

For Figure 10.5, high opening prices of soybean meal were compared to the previous day's trading ranges. The empirical data could be interpreted in the following way.

The previous day established a range of prices. The current day starts with a high opening price—one that is above the halfway

*R. Earl Hadady, *Opening Price Statistical Data on the Futures Markets* (Pasadena, CA: Key Books Press, 1984).

Figure 10.5
Soybean meal opening prices compared to previous day's high. (Courtesy of Hadady Corporation, Pasadena, CA.)

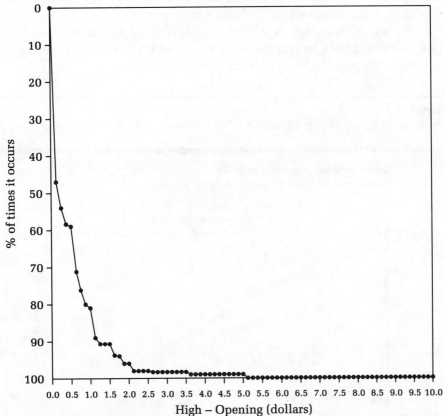

Soybean Meal, Nearby Contract
Time period: April 1, 1983–March 30, 1984
Frequency: Opening Price from High
(for opening nearer the high)

mark of the previous day's high. The chart shows that the high of the current day—which hasn't been established until the close of the current day's trading action—will not be X dollars higher than the opening price.

Once the opening is higher than the previous trading day's close, there is then a 98% probability that prices will go to at least $3.50 higher from the opening price. The conclusion to be drawn from this is that the high of the current day, when the market is closed, will be at least $3.50 higher than the previous day's close. This does not mean that the *close* of the current day will be $3.50 higher, but merely that, during the course of the trading day, prices will move to $3.50 higher where it settles. Prices can settle unchanged or slightly higher, and cannot be forecasted from this behavioral observation.

The trader who watches soybean meal can buy when prices go $3.50 higher than the opening, with the assurance that he has only a 2 percent chance of losing money (a 98 percent chance of making at least 1-cent profits). Of course, this fact does not ensure that prices will stay higher. Prices could go to $10.00 higher than the opening and then drop back to a close price only $3.50 higher than opening, to give the trader a scratch trade.

Figure 10.6 is the expected probability of occurrence and degree of occurrence in the soybean meal contract with a lower opening than the previous day's midway range price.

Figure 10.6
Soybean meal opening prices compared to previous day's low. (Courtesy of Hadady Corporation, CA.)

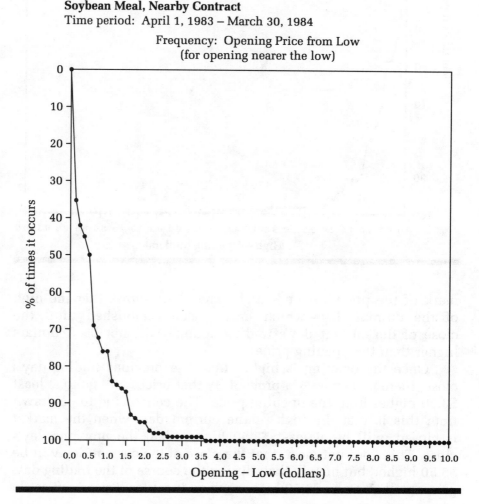

Soybean Meal, Nearby Contract
Time period: April 1, 1983 – March 30, 1984

Frequency: Opening Price from Low
(for opening nearer the low)

SEQUENTIAL PATTERNING
FROM VARIOUS PRICE POINTS

A recent work by Toby Crabel, *Day Trading with Short-Term Price Patterns & Opening Range Breakout,** explores the relationships of opening, closing, high prices, and low prices on an interday basis. Using such prices, Crabel attempts to find forecastable events. The observations are removed from day trading techniques, but they can be classified as short-term trading. Day traders may find these observations beneficial to the extent that they have a high-probability forecast rate.

The only difficulty with Crabel's observations is that the short-term outlook does not consider the cost of entry and exit of positions, that is, commissions and slippage on trades. Crabel leaves the application of his observations to the trader's discretion. Because certain empirical observations have a high degree of forecastability and high entry and exit costs, traders who have access to low commissions and excellent trade executions (for example, bank traders, exchange traders, insurance fund managers) can benefit.

In a series of studies Crabel sequentially evaluated sets of opening and closing price conditions for one to four days. From these set days, Crabel attempted to find the probability of directional opening or closing prices. The markets studied were strictly futures: U.S. bonds, soybeans, soybean meal, soybean oil, S&P 500 Index, live cattle, live hogs, pork bellies, gold, silver, copper, Deutsche marks, Swiss francs, Japanese Yen, crude oil, wheat, corn, and Eurodollars.

The number of trades based on how the markets sequentially opened varied from as few as 4 trades to as many as 1390 trades. One unique study developed by Crabel broke the range of the day's trading into five equal divisions and attempted to discern possible forecastable events based on how prices settled or opened into any of those segments of the trading day.

Under the four-trade conditions, U.S Treasury bonds gapped open 32 ticks and proceeded to go up another 16 ticks. Using a countertrend approach, a sale resulted in 50 percent profitability. Average gain was $728 and average loss was $370, resulting in a total gross profit, before commissions, of $2,500.

The cattle futures market was evaluated under conditions where the maximum number (1390) of trades were executed. Let's take a look at the results of a two-day trading signal. On day one, the opening price is higher than the previous day's closing price. On the second trading day, the opening price is higher than the closing price of the first day. A sale made in the second day and closed

*Toby Crabel, *Day Trading with Short-Term Price Patterns & Opening Range Breakout* (Greensville, SC: Traders Press, 1990).

out around the closing price of the second day will result in profits 46 percent of the time. The average winning trade is $173 and the average losing trade is $135. Total gross profit is $10,389. Because the gross profit is so minimal for the efforts, and the number of trades so relatively high, paying more than $7.80 ($10,839 gross profits divided by the number of trades, 1390) per round-turn trade will result in net losses. As you can see, such a set of conditions — when acted upon in the manner discovered by Crabel — would be ideal for the floor trader who pays around $2.50 per round-turn transaction.

Crabel goes into detail on other price patterns. If you are interested in such detailed patterning, you may want to investigate it further. For our purposes, it is sufficient to say that Crabel's market approach using detailed patterning is valid.

Although Crabel's studies were not systematically constructed, the work itself is the most comprehensive of the group and has the most information for the day trader in our current trading environment.

SEQUENTIAL PATTERNING AND DAY TRADING

From the primitive patterning of William Moore's techniques to the advanced and detailed patterning found in Toby Crabel's work, the day trader is provided a myriad of patterns to investigate and to examine for viable conclusions. The obvious challenge for the practicing day trader is to find the right pattern and apply the filtering to current market action. There is such a wide variety of patterns to select from, *all of which are usable in extracting profits from the markets*. The problem at first may seem to be exactly that: There are too many patterns to choose from; which is the correct one? The less-than-obvious answer is that all patterns work: If the preconditions are existent for a given methodology, the expected pattern will result. This can be verified by examining the relevant statistical tests.

The trader reads the studies, but he must also perceive the correct conclusion: Each pattern works if and only if the trader follows the forecastability of that particular pattern.

Therein lies the route to successful trading: Find a game plan and stick to it. If one pattern — as simple and banal as it may be — has a high profit percentage, success is ensured only if the trader follows it. There is an abundance of patterns; each is different, but each shows a high degree of profitability. However, this does not mean that a trader can pivot on that percentage of profitability with the many different patterns. The selected patterns work, which yield a calculated profitability; the statistical profitability itself does not make the patterns work.

11

Elliott Wave Theory
and Day Trading

The Elliott wave theory is an arcane theory of market analysis developed by Ralph Elliott in 1932. This approach views price moves in waves of upmoves and downmoves. The theory was developed with daily bar charts of the stock market and it is only recently that the theory has been applied to futures price data. (For more thorough analysis, see *The Technical Analysis of Stocks, Options and Futures*.) Additionally, within this time period, traders have refined the approach on a more minute scale to encompass trade-by-trade price data.

Unfortunately, the reduction of the major analysis to smaller scales is subjective; that is, it is extremely dependent on the analyst's ability to see the "developing waves."

Several background paragraphs will prepare the reader for the application of Elliott wave theory to day trading.

IMPULSE WAVES, CORRECTIVE WAVES, AND SCALING

Ralph Elliott looked at market price action as working in an action-reaction framework. All upmoves are followed by corrective moves. All corrective moves are followed by upmoves. Within this continuum of the ebb and flow of prices can be found certain repeated patterns. The upmoves are termed *impulse* waves; downmoves are termed *corrective* waves.

The impulse waves are always composed of five lesser-scaled waves, three impulse waves and two corrective waves, with each impulse wave followed by a corrective wave. The sequence of the larger-scaled impulse wave is as follows: impulse wave, corrective wave, impulse wave, corrective wave, and one final impulse wave. Labeling such subwaves in the larger-scaled impulse wave, the analyst uses this nomenclature: Waves 1, 2, 3, 4, and 5 of a larger-scaled impulse wave. Waves 1, 3, and 5 are therefore impulse waves of lesser scale, and waves 2 and 4 are corrective waves of lesser scale.

Once this larger-scaled impulse wave ends at the end of lesser-scaled wave 5, the whole larger-scaled impulse wave is itself corrected with a larger-scaled corrective wave.

The corrective wave is generally composed of three waves in the following sequence: impulse wave, corrective wave, impulse wave. The impulse and corrective waves of the larger-scaled corrective wave are relative by definition. Because the corrective wave is itself a correction of the previous larger-scaled impulse wave, the corrective wave's subwaves are termed relative to the direction of the corrective wave. Being downward, the lesser-scaled downwaves are impulse waves because they are in the direction of the corrective wave; the lesser-scaled corrective wave is a corrective wave because it is in the opposite direction of the larger-scaled corrective wave. Figures 11.1 and 11.2 illustrate this type of fractionation.

Figure 11.1
The five basic waves to the upside. (Copyright© 1988 by William F. Eng.)

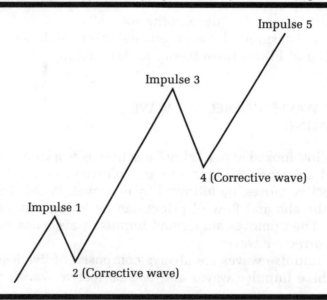

Impulse 5

Impulse 3

4 (Corrective wave)

Impulse 1

2 (Corrective wave)

Figure 11.2
The third wave is itself "fractaled" into a set of five smaller waves to the upside.
(Copyright© 1988 by William F. Eng.)

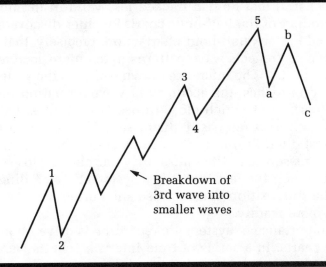

WHAT SHOULD BE RECORDED?

The problem of determining what is being recorded is a main concern when it comes to the correct application of Elliott wave theory. The charts drawn from the daily bar charts will suffice if the analyst views the larger scale. Ralph Elliott applied the theory to analyzing charts drawn from the last recorded price of a half-hour segment of market activity. He also applied it strictly to the analysis of the data derived from the Dow Jones Industrial averages.

The issue of how to draw the charts for correct Elliott wave analysis was not a problem until the New York Stock Exchange extended the trading hours on September 30, 1985. The trading day prior to the inception of the extension was 6 hours long: 10 A.M. to 4 P.M. eastern daylight time. The 6-hour trading day provided exactly 12 half-hour closing prices with which to plot the Elliott wave charts. After the trading hours were extended, the previously recorded charts could not be compared to the new charts, because the newer charts included the extra price point derived from the extra half-hour. The extra half-hour was added at the beginning of the trading day; thus the new trading hours were 9:30 A.M. to 4 P.M. eastern daylight time.

How is this problem to be resolved? The leading current practioner of Elliott wave theory, Robert Prechter (publisher of the *Elliott Wave Theorist*) concluded that the best solution would be to consider the additional half-hour as another point on the chart. Several months after the addition of the extra half-hour, Prechter acknowledged that the extra half-hour made the *hourly* charts (not half-hour charts) that he had tracked less valid in forming waves. As a by-product of the half-hour chart, Prechter discovered, while being forced to track half-hour charts more precisely, that the half-hour chart also "reflects wave patterns much more accurately than it did in the past."* The inference drawn is that as the scale of tracking action diminishes, the accuracy of wave formation increases.

The question of which close to use (15 minutes, half-hourly, hourly, bi-hourly) is not easily dismissed. The half-hour bar chart is used most often in filtering out price action into concise Elliott waves. The reason why the half-hourly bar chart's closes are used depends more on the fact that it is a systematic recording method than on the supposition that impulse and corrective waves will be disclosed more readily.

The importance of systematic recording is driven home by the following charts. In a series of time intervals, charts were created from the highs only, the lows only, and the closes only. As you can see in Figure 11.3, the obvious fact is that the closes-only chart is bounded by both the highs-only and the lows-only charts: It falls within the borders of the highs-only and lows-only charts.

Any chart created using prices between the highs and lows will be contained within it: The analyst can go to the extreme of creating charts from randomly selected times within the bars.

Because one of the problem areas in Elliott wave theory analysis is determining the correct count of the corrective waves, the analyst must filter out the noises from a strict application of the close-only half-hour line chart. If such a chart discloses muddled wave counts, the analyst must use the bracketed chart, which includes a path of prices from the high-low range, to perceive the corrective waves more accurately. Here is where subjectivity enters into the quasi-accurate Elliott wave analysis.

APPLYING ELLIOTT WAVE THEORY:
ITS FORECASTABILITY

In scientific circles, a theory is useful if it has predictability. If a set of observations can be repeated then the theory can be used to forecast identically produced events. In market analysis, there is no such thing as an absolute condition. What the analyst has is a set of probabilities of a set of repeatable conditions, each approaching maximum forecastability, 100 percent, but never reaching it.

---

*The Elliott Wave Theorist, January 1, 1986, page 10.

Figure 11.3
Line charts drawn from daily bar charts of the Dow Jones Industrial average, derived
from highs-only, lows-only, or closes-only data. (4/16 at 1:41 PM)

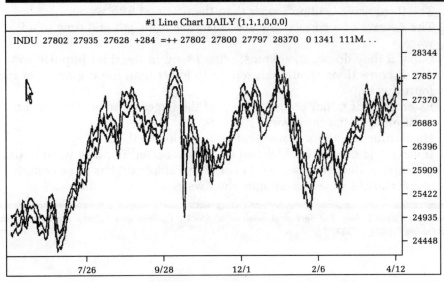

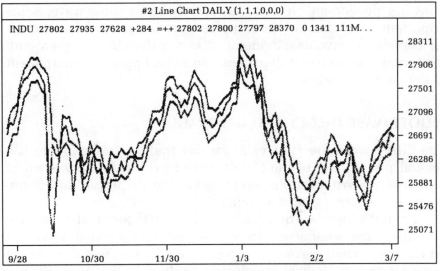

In Elliott wave theory terms, there are certain observations that
have more than a 50 percent probability of recurrence. They are
summarized as shown in Table 11.1. There are other summary behaviors with expected frequencies of occurrence, but their probabilities are less, so they are ignored.

It is interesting to observe that most of what is forecastable
centers around the impulse wave. The corrective wave observa-

---

Table 11.1
Salient Facts About Certain Elliott Wave Behaviors

---

1. The third wave is often longer than the first and fifth waves.
2. The A wave of a corrective wave is similar in length and time to a B wave.
3. Gaps, if they do occur, are most often found in the third impulse wave.
4. A-B-C corrections should not retrace to lower than the beginning of the fourth wave.
5. Extensions of minor scaled subsets of the larger impulse wave occur most often in the third wave.
6. High-volume activity is most often found in the third wave.
7. If wave 2 (a corrective subwave) of a larger-scaled impulse wave is simple in structure, then wave 4 (a corrective subwave) has to be complex. Conversely, if wave 2 is simple, then wave 4 has to be simple.

Source: William F. Eng, *The Technical Analysis of Stocks, Options and Futures* (Chicago: Probus Publishing, 1988), p. 387.

tions are dependent on some aspect of the impulse wave; some important component of the impulse wave is used as a benchmark for corrective wave development. It is not the other way around; the impulse wave is not dependent on some important component of the corrective wave.

ELLIOTT WAVE THEORY AND DAY TRADING

The Elliott wave theory is valid for day trading. In fact, there is a general practitioner of the Elliott wave theory (Abe Saperstein of *Compuwave* writes an electronic newsletter displayed on Futuresource) who has a good following.

From the premises on which Elliott wave theory is structured — that there are smaller-scaled waves and larger-scaled waves of which the current wave is composed and from which the current wave forms — the logical conclusion to draw is that if one could fractal the wave into smaller-scaled waves, then one could easily trade the forecastable wave structures.

The day trader merely applies the relative concepts of waves to smaller-scaled waves with the analytical freedom that the labeling of the waves need not be strictly ordered. The implied beauty of the practice of Elliott wave theory is that all wave endings are beginnings of new waves. For the purpose of day trading, this stricture is not required.

Why is this so? In the application of the Elliott wave theory, the greatest profits are made when prices move the most in absolute numbers. The wave in which prices move the most is always the third wave. Third waves have peculiar characteristics: longest, most volume, and the most gaps. First and fifth waves are not as long, not as volume-active, and do not have as many major gaps (the first wave can have gaps, but these gaps are not due to high volume, or lopsided buying or selling activity; they are attributable to low volume due to lack of trading interests). All the day trader needs to find is the longest run in prices on his 5-minute chart, 15-minute chart, or whatever. Once the longest run has been discovered, the tracking and labeling of the future waves is the next objective task. It is not even necessary to have an absolutely correct wave structure interpretation to make use of the Elliott wave theory at this point. Moderately successful labeling of following waves will offer insight on the next developing third wave of whatever magnitude. The day trader can trade the expected developing of corrective waves and the other two impulse waves, the waves labeled as 1 and 5.

The strategy described in the preceding paragraph, which stipulates that once a third wave is discerned, the tracking begins, would prevent the longer-term trader from making substantial profits. This is attributable to the fact that larger-scaled waves obviously take more time to appear. Waiting for the formation, development, and ending of a larger-scaled third wave, is a waste of profitable opportunities. As the day trader analyzes the data, he or she has more than ample opportunity to see the formation of various third waves of lesser degrees.

EXCEPTIONS TO THE RULES

If markets were perfectly forecastable, traders and writers (of which I am both) would soon be out of work. If there were such a fortunate trader who discovered the key to market forecasting, the lead time that he had would eventually evaporate because, as he controlled the market to a greater and greater extent and accumulated more and more of its wealth, there would be fewer and fewer players on the other side to take money from.

The markets are, in a perverse way, blessed by the fact that all forecasting techniques contain within themselves the seeds of self-destruction. The Elliott wave theory is certainly so blessed. The blessing benefits the wave theory because it shows that it is not perfect. Perfection, in any form, implies a homeostatic state of inertia.

Ralph Elliott was wise enough to have discovered large overall patterns in the market's behaviors, and inductive enough to recognize that these overall patterns could be "fractaled" into lesser-scaled patterns. In cases where his observations could not account for expected patterning, he developed a body of exceptions to his rules. The conventional statement, "If A happens, expect B to occur," now had the phrase, "unless C, in which case D must be factored in," tagged to the end of it.

Elliott wave theory is useful—when following its rules, the analyst is able to create accurate forecasts. When the forecasts, as based on previous rules, are no longer probably accurate (in market analysis, we are dealing in probabilities instead of certainties), then one must go back to the previous rules and modify them to account for the new sets of data.

Fortunately, Elliott wave theory has only two major components: the impulse wave and the corrective wave. When incorrect analyses result from applying the theory, the rules need to be modified. The best way to modify the Elliott wave theory is to modify only one set of rules, pertaining either to the impulse wave analysis or to the corrective wave analysis portion. To change the Elliott wave theory by attempting to modify rules pertaining to both sets of waves would increase the complexity of the task.

Herein is where the genius of Ralph Elliott really shone. Elliott modified the corrective wave analyses component of the theory and left the impulse wave analysis component intact.

In situations where there were questionable areas of wave counts within the obviously forming impulse wave, the analyst assumed that the areas with the questionable wave counts were caused by the lower-scaled *corrective* waves. So Elliott wave theory covered itself even in this manner: Within impulse waves, problematic counts are due to appearances of lower-scaled *corrective* waves. To the extent that Elliott wave theory could be applied to market analysis, it really begged the question of when the waves actually started to scale higher or lower. It is interesting that even here, the scaling problem is evident: When does the scaling begin?

In a sense, what Elliott did to make the theory more applicable was isolate the component parts, lump all the problem analyses into one such isolated part, and then dismiss this part as a problem area. In this manner, Elliott increased the chances that the remaining, unadulterated analyses would be correct. This was an extremely clever way of handling problematic analyses. It allowed the approach to work best when it was applied to impulse waves.

The isolated component part of the Elliott wave theory where everything was lumped together was the corrective wave. The corrective wave, in order to accommodate the holistic theory, evolved into tremendous complexity. Had the corrective wave simply been defined as being composed of three basic waves (impulse-corrective-impulse waves) and remained so, the theory's simplicity would have epitomized elegance. Seldom, however, is the categorization of real-world observations this simple.

The simplicity of the impulse wave was offset by the complexity of the corrective wave. (A note to Elliott wave aficionados: I believe I've found another rule of alternations, that simple impulse waves are always countered with complex corrective waves, and complex impulse waves are always countered with simple corrective waves!) Corrective waves can be composed of more than one set of three waves. These sets of waves constituting the larger-scaled corrective wave can be composed of 7, 11, 15, or maybe more such subwaves. If the count of the subwaves was not a multiple of three, then the creation of one singular subwave, identified as an X subwave in Elliott wave terminology, wherever it could be "seen" in the corrective wave structure, made the count "valid." With the inclusion of the X subwave, all the other waves could be lumped into sets of three waves (A-B-C corrective waves). The valid interpretation of the corrective waves, then, was reduced to the addition of the X subwave: Can anything, then, ever be incorrectly read?

The developer of the Elliott wave theory allowed another set of interpretations of the conventional wave counts in case the conventional wave counts were to be proven inaccurate in the future. The current leading practioner of Elliott wave theory, Robert Prechter, has taken the alternate count solution also.*

Other practitioners of Elliott wave theory have extrapolated further and have "discovered" additional patterns in the corrective waves.†

THE FRACTAL WAVE ALGORITHM
AND ELLIOTT WAVE THEORY

The concept of the Elliott wave comprising a series of lesser-scaled waves borders on fractionation and chaos. However, a very basic problem has prevented any solid effort to find fractals of market

---

*For more information on the purpose of the alternate count, see my article, "How to Always Be Right," *Intermarket*, December 1988.

†See Glenn Neely with Eric Hall, *Mastering Elliott Wave* (Brightwaters, NY: Windsor Books, 1990); and David H. Weis, *Trading with the Elliott Wave Principle* (Greensville, SC: Trader's Press, 1989).

price behaviors: There wasn't an objective way to find waves. In order to study possible wave developments in prices of markets, there must be ways to identify the wave structures objectively. Because one of the problems of applying Elliott wave theory to market prices is that it is difficult to discern when one wave is scaling to another dimension, no real attempt was made.

In a series of newsletter articles for *Technical Traders Bulletin*, Arthur von Waldburg wrote about his approach to objectively classifying waves, and E. W. Dreiss expanded on the concept. Von Waldburg's solution to wave identification eliminated the subjectivity of interpreting Elliott waves (and most other waves, for that matter). By his objective categorization, he dismissed one type of Elliott wave altogether: the irregular corrections. These corrections do not occur often, but when they do they take out the highs of the previous impulse wave up to that point. This is the problem with corrective waves—in this case, an irregular correction, as defined by Ralph Elliott, could even make new highs for the move!

Von Waldburg merely stipulated that an upward wave was to be identified by the fact that it closed higher than the previous day's close. However, within this type of labeling, the series of such moves was classified as one set until one move downward penetrated the last prior sets of labeled waves. In this manner, von Waldburg "fractaled" the larger waves. This approach is not as elegant as a chaos scientist would want to see, but it is certainly very systematic in labeling waves and their respective larger waves. Note that, by von Waldburg's definition, the labeling starts at the smallest-scaled wave available and progresses to larger-scaled waves. He cannot take large waves and sublabel the structure without first having accommodated for subwaves in the creation and monitoring of the subwaves.

What the chaos-theory-applying day trader sees here is the fact that by using a daily bar chart, he or she can label objectively larger-scaled waves with continuously created market data—a sort of artificial intelligence approach to market analysis. The waves are limited by the fact that they are all composed of daily bar data and that, looking at certain structurings of those bars, one can observe waves within waves. This is all accomplished within the context of daily bars.

An approach that I have used with a good amount of success in looking at smaller-scaled "waves" (waves and subwaves as defined by time shifts) is found in an article that I wrote for *Stocks and Commodities* magazine (June 1986) and later reprinted as a chapter in *The Technical Analysis of Stocks, Options and Futures*.

In this article four sets of charts are used in analyzing one market: The daily bar chart, the 60-minute bar chart, the half-hour bar chart, and the 15-minute bar chart. The same pattern-filtering approach is applied to all four of the variously timed bar charts, and when they all point to the same action (either all buys or all sells), then that action is taken in the markets.

There are two ways of using daily bar charts and looking at larger wave structurings. The first case involves a systematic way of looking at market action by taking in market action on the fly. The waves form in larger and larger scalings with the new data that comes in. In the second case, the trader has predetermined the parameters of the scaling and watches market action within the context of such fixed parameters. Which is better? Both are useful, depending on how much control the trader wants in the markets, because both approaches would engender buy and sell decisions. The first case shows that control is dictated by the markets. The second case shows that the market's action has to fall into the parameters set by the trader before action is called for.

A hunting analogy would best explain the two different approaches. In the first approach, the hunter is following the prey with a rifle; when the time is right, he attacks the animal. In the second approach, the hunter designs his own traps, systematically places them around feeding grounds and watering holes, and waits for the prey to approach. The two approaches attain the same goal— catching the prey—but from different angles.

The objective classification of waves by von Waldburg is a first attempt at fractioning out price waves. Its success has yet to be determined.

However, an interesting note to readers should be made here. In the course of working with chaos and fractals, Mitchell Feigenbaum discovered a unique property of a universal scale to a class of nonlinear equations. Feigenbaum was a student at the Massachusetts Instutute of Technology when he started thinking of a possible universal constant for physical matter. While working on solutions to nonlinear problems (it is my belief that the forecastings of price and volume activity in markets are categorized as nonlinear problems and, as such, the developments in chaos and fractionation can be used to analyze them) he discovered that this universal constant was 4.6692016090. I would like to write a section on how Feigenbaum discovered this but it is beyond the scope of my own comprehension. A comparable, but less important, concept is the Fibonnacci ratio and its various derivatives that can be found in various relationships between different price swings and time moves in the markets. John Briggs and F. David Peat, in *Turbulent Mirror,* discuss the universality of this constant:

> Feigenbaum showed that the fine details of these different systems
> don't matter, that period doubling is a common factor in the way or-
> der breaks down into chaos. He was able to calculate a few universal
> numbers representing ratios in the scale of transition points during
> the doubling process. *He found that when a system works on itself
> again and again, it will exhibit change at precisely these universal
> points along the scale.*[*]

Von Waldburg took the various degrees of waves and compared
them to previous ones; that is, when waves of degree one begat
waves of degree two (albeit in lesser frequencies), he compared the
ratio of the second set of waves to the first set of waves. What he
discovered in averaging out the ratios of 13 markets is shown in
Table 11.2.

The ratio numbers that he obtained came nowhere near the
Feigenbaum constant of 4.6692016090. If Feigenbaum's discovery
is universal, then I acknowledge that the Feigenbaum constant has
to be found somewhere in market price action. As von Waldburg's
work is only an initial attempt at an objective classification of
waves, the solution to finding the Feigenbaum constant in price
action most likely rests in how the observer can classify wave structuring. The problem is similar to the approach that made Benoit
Mandelbrot a reknowned scientist associated with chaos theory
and fractals: The observer's viewpoint must be great enough to
unite the wave structures into a cohesive unit. The von Waldburg
structuring and classification of waves, as good as it is, is only a
starting point.

Table 11.2
Average Fractal Wave Count Ratios—13 Markets

FWA Model	TD:L0	L0:L1	L1:L2	L2:L3	L3:L4
Weak	2.02	3.96	3.79	3.46	3.73
Hybrid	2.02	4.38	3.93	3.84	4.02
Strong	2.02	6.89	6.06	5.99	NA

Reprinted by courtesy of *Technical Traders Bulletin*, October 1990.

[*]John Briggs and F. David Peat, *Turbulent Mirror* (New York: Harper &
Row, 1989), p. 640.

PART 3

THE ART OF DAY TRADING

Introduction

In Part One, you learned the theory of day trading. In Part Two, you learned the mechanics of the techniques actually used by day traders. In this final part, you will learn the reasoning behind certain decisions that are made in day trading.

The decision making described here in Part Three is not "etched in stone"—you should not see it as being rigidly and systematically defined: Herein lies the *art* of day trading. What is it that causes a trader to make the right decision at the right time? Certainly, there must be an element of knowing whether a trend will continue or will reverse. However, the trader must acknowledge, if only momentarily, that anything can happen given the right circumstances.

The cases you examine will include losers as well as winners. Winners are easy to deal with because the outcome is always so beneficial to the participants. Losers, however, are very hard to deal with because the outcome is so damaging. If the trader doesn't know how to deal with the trades that might become potential losers, she won't be able to profit when an opportunity presents itself. Losers can cause the margin clerk to close out the trader's positions. Losers can damage the trading equity to the point that the trader can never come back to the trading game. Losers can cause psychological stress and even destruction.

If you find that I spend an inordinate amount of time discussing losers, you should bear in mind that knowing how to handle losses will continue a trader's career. Knowing how to handle profits merely gratifies the ego. This is one of the most important rules of successful trading.

Part Three is composed of case studies that I have come across in day trading. Each case includes a thorough explanation of the trading techniques and reasoning that I used in making the decisions. Hopefully, you will benefit from a detailed reading of the examples and, in your own way, implement the reasoning in similar scenarios that you encounter. My approach relies heavily on the forecastability of market-trading techniques.*

* I did not execute on every signal as indicated in the text. For fluidity of content, I wrote the text from the perspective of a trader using every signal. For a majority of the case studies I did execute a large portion of the signals based on my analysis.

CASE 1   A Gift in U.S. Bonds

This is one of the rarest trades to date. This trade was a virtual gift, a guarantee of at least 16 ticks of profits. In this trade, I was using the Market Profile (copyright Chicago Board of Trade) approach.

Figure C1.1, 11-2 @ 8:30 A.M., shows one full day of trading (the leftmost profile) and the first three half-hour periods of the second day.

Figure C1.1

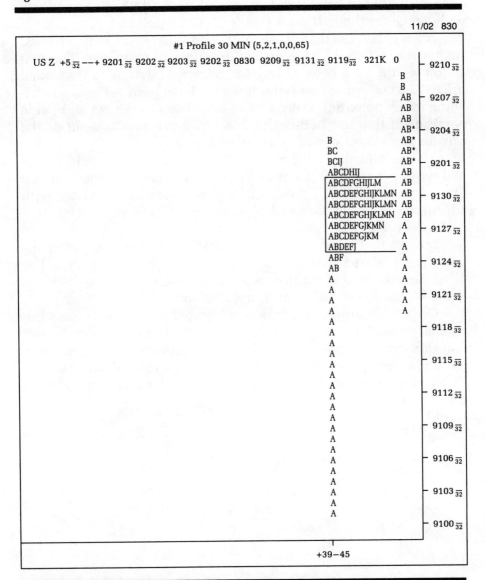

One significant detail in the first day of trading is the long tail that formed between the low price of 91 and about $91\,^{24}/_{32}$. The tail formation suggests that a balance will be created in the future price action with a tail formed on the opposite side. That is, if a tail forms between 91 and $91\,^{24}/_{32}$, then another tail will have to form between 92 and $92\,^{24}/_{32}$ before the price action is considered complete! In this case, I merely had to buy on the next day at any price in the value area (between 92 and $91\,^{24}/_{32}$) and watch the price go higher.

The second day's trading activity in Figure C1.1 showed an opening half hour bracketed between $91\,^{19}/_{32}$ and $92\,^{7}/_{32}$, a relatively wide range for the half hour (that's $^{20}/_{32}$ of a point).

Acknowledging that the second day's first period encompassed such a range, I could have reacted in either of two ways. The first action would have been to buy the bonds, oblivious to the actual price. The second action (which would have been safer, but sacrificing much potential profit) would have been to buy on an upside breakout of the first half-hour's bracketed price: A takeout of the upside $92\,^{7}/_{32}$ high would warrant purchase.

The second day (still Figure C1.1), 11-3, evolved into a normal day's pattern with balance throughout. However, the long tail formed on the first day, 11-2, still had not been balanced out with additional price workouts at higher levels. This was a sign that prices had to move higher.

Inspecting Figure C1.2 (11-6 @ 8:16 A.M., four days after the first figure), shows that prices had moved as high as $92\,^{16}/_{32}$. The initial forecast was that prices would eventually go up to $92\,^{24}/_{32}$ in order for the lower tail to find price balance.

On 11-6, initial price action suggested a very good possibility that price would move up to the $92\,^{24}/_{32}$ level. Despite the fact that this trade lasted over one day, price action never showed any particular weakness. It was safe to carry positions overnight.

This trade wound up making about 18 ticks over the span of three days.

Figure C1.2

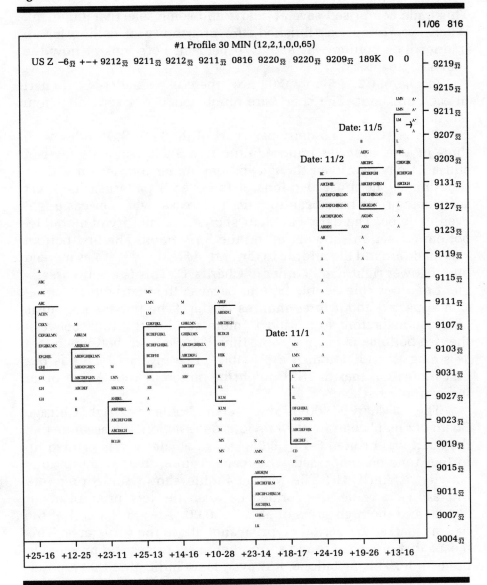

CASE 2 Seeking an Intermediate Bottom in the S&P Index

This trade comprised several charts and some selective judgment. When everything was finished, the probability of calling for an intermediate bottom was about 70 percent. Let's look at how the analysis progressed.

In Figure C2.1, 5-1 @ 6:03 A.M., there is a smaller-sized chart in each quadrant. The charts are numbered 1 to 4 vertically from left to right.

The #1 Chart is a daily bar chart of the June S&P Index with three moving averages imposed onto it: a 5-day bar, a 13-day bar, and a 21-day bar. Even though the day trader focuses on a short time frame, she must also look at the overall patterns. She must see where prices have been in order to forecast where prices might eventually be. The daily bar chart shows a possibility of a double-bottom formation showing up on the S&P Index. The first bottom was made around the middle to the end of February (2-14 as marked on the lower right-hand corner of Chart #1). This is a valid assessment of a possible double bottom because the first bottom formation appeared about three months earlier. (The trader's prognosis of a double-bottom formation is more valid if the time between the two bottoms is large; a short time between two bottoms is not as strong an indication of a possible price reversal.) This is our first indication that the S&P might be bottoming out. What other indications are there?

The #2 Chart is a 60-minute Market Profile (copyright Chicago Board of Trade) chart for the previous day's action. (Please note that the chart was printed 5-1 @ 6:03 A.M., so whatever was printed up to that time encompassed what came before, that is, the trading activity of April 31.) The Market Profile shows something very interesting: a value area formed between the low price of about 328.80 and the high price of about 330.00. Toward the end of the day, as marked by Period G, price shot above the value area. This means that price had found support at lower prices and reversed to the upside. This fact alone, however, is no indication that a possible bottom had formed. What other indications showed a possible bottom?

The #3 and #4 Charts show bar charts of 60-minute and 15-minute duration, respectively. What I was looking for here was the same thing that I had found in #1 Chart: a possible double bottom! Were there double bottoms here?

Upon further inspection of #3 and #4 Charts, I was disappointed in finding that the second bottoms in both charts are *lower* than the first bottom! From a strict technical interpretation of double bottoms, the second bottom must be higher than the first in order to show strength as a reversal pattern. Double bottoms are

Figure C2.1
(a) Perhaps a double bottom? (b) This formation balances bottom (c). (d) First bottom. (e) Last bottom. (f) First clue that bottom was being made. (g) First bottom. (h) Second lower bottom.

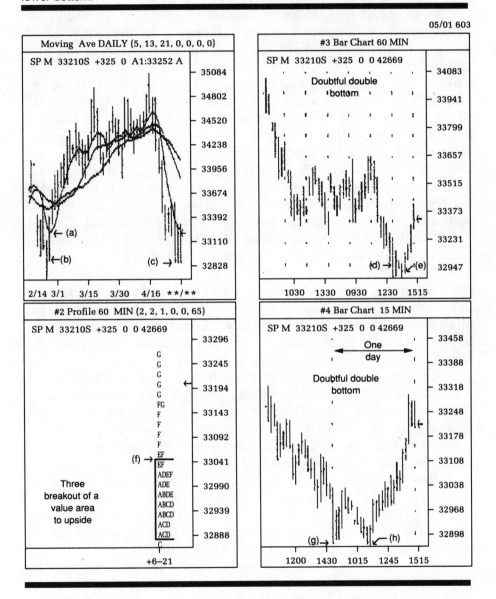

formations showing that prices have found support. It is not likely that a secondary bottom will find support at a lower price than the first bottom.

What should the trader do in such a situation? There are cases where valid double-bottom formations develop when the second bottom is lower than the first. These cases exist when the selling into the second bottom is great enough to force prices down to hit stop-sell orders just below the first bottom. At this point, some breakdown traders will enter stop-sell orders to either protect their long positions or to initiate short-sales positions.

As a general rule, however, market professionals use limit orders entered by the public to buy just above the lows of the first bottom as orders to "shoot" against. This means that, if the first bottom's low is 320.00, the public would enter orders to buy at 320.05. The market professionals would step ahead of these orders to buy at 320.05 and buy for their own accounts at 320.10. These traders know fully well that, if there appear to be massive market sell orders, they can immediately unload their own proprietary trading positions onto the limit orders to buy at 320.05, and limit their losses to 0.05. This is a great strategy for the market professionals. They have virtually unlimited profits if the market happens to turn around immediately after it touches 320.10, and very limited losses if the market continues to sell through.

Now the day trader should see how invalid or valid the double bottoms on the 60-minute and 15-minute charts are.

Figure C2.2 was created 5-3 @ 9:38 A.M., about 3½ hours after Figure C2.1 was created and about an hour after the S&P Index started trading. Figure C2.2 is a line chart created from a 15-minute bar chart. To create this line chart, I took #4 Chart from Figure C2.1 and, looking only at the last price of each 15-minute bar, connected these prices with lines.

What are the advantages of line charts? Line charts eliminate a lot of market noise. Only closing prices of the bars were used to create this line chart. There are situations where line charts are created from high-only prices or low-only prices. In such situations, each chart is used specifically to filter out any biases of that particular market at that particular market stage.

Upon inspection of Figure C2.2, the day trader finds that there is a valid double bottom, with the second bottom showing a higher price support level than the first bottom. The day trader, having viewed the 15-minute bar chart through the filtering of line charts, now realizes that a market reversal is imminent!

As a quick, additional confirmation of a possible bottom the day trader looks at the previous swing and notices that the price drops from the 335.54 level to the lowest bottom of 332.80. This is a straight drop of over 2.75 points in one trading day! Could this be an Elliott impulse wave to the downside? Impulse waves are long and dramatic! If so, this has to be some sort of C wave. (C waves must be five waves down, and *not* three waves down!)

The day trader starts to look at the supposed impulse wave and tries to throw on a five-wave sequence. The impulse wave is fitted into the line chart. The fourth wave fits nicely into a collaps-

Figure C2.2

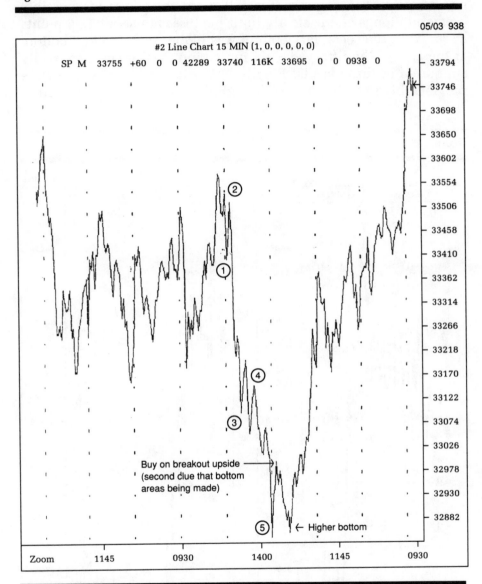

ing market. It is a running correction that shows dramatic *weakness* because the corrective wave of this fourth wave fails to reach back to some previous levels. Collapsing markets are characterized by rushes to unload at any time and at any price! Here is yet another confirmation that this could be a blowoff sell-off!

Armed with this type of background analysis, the day trader looks for a price level to enter the market from the long side. Around the 330.00 level the day trader is comfortable with going long. Why? First, if he enters longs here, he can use the low at the end of the fifth wave as a stop-sell point to unload his possibly premature longs and basically limit his losses to about 1.75 points or so. Also, the secondary bottom was higher than the first bottom at the end of the fifth wave, an indication that prices were really supported at these levels! Finally, the price action taking out the previous high at 329.50 or so would warrant additional strength.

Figure C2.3

05/03 1026

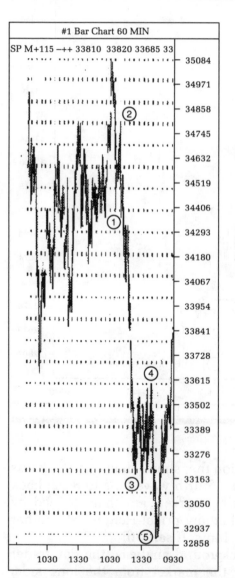
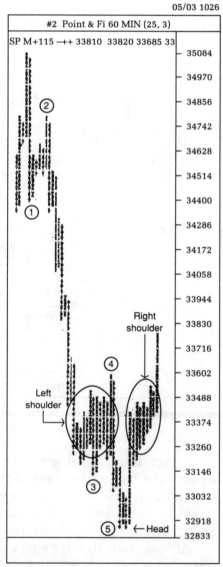

Figure C2.3 (5-3 @ 10:26 A.M.) shows the price action of the S&P Index in a 60-minute bar chart and in a 1 × 3 reversal point-and-figure chart. This point-and-figure chart could be used to determine whether the impulse wave down was correctly analyzed.

As you will notice, each mark on the point-and-figure chart equals 0.25 of a full S&P Index point. Each reversal required three such points. Within the third wave of the impulse wave, note the details that could easily be classified as extensions.

The double bottom formed at the end of the fifth wave eventually gave way to a pretty valid head-and-shoulder bottom formation. Note that the left shoulder and the right shoulder are about equal in congestion development. This fact offers further confirmation that a major bottom has occurred.

Figure C2.4 was created 5-3 @ 10:30 A.M. I was interested in looking at the point-and-figure chart through a broader filter; this was made possible by changing the value of each mark. Each mark on the point-and-figure chart was changed from a representation of 0.25 of a point to a representation of 0.50 of a point. By adjusting the valuation to a larger scale, I was able to see the previous analyses in a different light.

First, what had looked like an obvious head-and-shoulder bottom on a 0.25 × 3 reversal chart now seemed less so. The right shoulder of the formation did not appear as well formed in the larger 0.50 × 3 reversal chart. The lesson to be learned here is that any congestion area can be made to look very formidable by viewing it on a smaller scale. On the other hand, it can be made to look practically nonexistent by viewing it on a larger scale. As you can see, an element of subjectivity enters into the analysis.

Second, the impulse wave to the downside, originaly labeled in five waves with greater detailing, now looked a lot cleaner—there were fewer jiggles to confuse me with labeling. You can see that the third impulse wave with the longest subwave between 336.00 and 340.00 is also the cleanest! The existence of the gap around the 338.00 level further confirms that this was a third wave.

In this case, I was essentially provided with several situations that suggested the same high-probability conclusion: The S&P Index was bottoming out.

Here is a summary of the factors that led to this conclusion:

1. The daily bar chart showed a possible double bottom.
2. The 60-minute Market Profile showed a definite reversal.
3. The 60-minute and 15-minute bar charts showed only questionable double bottoms, but this doubt was removed upon inspection of the line chart.

Figure C2.4

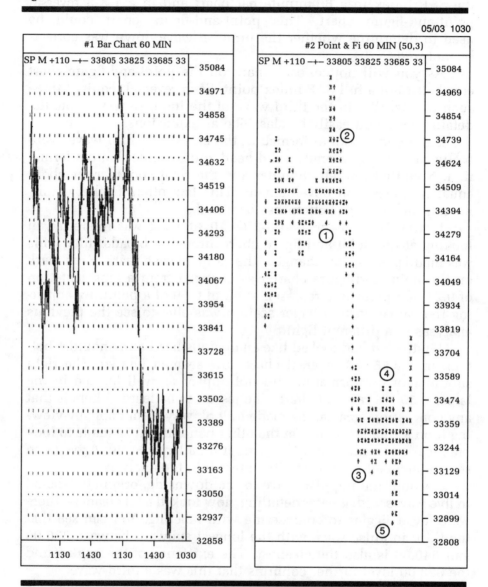

4. The correct Elliott wave analysis of the last impulse wave to the downside suggested that the sell-off had been completed.

5. The line chart gave a price entry level for longs and a stop-sell point in case the analysis was incorrect.

6. The two point-and-figure charts served to give a better wave count of the impulse wave, revealing a possible bottoming action.

In this trade, I entered around the 330.00 level. The final charts show a last sale of 338.05, or an 8.05 gain from the first long positions! Because this trade extended throughout several days, it is not a strict application of day trading principles. Nonetheless, it proved to be a good trade. The lesson learned here is that, if the winner is held and the day trader knows where his exact exit points are, he is sure to make money!

CASE 3   Using RSI with January Soybeans

After the detailed reasoning that was given for Case 2, this little example is a brief respite. It has only one chart! Figure C3.1 was created on 11-28 @ 10:11 A.M. and illustrates a 5-minute bar chart of the price action of January soybeans spread out to a little over 4 days. The last sale of the soybeans was 5.76 1/2, up 1/4 cents. Superimposed on the chart is a Relative Strength Indicator (RSI)

Figure C3.1

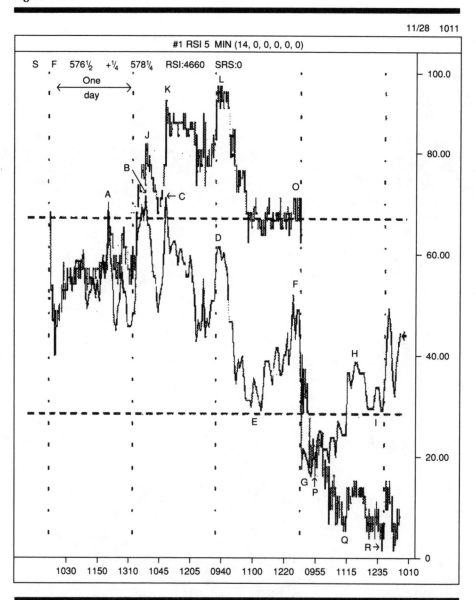

chart with a 14-day analysis. The RSI chart is a line chart so it can be read easily.

Relative Strength charts purport to show momentum of price movements. Here the day trader attempts to determine whether or not a market is finished with any runups or is exhausted on the downside selloffs. The momentum studies, as a general rule, measure the rate of change of any given block of time: Is the rate of change slowing or increasing? If the rate of change is slowing, then an impending reversal is near; if the rate of change is increasing, then the reversal is not here yet. This is all that momentum studies can reveal. The block of data sets is moving forward in time to encompass the most recent series of data sets. This block of time can be anywhere from three time periods to an infinite number, but for practical purposes analysts have concluded that a 14-block set is a good starter for analysis.

All points labeled on the RSI chart (A, B, C, D, E, F, G, H, and I) correlate with price bar reversals on the 5-minute bar chart points (J, K, L, O, G, P, Q, and R). The right Y-axis is the normalized percentage key: From 0% at the bottom, it ranges all the way up to 100% at the top. Conventional RSI studies teach that any RSI movement into the 70%-or-higher level indicates overbought conditions and a movement into the 30%-or-less level indicates oversold conditions. Overbought signals warrant selling; oversold signals warrant buying.

There's a flaw with the conventional analysis, however. Please note that points A, B, and C correlate with price peaks at an unlabeled price, points J and K. Selling at point A of the RSI overbought area warrants additional selling at point B and even more selling at point C. Fortunately for the seller, prices reached a maximum high at point L. Unfortunately, no overbought signal was generated at the correlating RSI point of bar chart point L or RSI peak D.

I have determined that RSI peaks and troughs correlate well only with the full understanding of the current stage of market action: If the markets are bearish, sell on any overbought indicators, even if the RSI does not enter into the overbought areas; if the markets are bullish, buy on any oversold indicators, even if the RSI does not enter into oversold areas.

What does this mean? It means that overbought indicators at points D, F, and H are valid even though they never reached into the 70% overbought area because the market was bearish! These RSI points correlated with points L, O, and an unlabeled point. Selling at these price points never placed the day trader at risk, because prices never reached higher than any of these points. Day trades were actually initiated at all these points of RSI "overbought" levels. Conversely, selling at points A, B, and C was never warranted because the market was actually bullish!

CASE 4   Lazy Profits in Ten-Year Notes, Bonds, Gold, and Soybeans

Every so often the strain of trading gets to me and I look for the simplest way to make trades and get out of them before the day is through. Well, this series of trades was made in one day.

This is a complete Market Profile (copyright Chicago Board of Trade) approach; it did not require any other type of analysis. Of course, most days do not fall into place as well as did this example.

Figure C4.1

01/31 1253

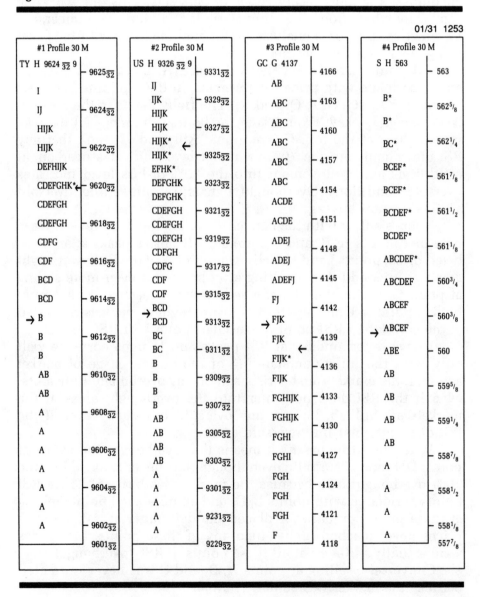

Figure C4.1 was created on 1-31 @ 12:53 P.M. and is composed of four charts, labeled from 1 to 4. All charts are 30-minute Market Profile charts.

The analysis up to this point was that #1 chart, March 10-year notes, was bullish; #2 chart, March U.S. bonds, was bullish; #3 chart, April gold, was neutral to bearish; and #4 chart, March soybeans, was bullish. Buy 10-year, bonds, beans, and sell or stay out of the gold. Nothing could have been simpler.

Why was this analysis so made? The buys were generated from

Figure C4.2

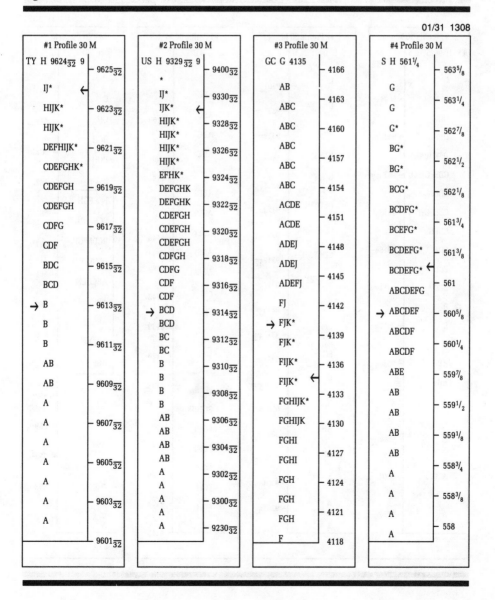

the formation of a tail created early in the trading day followed by a value area formation during the end of the first half of the trading day. What does this imply? The uppermost tail had to be formed before the day's end.

Buy 10-year at 96 $^{20}/_{32}$, bonds at 93 $^{26}/_{32}$, soybeans at 5.63, and maybe sell some gold at 413.70!

Figure C4.2 is the same chart as C4.1 except that it was created 15 minutes later. Ten-year notes was challenging the highs of the

---

Figure C4.3

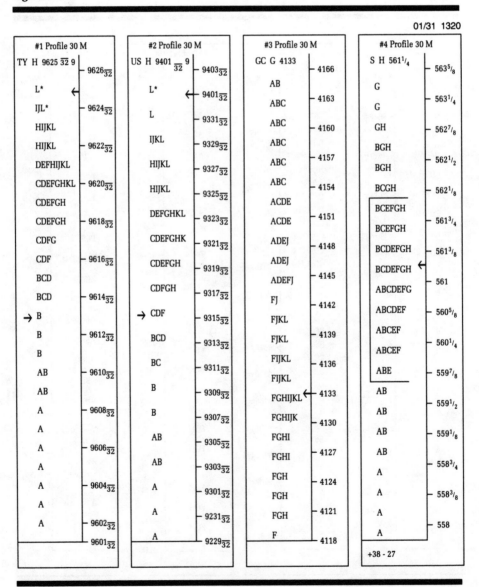

day at 96 ^{24}/$_{32}$, U.S. bonds made new highs for the day at 93 ^{29}/$_{32}$, beans had made new highs for the day at around the 563 ^{1}/$_{2}$ area and had backed off to 561 ^{1}/$_{4}$, and gold hadn't gone anywhere to the downside.

The strategy was to buy the bullish markets and sell anywhere between the start and completion of the high-priced tail. So selling at any higher price would be warranted for this no-brainer type of trading.

Figure C4.3 is a chart from the same day, but created at 1:20 P.M. Ten-year notes had gone up to 96 ^{25}/$_{32}$ (from entry price of 96 ^{20}/$_{32}$, a 4-tick profit), bonds up to 94 ^{1}/$_{32}$ (from entry price of 93 ^{25}/$_{32}$, 8 ticks of profit), soybeans down to 5.61 ^{1}/$_{4}$ (from entry price of 5.63, a loss of 1 ^{3}/$_{4}$ cents), and gold down to 413.30 (from entry price of 413.70, a minimal profit of 40 cents).

Overall, this was not a bad trading day; the profits on the financials more than offset the one loss on the soybean trade. If you had counted on allowing a tick on either side of the trade to enter and exit, the profits would still have been for one day of trading. And this was one of the laziest trading days I have ever had. Trades lasted less than half an hour. The problem was then to try and find something to do for the rest of the trading day without getting into trouble!

CASE 5   A Long Campaign in Gold
with Day Trading Opportunities

This trading campaign lasted less than a month but was interspersed with a large number of profitable day trades. Because the last few examples contained only a few charts, this example contains 16 charts! This is the author's way of using the Law of Alternation: one simple one followed by one complex one.

Figure C5.1 is a daily bar chart, created on 12-11 @ 9:44 A.M., of April gold from May to December. Superimposed onto the chart are three moving averages: 5, 13, and 21 days.

I have often been asked why I use Fibonacci numbers (rather than other numbers) for length of moving averages. In fact, I do use other numbers, such as 14 for RSI and 7 for stochastics. In moving averages, I have discovered that the length of the block of data averaged basically reflects how short-term or long-term oriented the trader is. Because there are no hard and fast rules to use in applying moving averages, I have arbitrarily picked Fibonacci numbers: A constancy of analysis is better than randomness. Constancy allows the analyst to reconstruct analyses. If randomness is used to select the length of moving averages, it would be difficult to take the same analysis of one market and apply it to another market without first having to establish some sort of base approach!

The chart shows that the price has moved above the moving averages, and that, on this date, December 11, a correction is in store. Why? When markets are moving straight up as this market is, price has less of a tendency to cross the moving average lines to the downside. However, once price does cross the moving average to the downside, the day trader can make one of two conclusions: Either the market has topped out and is headed downwards, or the market hasn't topped out but is vulnerable for a correction.

Minimally, price moving past the moving averages show a correction; maximally, such price action indicates that a top has been made.

The price of gold took about two months to move from the $373 per ounce level to $425 per ounce level, a pretty good move. How does one play this market? Should one go long? Should one go short?

I assessed the situation and decided to try and sell weakness and not buy strength. I saw that the completed move to the upside had not been finished. A simple wave count showed that a five-wave impulse wave had not been completed, with a fifth wave yet to form. The third wave that appeared probably ended at the marked ③. Was this move, from $407.20 to the current pricing at $421.90, part of the fifth wave, or was it still part of the A-B-C

Figure C5.1

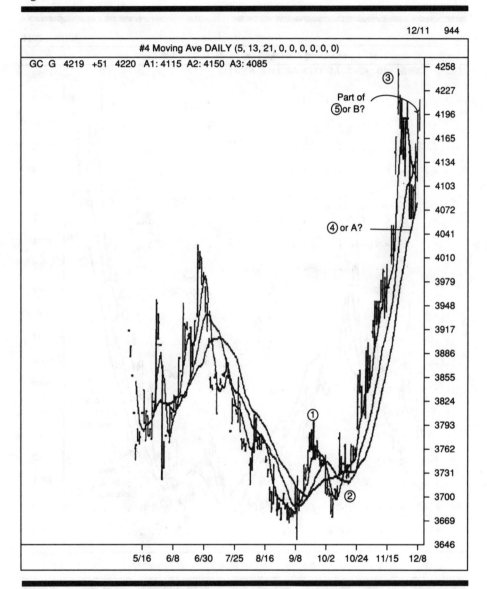

correction, with the C wave yet to form to the downside? A correct interpretation of this would yield the right day trading strategy.

I exploded Figure C5.1 so that it would fill the screen completely. In doing so, I was able to see more details. The lengths of the moving averages were maintained.

Figure C5.2, created the next day (12-12 @ 8:56 P.M.), showed that gold prices had closed $1 higher to $422.80 and was within reach of the previous wave ③ top at around the $425 level. Upon

Figure C5.2
(a) 411,00.

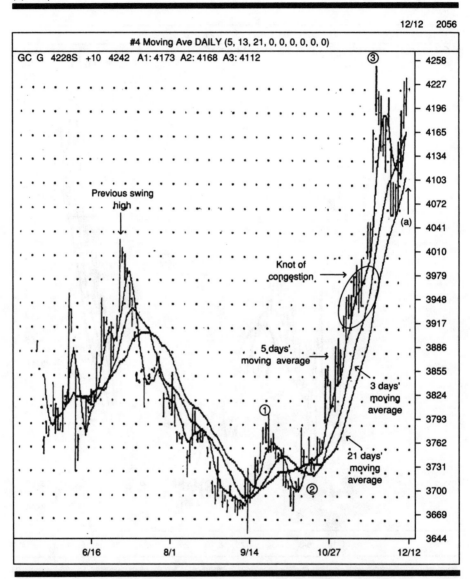

further inspection, the first wave down from the wave ③ top showed prices moving from $425 down to $407.20. The wave, definitely a correction, was either an A of an A-B-C or the completed A-B-C wave ending at the $407.20 level. Why was the latter such a probability? If you inspect the move downwards, you will see that it could be broken down into an A-B-C wave correction that lasted about 8 days (8 is a Fibonacci number in itself).

Somewhat subjectively, I concluded that the move downward was only the A of a yet-to-be-finished A-B-C larger corrective wave.

Why? Take a look at the previous move, the third impulse wave. It was a long move and shot up in less than 2 months. Such a strong move upward had to be corrected downward by a similar length. The correction, if it was from $425 to $407.20, was awfully short. I eyeballed the pattern and concluded that the correction should at least move down to the $401 level to test the previous swing high made around July. Also, in the third impulse wave up, there was a knot of congestion between $391.70 and $400.00. What better place than this for prices to come back to and test these levels before charging on to new highs?

In fact, because the previous swing high was made in July, gold prices had to chew around the $391.70—$400 area in the knot. It was like a visitation line passing an open coffin: everybody had to stop and pay their last respects on the way out. My feeling was the same: Let prices chew around this level before charging on to new highs. Let prices come back to these levels and pay their respects one more time!

With such a conclusion, I fully prepared to play the gold market from the short side, looking for weakness. Also, I sensitized myself to the intersection price of the 21-day moving average. On this particular chart, I was on guard to note price behavior around the $411 level. If prices took out that level to the downside, then all hell would break loose!

Figure C5.3 was created 12-13 @ 3:02 P.M., the next day after the close. Price had dropped $9.90 an ounce to a $412.90 settlement. This served as confirmation to me that this was the C wave of the A-B-C correction.

Also, please remember that the previous day's crossover price of the 21-day moving average was about $411. Today's selloff didn't get there, but gold was certainly weak enough to sell off close to $10 an ounce! This little downside action was a tease—it got low, but not low enough to warrant a grand selloff.

What could I have done if perchance my analysis was incorrect and that instead of this being the final part of a correction—the C wave of an A-B-C movement—this was a correction of another wave into the fifth wave—that the fourth wave correction really ended at the $406 level, that the move down from about $423 to $412.90 was the second wave correction of the fifth wave?

Glad you asked!

First, the extended move upward warrants a longer downward correction, so that the correction from the highs was too short in duration (only 8 days or so) and too short in price correction (from $425 to $406, or $19) to offset the extended upside movement. Of course, there are always exceptions, and it is possible that perhaps the extended upward move needed only a weak correction.

Figure C5.3

#	Time	High	Low	Last	Open
142	12/5	4107	4066	4089	4066
>143	12/6	4104	4065	4101	4078
144	12/7	4160	4075	4150	4108

Second, if this move from $406 to $423 is indeed the first impulse wave of a larger fifth wave, then the first wave is pretty darn long! Remember that first waves are similar in length and duration to fifth waves of the same scale, so if the first wave is about $17 in price move length in our situation, then the fifth wave should be about $17 in length also, *and* the third wave, being the longest of the impulse waves, must be greater than $17 in length! If this holds true, then the fifth wave will run out of gas at around the $460–$470 level. This level is calculated using $17 as the average length of three waves—first, third, fifth—or $3 \times \$17 = \$51$; then adding about $51 to the suspected beginning of the fifth wave of $406 to give $457 as a possible final objective. Of course, I used a bit of rounding upward to get the $460–$470 objective, because the third wave must be greater than $17 in length.

So it appears as if this correction has yet to be completed. As an interested trader, I awaited the completion of the C wave! Hopefully, I waited for entry points in my short-sales.

Figure C5.4 was created on 12-19 @ 8:03 A.M. and is composed of five separate charts: #1 is a 5-minute bar chart; #2 is a 30-minute Market Profile (copyright Chicago Board of Trade) chart; #3 is a 15-minute bar chart; #4 is a 60-minute chart; and #5 is a daily bar chart to give me a larger perspective.

You may have started to wonder why I have not applied any extended moving averages or momentum analyses to this trading example. Moving averages and momentum studies have their places in day trading, but because the length of data is so arbitrarily defined, they are very imprecise. When I day trade, I consider precision to be a very important factor. The use of arbitrarily defined factors in relatively precise mathematical tools gives a false confidence to the trader. Instead of relying on faked precision, I use these studies as basic guides, but when the execution points are required I use more precise techniques.

In the chart, you can see from the daily bar chart that the price congestion at the upper ranges still provides for a possible correction to lower prices. On this particular day's trading activity, the Market Profile chart shows a long first half-hour of trading activity from period A, bracketed from a high price of $419 to a low of $415. It appears as if the prices might go up for the rest of the day. There is still no entry of shorts.

Figure C5.5 was created on 12-21 @ 11:11 P.M., rather late in the trading day. I had a restless day and was up late to analyze the markets. After waiting for such a length of time for the hunt to begin, I sensed that something major was about to happen. Again this chart is basically composed of the elements found in Figure C5.4 with the five types of charts.

What is interesting in this day's analysis is that the gold market appears to be heading into some sort of tailspin to the downside. How does this appear?

The first signs of some setup situation for a major collapse appear. The daily bar chart (#5) shows a coiling price action reaching to an apex price of about $415. This in itself does not show the direction of the imminent breakout—either upside or downside. Remember, though, that I am expecting a sell off to the downside. Now, all I need is confirmation of such action and I can jump on board.

Figure C5.4

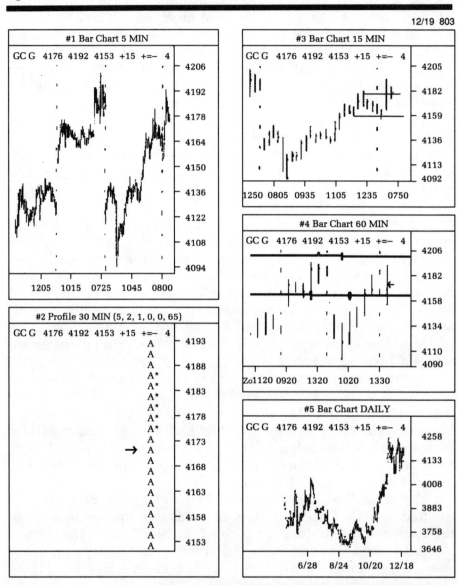

The 60-minute (#4) and the 15-minute (#3) bar charts indicate continually lower tops, especially the former chart. The 60-minute chart shows continually lower tops, whereas the high bottoms are fewer in number and are spread out to a greater degree. The lower tops can even be seen to appear sequentially, one right after the other. This is another good sign for bearish strategies!

The final sign comes from the Market Profile. The rotation of price activities is downward. In any major reversal area the trader

Figure C5.5

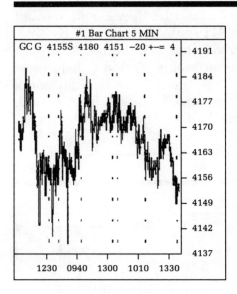

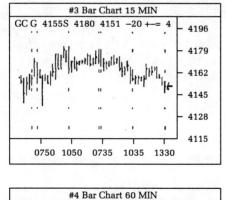

12/21 2311

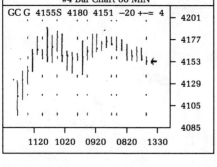

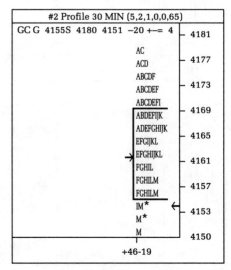

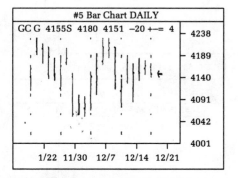

can expect some rotational activity spread out over several days before the price reversal is imminent. Because this profile didn't look like a fully normal day or a nontrend day, a hybrid form was created by market action. This is the only "go slow" sign that I saw. This type of action had to work itself out more before I could get on board to the downside.

The way the 5-minute chart (#1) showed a selloff into the close—but with a slight rebound off the lows made minutes before the close—reflected the *fact* that there were still buyers of the gold.

Not yet...not so soon. I must wait a bit more before I start to sell gold.

Figure C5.6 was created on 12-22 @ 10:59 A.M. and showed additional movements around the $415 price level.

This was a tough one to justify in terms of bearish analyses. The only bearish sign was the Market Profile. Period A held most of the day's trading range and it was toward the half-day mark that prices started to move out of the range bracketed by A period. However, I did not expect prices to challenge new highs by much,

Figure C5.6

12/22 1059

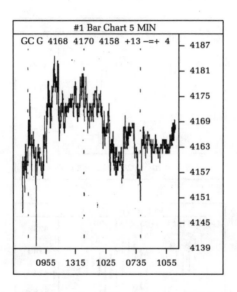

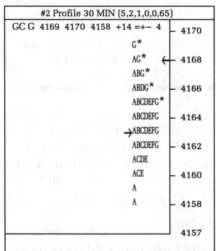

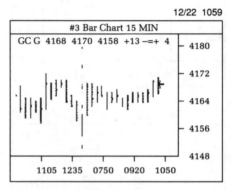

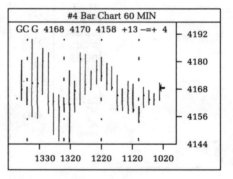

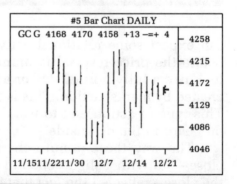

because the Value Area was made at around the $416.50 area. Additionally, the range of prices was too small to be of any significance in any forecastable price move: Price probes to the upside or the downside could not effectively discover whether there were sellers or buyers waiting in the wings.

This was, in effect, an uninformative day.

Figure C5.7, created on 12-23 @ 37 minutes past midnight, showed exactly the same information as Figure C5.6.

Figure C5.7

12/23 1237

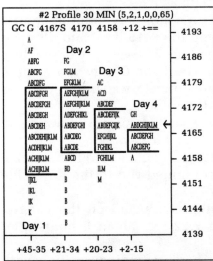

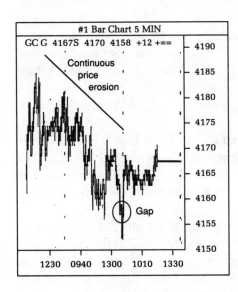

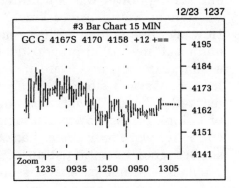

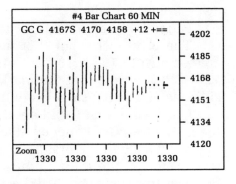

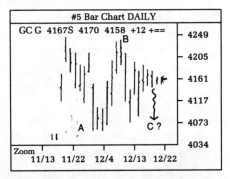

There was one major exception: In the profile chart, four days' trading activities were compacted. In Figure C5.5, you saw price rotation that formed a somewhat normal profile. In Figure C5.7 the four days' activities showed even more rotation spread out over a greater number of days and prices converging to an apex.

In Chart #2, Day 1 showed price rotation to the downside. Day 2 showed rotation to the upside. Day 3 showed rotation to the downside. Day 4 showed rotation to the upside. The four days' price activity showed an alternating down-up-down-up pattern. Even more interesting, though, is the fact that each day's price range narrowed from the previous day's range! This showed that prices had reached a balance level and a battle between buying and selling power was unfolding.

Where would prices break? Up or down? Down, of course! How was this evident? Please note Chart #5, the daily bar chart, and recall my initial prognostication that gold prices had reached a temporary top and were in an A-B-C correction. Wave A had formed. Wave B stopped going up at a top lower than the level reached at $425. Wave C was not forming. The first impulse wave of C took prices down to around the $407 level, and a second corrective wave took prices back up to the $420 level; if I had only shorted gold in anticipation of tomorrow's opening! This is the problem with market analysis—by the time the trader has had the time to digest all the information, the markets could have moved away from the trader.

Patiently, I had to wait for the next day's opening.

The eighth chart of this trading example (Figure C5.8) was created on 12-27 @ 2:18 A.M., after the day's trading had ended on 12-26. Please note that the markets closed for Christmas and had abbreviated trading sessions on Christmas Eve.

On the opening I sold short, with a stop buy order at around the $417 level. Gold opened at around the $415 level and dropped to around $409 in the first hour of trading. The velocity of the drop surely created the third impulse wave of the C wave correction. Because this appeared to be a third impulse wave, lower prices had to be made after a corrective rally to the upside.

Bracing for a sharp correction, I waited for new lows to be made on either the twenty-sixth or the next day.

Now that I had a profitable position, I could afford to risk some of the profits for more profits if a continued run to the downside occurred.

Figure C5.9 is the actual trading conducted on the twenty-seventh; the printout was made at 7:22 P.M., about 5 hours after trading had stopped.

This is essentially the hardest part in trading: waiting with positions when the trader is just itching to close out profitable

Figure C5.8

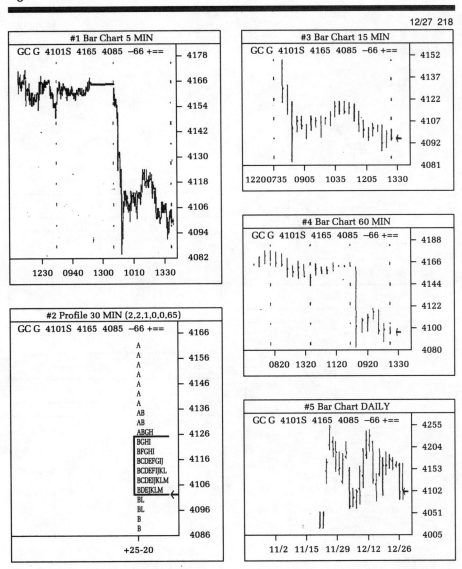

trading and count the profits! My cautionary advice is as follows: Don't, unless your life depends on closing out profitable trades. The beauty of trading is that there really isn't much work that a trader has to do once a profitable position is established. No matter what the trader does to his position, he cannot really mastermind the direction and duration of the markets. The only actions that a trader can execute are exit orders of already existing positions. He can execute exit orders to cut his losses if the positions are losing money; *or he can execute exit orders to cut his profits.* And

Figure C5.9

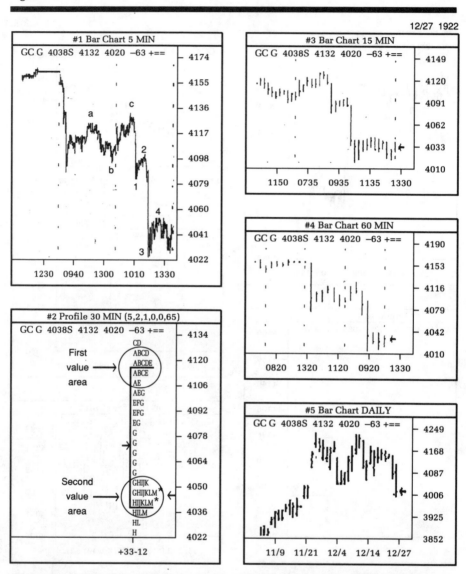

surprisingly, a very large number of traders will look for whatever reasons to cut their profits short!

Chart #1 appears to have an incompleted impulse wave to the downside; that is, the fifth wave hadn't been formed yet. Price had to reach new lows yet.

Additionally, Chart #2, a profile chart, looks extremely bearish: It is a downside profile with *two* Value Areas. The first Value Area was formed around the $412–$410 level. The second Value Area formed between $404 and $403. Double Value Areas were indications that prices hadn't reached levels of support or resistance and that new lows or highs had yet to be reached. In this case, the $400 low level would not hold! Why cover shorts at $400 when they can be covered at lower prices?

Figure C5.10, was created on 12-28 @ 3:47 P.M., after the gold market had closed. Several forecasts were fulfilled.

In Chart #1, the 5-minute bar chart, the fifth wave of the five-impulse wave punched through to new lows. From the 60-minute

Figure C5.10

12/28 1547

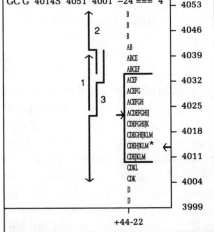

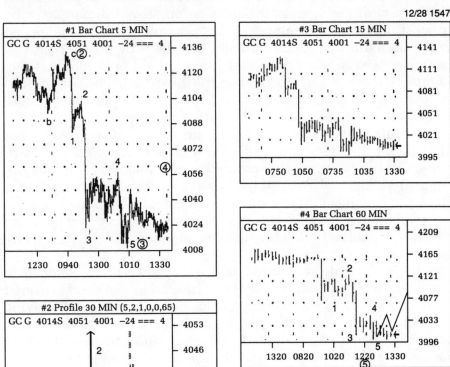

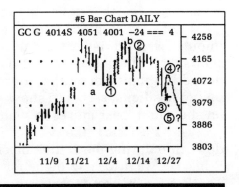

bar chart, #4, the new lows for the move were made in the second hour of trading.

Shorts initiated at around the $416 level were covered at around the $400 level. You may ask why shorts were covered at such an opportune price. Because I was looking for new lows in this move, any move to below the end of the third wave was considered a new low. Once prices punched out the lows made at the end of the third wave, at around the $401 level, *any* tick below that warranted short covering. Of course, I could have done further analysis by taking a look at the length of wave 1 and measuring the fifth wave and approximate the distance of travel (first and fifth waves are similar in length), but this precision would have been wasted, because the returns on spending so much time on this aspect of the analysis would have improved performance by at most only $1-$2 an ounce. In this example, it just so happened that prices did not punch through $400 level by much, so it was within a $400 to $401 price range that I could only have covered shorts. Had prices gone to $370 on the downside, the shorts would still have been covered around the $400 level. The result is a profit of $16 per ounce on a day and a half of trading.

At this critical juncture, I was still unsure of whether or not the low for the move was made. For a clue, I inspected #5 Chart, the daily bar chart, and discovered a probable count. It was obvious that the third wave of the C wave correction was in effect. I drew the conclusion that a probable low hadn't been made for the complete move, because it was very possible to ink in a probable fourth wave correction to the upside and a final fifth wave to really new lows.

What did I do? I covered part of my shorts and held on to the balance for a possible new low. The amounts of shorts covered run between ½ to ⅔ of the total position. The object of leaving so relatively few contracts open is to minimize possible losses that may come about with a totally intact position in case the lows around the $400 level held and the market reversed to the upside, yet at the same time there were positions open that could take advantage of further downside moves.

For more risk-prone traders, especially day traders, because the impulse wave started around the opening of the previous day, more shorts could have been added on any strength! The fact that I did not add to shorts, but rather looked for opportunities to lighten up on my positions, serves to show my conservative stance to trading on short-term bear moves in viable bull markets!

The #2 Chart, the Market Profile, showed weakness to the downside during the C time bracket. A bracket opened higher, the B bracket went to new highs for the day, and then rotated down. The C time bracket took out new lows for the day. This showed still more selling. The fact that prices then churned around the range created in periods A, B, C, and D showed additional doubt as to whether or not prices were going to hold at these levels or continue downward. The educated guess was that prices would go still lower: The last trade in M period was below half of the day's range, and the Value Area did not look evenly balanced but was skewed to a teardrop shape toward the downside—this was inferred to be continued erosion of price supports. The prognosis was that prices were to go still lower.

Figure C5.11 was created on 12-30 @ 1:35 A.M. This was another sleepless night for me and I looked at the gold chart again to forecast what would happen the next day.

Please note that this day was also preceeding a holiday, New Year's Day; this warranted caution and care trading the gold market. Volume is much lighter around the holidays, so price movements are not as valid as ones made on normal-volume days.

From #1 Chart, a 5-minute bar chart, it appears as if the fourth wave had been completed and that a fifth wave was going to punch through $400 on the downside. This C wave correction (C waves are always composed of five waves, never three waves) to the upside was a perfect five-wave sequence: Note that the third wave of this C wave had a gap from the previous day's action (another confirming indicator that the third was the third wave).

The #2 Chart showed an interesting profile pattern. Note that the auction line (the leftmost letters) showed continually higher prices, yet a Value Area formed once D period had been made on the auction line. The market was strong to the upside, but somehow, selling came into the market and pushed it down to a comfortable level where buying and selling entered to form a Value Area. If this was indeed to be a strong reversal, the auction line would have continued upwards to form probably a double distribution trending day pattern. This didn't happen. Instead, prices found *support* at prices off the day's high. Support levels are indicative that selling is in progress; why else would prices stop at some level *after* the selling? Prices did not find additional buying at higher prices.

The #3 and #4 Charts showed confirmation of the C wave count and the possibility that the fourth wave had been completed.

I decided against selling more at these levels but instead looked to cover the balance of my positions on any new lows.

Figure C5.12 was created on 1-2 @ 3:48 P.M. and showed an attempt at new lows. I was not vindicated in my analysis but was considering that I had spent too much time on the analysis. I had already taken out $16 on the trade on part of my positions, but I wanted to squeeze out some extra dollars on the balance of my positions.

Figure C5.11

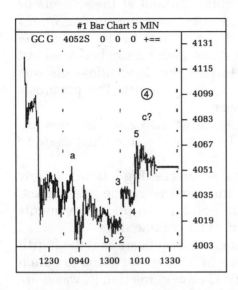

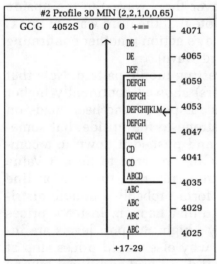

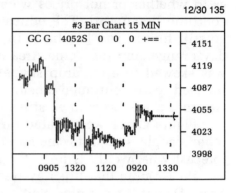

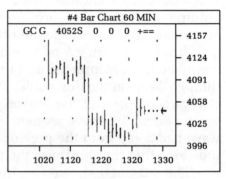

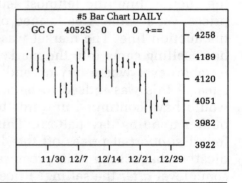

Figure C5.12

01/02 1548

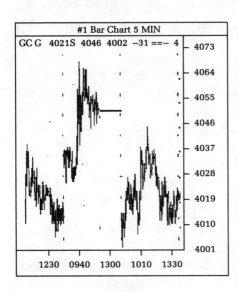

#1 Bar Chart 5 MIN

GC G   4021S   4046   4002 −31 ==− 4

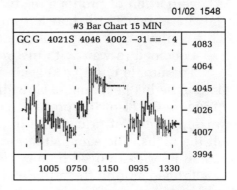

#3 Bar Chart 15 MIN

GC G   4021S   4046   4002 −31 ==− 4

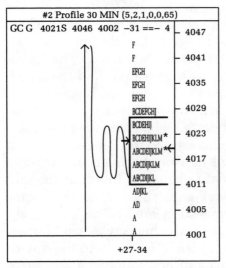

#2 Profile 30 MIN (5,2,1,0,0,65)

GC G   4021S   4046   4002 −31 ==− 4

+27-34

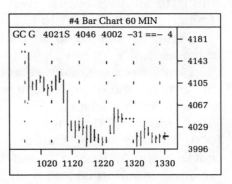

#4 Bar Chart 60 MIN

GC G   4021S   4046   4002 −31 ==− 4

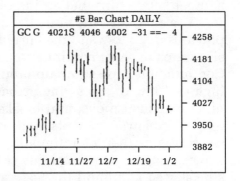

#5 Bar Chart DAILY

GC G   4021S   4046   4002 −31 ==− 4

In a sense, the taking in on such hefty profits eventually contributed to this series of profitable nonplays. Because I had banked a large portion of profits already, I figured that I could hang on to the shorts that I still had left and wait for the end of the world. This is playing from a position of power.

I decided to wait with my profitable positions.

The profile chart (#2) again showed disturbing signs that the bottom hadn't been made. How did it show this? Note the analysis of Figure C5.11 of the profile chart when I noted the auction line was upwards, yet prices sold off and found a Value Area at levels off the highs. The same situation occurs here. From periods A, B, E, and F, prices moved higher, yet towards the close, a Value Area was formed around the middle of the range. Again, there was more selling to support levels, even though there was initial obvious strength from periods A to F! Look out below!

Figure C5.13 created on 1-3 @ 9:39 P.M. vindicates my analysis of the necessity for new lows to be made.

New lows were made at around the $394 level, about $6 from the previous end of the 5 wave at $400. This means at least another $4 profit on the balance of my positions.

A possible bottoming action showed in the Market Profile chart (#2). The day trader would have noticed that the auction line moved from A, B, and L and then rotated upwards. The Value Area was found to be just slightly a bit higher than half the range, another subtle hint that an intermediate bottom had been formed.

The #5 Chart, the daily bar chart, showed a wide gap from the previous day's low and the current day's high. There are three classifications of gaps: continuation, exhaustion, and breakaway gaps. Continuation gaps show up around halfway between the extreme high and low of the swing, exhaustion gaps are found at the end of an extended move, and breakaway gaps show up at the beginning of runaway markets from congestion areas. The gap in #5 Chart was neither a continuation gap nor a breakaway gap, but an exhaustion gap. How was this concluded? The move to the downside started at around the $425 area and had touched a low price of $394, a drop of about $31. The move to the upside started at $364 and hit a top at $425, a move of $61 (see Figure C5.1). A $31 move to the downside was an approximate 50 percent correction. Because I believed this selloff to be a correction before new highs were to be made, a correction of about 50 percent was perfectly acceptable. Once prices reached the $394 level with a gap, I had to conclude that prices had touched bottom.

What to do? Cover all shorts. What about going long at these levels? I have always found it hard to double up at reversal points. It isn't a question of a lack of trading skills, but more a problem with getting the mind reorganized. Because I had played this move

Figure C5.13

01/03 2139

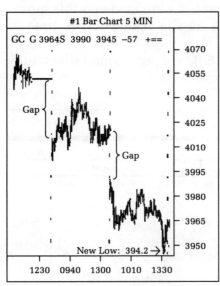

#1 Bar Chart 5 MIN

GC G 3964S 3990 3945 −57 +==

Gap

Gap

New Low: 394.2 →

4070
4055
4040
4025
4010
3995
3980
3965
3950

1230 0940 1300 1010 1330

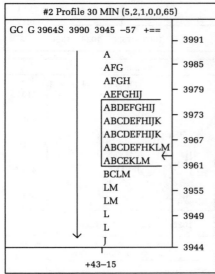

#2 Profile 30 MIN (5,2,1,0,0,65)

GC G 3964S 3990 3945 −57 +==

A	3991
AFG	3985
AFGH	
AEFGHIJ	3979
ABDEFGHIJ	
ABCDEFHIJK	3973
ABCDEFHIJK	
ABCDEFHKLM	3967
ABCEKLM ←	3961
BCLM	
LM	3955
LM	
L	3949
L	
J	3944

+43−15

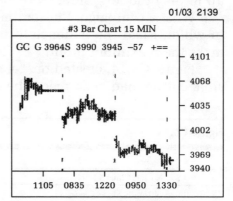

#3 Bar Chart 15 MIN

GC G 3964S 3990 3945 −57 +==

4101
4068
4035
4002
3969
3940

1105 0835 1220 0950 1330

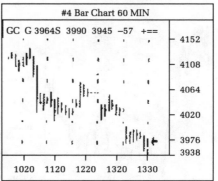

#4 Bar Chart 60 MIN

GC G 3964S 3990 3945 −57 +==

4152
4108
4064
4020
3976
3938

1020 1120 1220 1320 1330

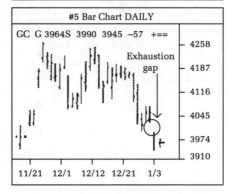

#5 Bar Chart DAILY

GC G 3964S 3990 3945 −57 +==

Exhaustion gap

4258
4187
4116
4045
3974
3910

11/21 12/1 12/12 12/21 1/3

to the downside for such a relatively long time (about 3 weeks), it would take at least about a week or two before I could set my mind up to play the long side.

What a campaign. Substantial profits were made on this move, in which I had the patience to wait for the right point in time to make the maximum profit.

Figure C5.14, created on 1-4 @ 5:03 P.M., confirmed that a possible bottom had been made the previous day.

Figure C5.14

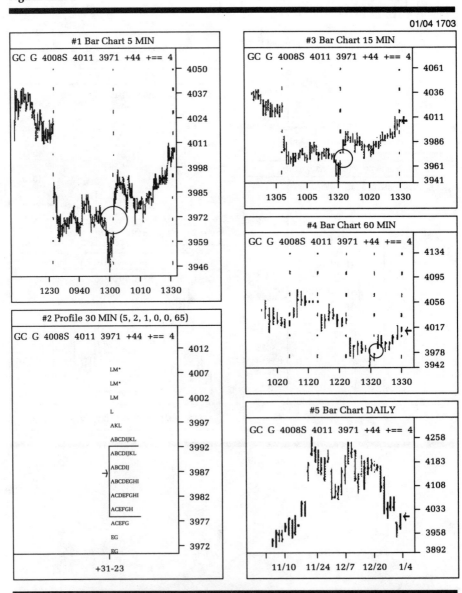

Figure C5.15

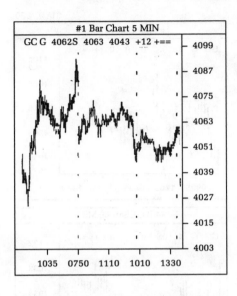

#1 Bar Chart 5 MIN

GC G 4062S 4063 4043 +12 +==

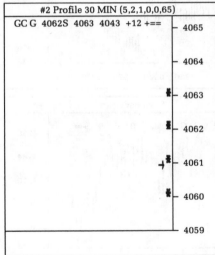

#2 Profile 30 MIN (5,2,1,0,0,65)

GC G 4062S 4063 4043 +12 +==

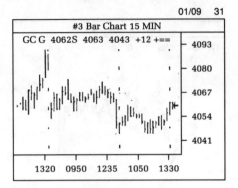

#3 Bar Chart 15 MIN

GC G 4062S 4063 4043 +12 +==

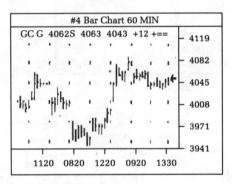

#4 Bar Chart 60 MIN

GC G 4062S 4063 4043 +12 +==

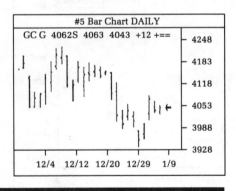

#5 Bar Chart DAILY

GC G 4062S 4063 4043 +12 +==

Figure C5.16

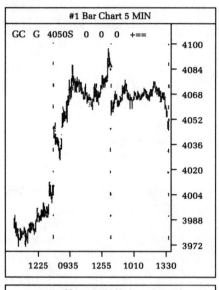

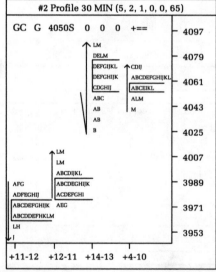

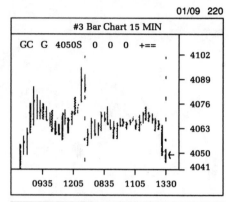

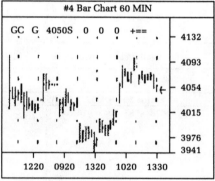

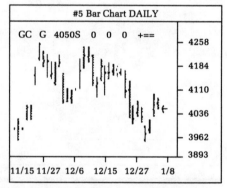

The #1 Chart, the 5-minute bar chart, showed a breakaway gap to the upside from a one-day reversal. This gap was not shown on the daily bar chart, however. I offer a word of caution in looking for and evaluating gaps for possible directional moves: Always consider the charts discovered within the context of the type of bar charts. If you were looking at 5-minute bar charts and saw a gap forming, it would be incorrect to apply the conclusion drawn to a daily bar chart, where the gap is not evident. Within the context of the 5-minute bar chart, the gap is valid, and any counter signals within this 5-minute bar chart must be heeded.

The Market Profile chart initially showed a weak gap opening up: Prices opened higher, but as the day wore on, it started to sell off. The selloff was arrested at period E and then found higher and higher support until, in the last two periods (L and M), prices punched through to new highs for the day. This indicated to me that prices were destined to go higher. If shorts were still open, they had to be covered on this type of market action!

Because the market action of gold was moving higher, it wasn't necessary to illustrate the action with additional price charts. Figure C5.15 was created on 1-9 @ 31 minutes past midnight. As you can see, prices have now moved to about the $406 level, after touching $409 briefly, a $15 move off the lows.

If I wanted to, I could continue to trade from the short side, always on guard for any possible sharp rallies.

At this time, though, I looked elsewhere for trading opportunities. The only way I would have traded this gold market was to wait for prices to find price supports and go long for the final move to the upside, the fifth wave.

The final chart, Figure C5.16, shows the next day's trading activity. What is important is the Market Profile chart. The chart showed continued rotation at the first two patterns, with higher auction lines in the last two trading days. This served as further confirmation that prices had to head up.

In conclusion, I found a very profitable trading campaign to make substantial profits with a composite series of approaches.

CASE 6 Using Gann Lines with Japanese Yen

This case does not deal with any particular trade, but rather with how Gann lines work compared to regular trend lines. This case uses only four figures, so you should be able to digest the analyses more easily.

Figure C6.1 was created on 11-22 @ 1:49 A.M. and comprises four 5-minute bar charts. Each chart shows trend lines drawn onto

Figure C6.1

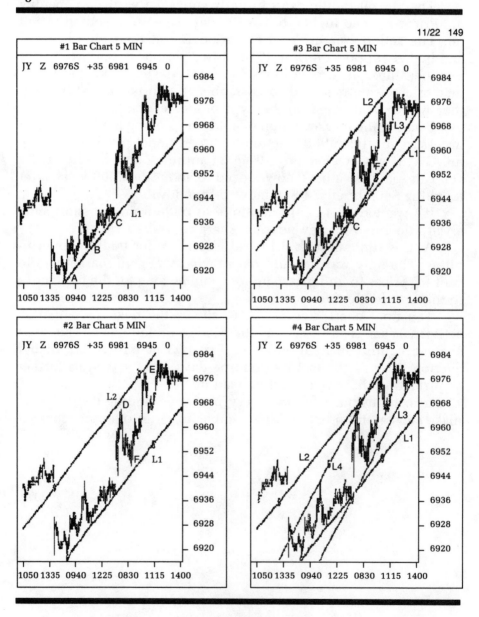

it. Trend lines are lines drawn on bar charts or tick charts that connect at least two points. These trend lines show support or resistance that has been projected out into the future. The trader who trades with these lines expects to go long on sell-offs to these critical lines or short on rallies to these critical lines.

The #1 Chart has an uptrending trend line drawn and identified as L1. Line L1 was created by connecting two points, A and B, which were sell-off lows of the Japanese yen contract. Coincidentally, point C is very nearly included in the drawn line L1. This gives further indication that L1 is a valid trend line: On the third sell-off, prices reversed off point C!

The #2 Chart has an additional line, L2, drawn on it. L2 is a parallel trend line to L1. From empirical evidence, analysts have determined that price oscillates between an upper trend line and a lower trend line in its movement through time. L2 is used as a gauge to determine where prices will find resistance. As you can see, L2 is not quite drawn to connect points D and E. I have moved L2 slightly higher than the actual intersection points so that it is easier to see. The #2 Chart now contains two parallel upward-sloping trend lines that contain the actual price moves of the 5-minute bar chart.

An axiom proposed by William D. Gann stipulates that, as prices start to move higher and higher, prices will move with greater velocity to the upside. Conversely, the higher price goes, the sharper it will break when it does sell off. Because prices behave in such a manner, Gann used sharply sloping lines to serve as reversal points. If the sharpest-angled line was broken to the upside, Gann would use this as a sell signal to get rid of long positions. For initiating shorts, he was considerably more conservative in assessing reversal points—that is, he would use double-top formations, which naturally take a longer time to evolve. There is evidence that empirically drawn trend lines correlate to a high degree with some of the important Gann lines.

Figure C6.2 is #4 Chart of Figure C6.1 blown up to fill a complete page. In the upper left-hand corner is a group of lines labeled as "Gann Lines." Some of these lines have been marked in the G-series: G1, G2, G3, and so on. The point from which these lines originate is labeled G. Each line has a significant numerical ratio. All lines are sloped in the following ratios:

1×8 has a $82\frac{1}{2}$-degree slope.

1×4 has a 75-degree slope.

1×3 has a $71\frac{1}{4}$-degree slope.

1×2 has a $63\frac{3}{4}$-degree slope.

234 THE ART OF DAY TRADING

Figure C6.2

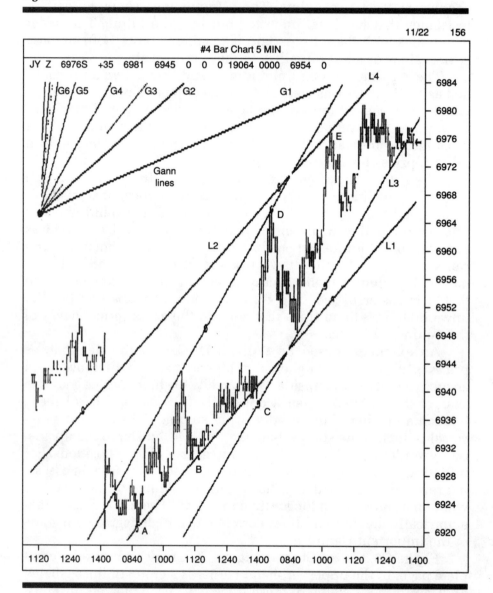

2×1 has a $25\frac{1}{4}$-degree slope.

3×1 has a $18\frac{3}{4}$-degree slope.

4×1 has a 15-degree slope.

8×1 has a $7\frac{1}{2}$-degree slope.

Each Gann line is correlated with certain planetary phenomena. You may wish to consult my book *The Technical Analysis of Stocks, Options and Futures* for additional information on the use of Gann lines.

The 8×1 line has a $7\frac{1}{2}$-degree slope: For every eight units that the analyst moves over on the X-axis, he moves up one unit on the Y-axis. The line slopes upward at an angle of $7\frac{1}{2}$ degrees. The 1×8 line has an $82\frac{1}{2}$-degree slope. If you were to add the two angles together, $7\frac{1}{2}$ and $82\frac{1}{2}$ degrees, you would get a 90-degree angle, where prices would go straight upward.

Knowing where to start from is important when considering the angled lines, but it is not necessary for understanding how to use Gann lines. Consider the situation where the Gann lines are based off the Y-axis, instead of the X-axis. In this case, the 8×1 line would have an $82\frac{1}{2}$-degree slope instead of a $7\frac{1}{2}$-degree slope. Conversely, the 1×8 line would have the $7\frac{1}{2}$-degree slope.

It is important to recognize the relationship each line has with the other lines, not the absolute numbers! Gann indicated that, if a price in a bull market broke past a sharply sloped line, it would find support from the next-sharpest-sloped line all the way to the least-sloped line (a horizontal line). Seeing price break the least-sloped line in a bull market, Gann would draw a new set of Gann lines from the high of the move, with the lines sloping downward. Each of these set of lines indicated that the slopes of the lines were again important indicators of the weakness of the market: Eventually breaking the sharpest-sloped line would indicate an imminent reversal to the upside! Breaking of sharper-sloped lines is also the way that markets must be analyzed using regularly created trend lines.

Figure C6.3 shows the same data as Figure C6.2, with the exception that the set of Gann lines has been moved to point A. In this figure, I have taken the complete set of Gann lines and imposed point G onto point A. It is interesting to note that line G3, shifted a bit off to the right so that you can see the line, is right on top of line L1. The market has found support at trend line L1, which happens to be Gann line G3!

Figure C6.3

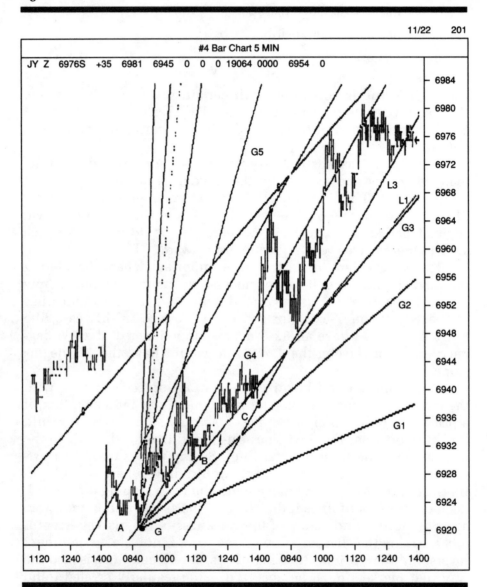

Figure C6.4 shows the same blown-up 5-minute bar chart from Chart #4 of Figure C6.1, except that this time the author has shifted the set of Gann lines from point A to point F.

Now, the Gann line that is imposable onto the sharper-sloped trend line L3 is not G3, but G4! This is consistent with the concept of sharper-sloping trend lines: the more sharply the actual price moves, the more vulnerable it is for price corrections. Using the

Figure C6.4

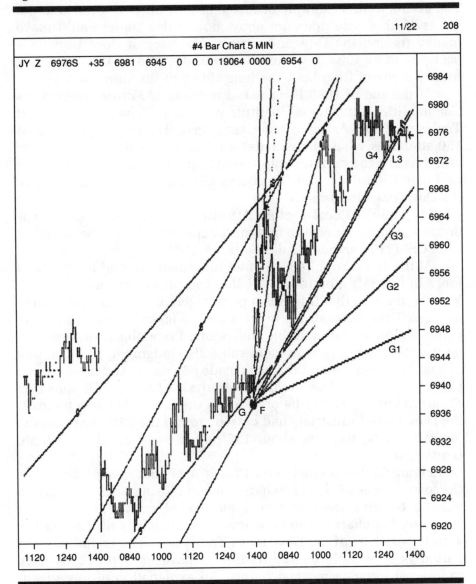

crossover of price past the sharpest viable trend line results in a continued sell-off.

Using Gann lines in place of trend lines drawn from empirical evidence allows the day trader to standardize his analytical techniques. The Gann lines were evolved from natural planetary cycles; however, it is beyond the scope of this volume to explain at length how these lines were mathematically derived.

CASE 7   Forecasting the Dow Industrials

The events in this example occurred at the end of December 1989. By itself, this case does not show how a day trader could make money trading the Dow Industrials. However, it does provide a background for Case 8, which illustrates day trading the S&P Index futures contract from both the long side and the short side.

At the end of 1989 I was asked to speak at *Futures* magazine's Commodities Educational Institute workshop, "The Best Tools and Trades of 1990." As a guest speaker I was asked to present to about 150 attendees what I considered the best trades for the upcoming year. Sharing the podium with David Caplan, Dennis Gartman, Bob Coffman, Glen Ring, and Jake Bernstein, I gave a price analysis of the Dow Jones Industrials.

My topic, "Global Factors Affecting Foreign Currencies," was documented on videotape and audiotape, which may be obtained from CEI (219 Parkade, Cedar Falls, IA 50613).

At the workshop, I spoke of an imminent reversal for the Dow Jones Industrials around the "2836 level, plus or minus 5 points." You should note that this was a price objective forecast, not a time forecast. Time forecasts are much easier to make because of the dependence on already reliable indicators. Price objective forecasts, on the other hand, require more subjective judgment. (An example of a perfect time forecast that was made 660 days in advance can be found in my book *The Technical Analysis of Stocks, Options and Futures*.) On the Friday before I made the price objective forecast, the Dow Jones Industrials had closed around the 2700 level, so the forecasted objective was about 136 points away, an all-time high, if attained.

Figure C7.1 was created on 12-8 @ 4:21 A.M., several days after the forecast was made. The chart shows a closing price of 2720.80, about 116 points away from the forecasted objective. The #1 Chart is a daily bar chart of the Dow Jones Industrials, and #2 Chart is a daily bar chart of the Dow Jones Transports. The technique that I used is applicable to day trading—I have used it successfully to forecast intraday reversal points. An explanation of these techniques was offered separately as a trading seminar; however, such an explanation would be too lengthy for this chapter. In the lecture, I went to great lengths to compare the mechanics of William D. Gann's "square of nine" chart with the workings of deoxyribonucleic acid molecules! For the reader who is unfamiliar with the Gann techniques, I should explain that Gann techniques are directly related to natural laws of oscillations and vibrations. The most-often-used function in Gann techniques is the sine wave.

In #1 and #2 Charts I wished to analyze averages from the perspective of Dow theory. For an explanation of Dow theory, see

Figure C7.1

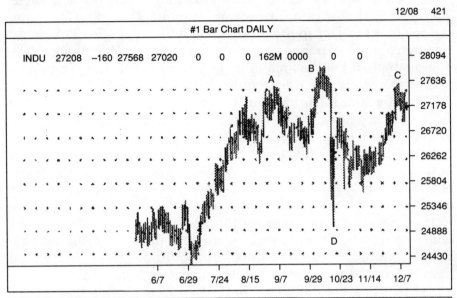

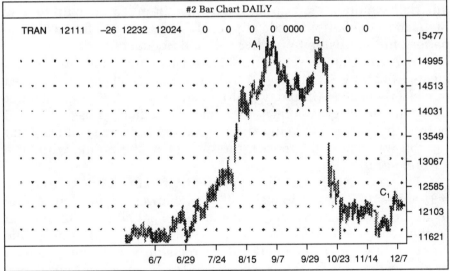

my book *The Technical Analysis of Stocks, Options and Futures.*
The crux of Dow theory is confirmation or nonconfirmation of one
of the Industrials with the Transport averages.

   At point A of #1 Chart, the Industrials made new highs. This
was confirmed by the action of the Transport averages at point A1
of #2 Chart. Such a phenomenon was in line with Dow theory: One

average's move to new highs must be confirmed within a short time by the other average.

At point B of #1 Chart, the Industrials surged to new highs after a normal correction. However, at point B1 of #2 Chart, you can see that the Transports did not surge to new highs. This was a classic example of nonconfirmation according to Dow theory: The intermediate, if not the long-term, bull market was over. The signal to traders everywhere was to unload longs and possibly go short.

Shortly after the price points B and B1 were made, I forecasted an upside objective of the Dow Industrials at 2834. The move of prices to point C for the Industrials and point C1 for the Transports indicated that the Industrials had to be very strong to even try to transfer strength to the tremendously weakened Transports. At points C and C1 the buyers were coming in to push prices higher, but the buying could not be mustered in the Transports. This gave further credence to my forecast that the Industrials' move to new highs would not be supported by strength in the Transports. That is, the new highs in the Industrials would be bogus and would have to be used as cover to unload longs and to go short.

Consulting the daily bar chart, it appeared to me that the Industrials would attempt to form a 5-wave impulse wave up to new highs from the bottom made at point D. Now I had to find a 5-wave pattern to the upside to further validate my conclusions.

In April 1990 I went back to the Dow Jones Industrials and created Figure C7.2, 4-16 @ 1:35 P.M. The Industrials had topped out exactly at 2834 (intraday high) on January 3, 1990—32 calendar days after the original forecast of a reversal at 2836, plus or minus 5 points, that was made to the audience at the *Futures* seminar. After the top was made, the market dropped over 300 points without a sustained rally.

Figure C7.2 contains three apparently identical line charts: #2, #3, and #4. For the precision that I required in my forecasting technique, it was necessary to examine the actual price in relation to the type of chart used: closes-only line chart, highs-only line chart, or lows-only line chart. Such precision may be glossed over by the reader, but for those who are in the business of forecasting, it is imperative. If an imprecise base is used, then future events are imprecise. Sloppiness begets sloppiness.

Please note point D2 of #2 Chart, point D3 of #3 Chart, and point D4 of #4 Chart. Points D2 and D4 are lower than point D3, even though the first two points were derived from the same data of the same day! Considered alone, this fact may seem unimportant, but when the analyst compares the points at G2, G3, and G4, it does become a matter of significance.

How is this so? If, for example, the analyst were to follow the closes-only line chart (Chart #2), point D2 would be lower than

Figure C7.2

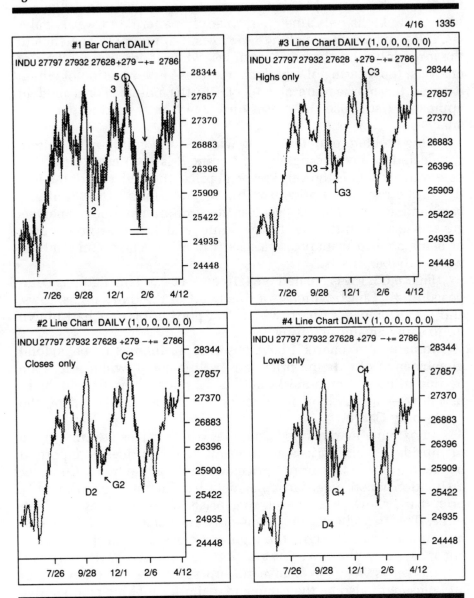

point G2. However, if the analyst were to follow the highs-only line chart, point D3 would be *higher* than point G3! I have used this apparent flaw of considering multiple line charts to add additional insight to market analysis.

The apparent problem can be resolved by applying pure Elliott wave theory to the closing prices of 30-minute bars. Even here, there are problems that may arise in analyzing the "correct" data.

I have a simple approach to analyzing extreme price moves to the upside or the downside. If the markets are making new highs, I look at the highs-only line chart to apply pattern and wave analysis. If the markets are making new lows, I apply more credence to the lows-only line charts. Oftentimes, when there are problems of analysis, the filtering of which charts to use as a function of which extreme the markets are at will clarify the points. For a median approach, I still use the closes-only chart as a starting point for analysis.

This problem of determining which is the *valid* top or bottom is reflected in day trading. In day trading it is even more critical to determine which is the valid reversal price, the high tick or the low tick of the respective price bars (that is, 5-minute bars, 15-minute bars, and so on). This is because the time frames under analysis are so short. With the day trader's time frame, there is no freedom of being able to reanalyze markets if one is *incorrect* in analysis with daily bar charts.

Figure C7.3 was created on 4-16 @ 1:41 P.M. This figure is composed of #1 Chart, which is a line chart of the daily highs, lows, and closes; and #2 Chart, which is a portion of #1 Chart blown up to show greater detailing.

In using line charts, I have observed an interesting behavioral phenomenon of extreme price moves. In general, when prices are trading in nonextreme markets—that is, not making new highs or new lows—the median price action can be encompassed by the closes-only Chart.

In extreme markets (for example, where prices are running to the upside), closing prices' relationship to high prices is important in predicting whether or not prices will follow the trend. Consider a situation where one particular data bar (in this case, the daily price bar), shows that the closing price is the same as the high price. The two charts, the highs-only line chart and the closes-only line chart, will show the high and close price at the extreme. For most cases the next day's action will be higher. If, however, the market is in an explosive run-up stage, the next day's high and close will also be the same and a similar-looking comparative analysis of the two line charts will reveal the same information: Prices closed on the high. The second day will have, in effect, hidden the close on the high of the previous day.

The day that the price does not close on the high will force the previous day's close on the high to "stick out like a sore thumb" in the two charts! This is a very *subtle* way of discovering an imminent price reversal to the downside. Such a situation occurs rarely, but, because of its rarity, its forecasting ability of an imminent reversal is nearly perfect. In daily bar charts, this method of analysis

Figure C7.3

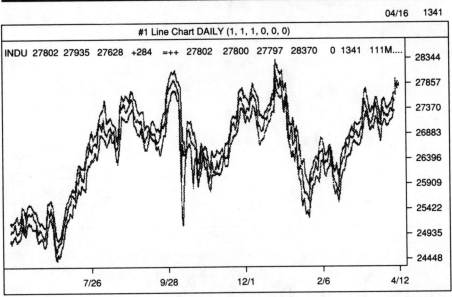

#1 Line Chart DAILY (1, 1, 1, 0, 0, 0)

INDU 27802 27935 27628 +284 =++ 27802 27800 27797 28370 0 1341 111M....

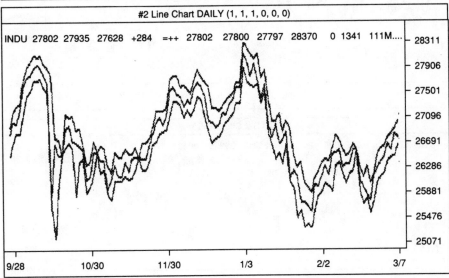

#2 Line Chart DAILY (1, 1, 1, 0, 0, 0)

INDU 27802 27935 27628 +284 =++ 27802 27800 27797 28370 0 1341 111M....

will not disclose too many reversal signals; in intraday charts, however, the situation occurs with greater frequency, depending on the length of the data bar.

Figure C7.4 was created on 4-20 @ 11:52 A.M. and is a basic overview of the daily price action of three markets: #1 is the Dow Jones Industrial Average; #2 is the June bond futures; and #3 is the Dow Jones Utilities Average.

Figure C7.4

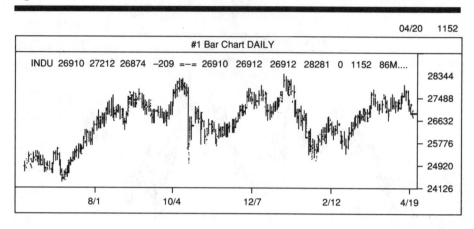

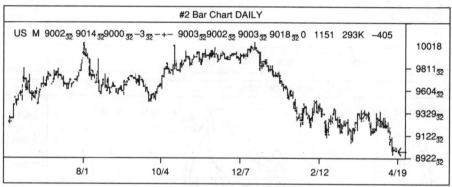

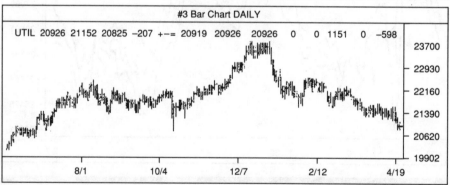

There are no forecasting or trading ideas in these three charts. These charts are provided solely as background materials depicting where the markets eventually headed. I had attempted to discern whether or not the U.S. bond futures had sold off, and I was about to make some investigations of bottoming action.

CASE 8   Day Trading the S&P Index
from the Long and Short Sides

Case 7 was presented as background for the following series of market plays with the March S&P futures contract. I forecast the Dow Jones Industrials to top out at 2836, plus or minus 5 points, in the previous example. Because there was no possible way to play the top in the Industrials as the Industrials, I decided to play the possible S&P top. I also decided not to use the Major Market Index, because there was less active trading in this market and it might have been difficult to get in or out of positions at the time and price that I wanted. The author's reasoning was that the Dow Industrials and the S&P Index should top out at the same time, but not necessarily at the same price levels.

This example uses an extensive array of charts. There are 34 figures, and each illustrates several particular points of analysis. It would be best to study these charts in three different sessions, at about eleven charts per session. The campaign created bullish plays until the top was made, and then a vicious bear campaign started that capitalized on the severe market drop.

Figure C8.1 was created on 12-19 @ 12:28 P.M., partway through the trading day. I used the S&P Index instead of other indexes to trade. My reasoning was that the Dow Jones Industrials were forecasted to top out at around 2836; because the Dow Jones Industrials had not moved up to that price point, the S&P had yet to reach its top. I assumed that the move to the upside would top out in the S&P Index once the Dow Jones Industrials found resistance around the 2836 level. You may question the validity of this conclusion. At the time it appeared to be as valid as any other conclusion I could draw. As the Dow Jones Industrials reached closer to the 2836 level, I could refine my analysis further. Until that point, this early conclusion was the best that could be obtained.

The #5 Chart showed that the S&P futures had reached a top in the second to third week of December at around the 358.00 level and then proceeded to sell off to where it was on this particular day, around the 347.75 level. The drop was about 10 points in about four trading days. My conclusion was that if prices were yet to have found a resistance, then prices had to go up to reach those possible resistance levels. I prepared to go long, despite the fact that once price levels reached a resistance level I would then go short.

The #2 Chart showed the first signs that a possible bottom was forming. Why was this so? The Market Profile (copyright Chicago Board of Trade) pattern showed early weakness from the opening through the A, B, and C periods. This weakness was then followed by support and then higher range development. The Value Area then formed in the upper half of the complete day's trading

Figure C8.1

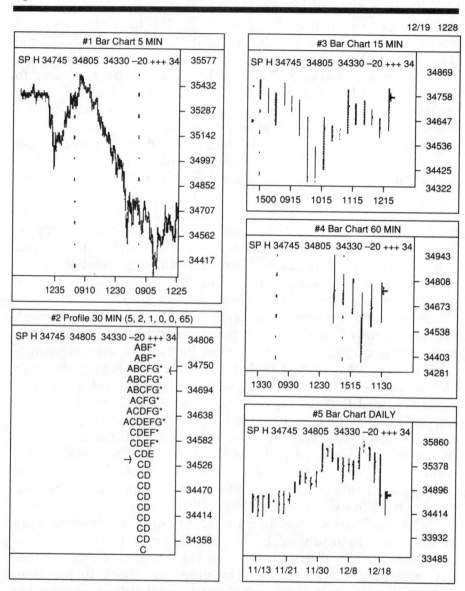

range. This pattern showed rejection of continued trading at lower prices and acceptance of continued trading at higher prices. The sequence of rejection and support is important: rejection of lower prices early, followed by support at higher prices later during the course of the trading day. I expected higher prices.

Buying around the 346.25 area was warranted. The only fly in the ointment was the two-period thickness of the tail: It was composed of price action in period C and period D. A much stronger tail would have been shown by one period, but not two. The rejection of lower prices was not quite that convincing to the market players, as was evidenced by the fact that it needed an additional second period to work off the excessive sell orders! Yet I was willing to risk the trade. In the back of my mind the objective in the Dow Jones Industrials had yet to be made, and consequentially, the S&P Index hadn't made its top either.

Figure C8.2, created 12-20 @ 9:33 A.M., an hour after the market had opened, shows five numbered charts.

Figure C8.2

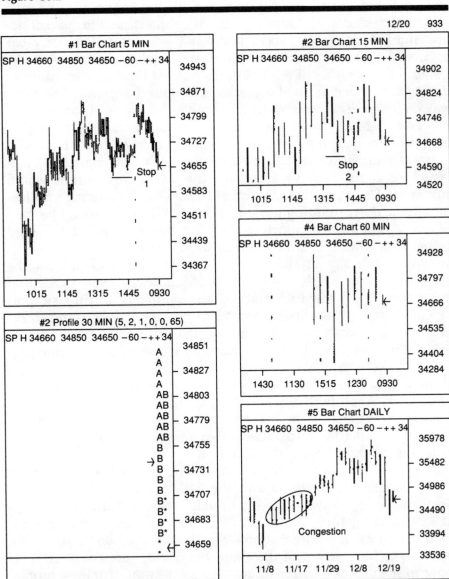

On inspection of #1 Chart, you will see that the market gapped higher. This shows strength, but let's wait and see what the other charts show.

The #2 Chart, the Market Profile chart, showed weakness immediately after the market opened. Period A's low was taken out by period B, and as the charts were even being prepared on hardcopy, period C was making new lows. This was a definitely weak and trending pattern to the downside!

Was my conclusion that a possible, intermediate bottom from the previous day had been negated by this particular Market Profile action? This is where the advances of personal computer technology are beneficial to the day trader. With the availability of various format charts, the analyst can filter questionable market action through other studies. I inspected #5 Chart, the daily bar data, and looked for some support area that would possibly be tested if the analysis of #2 Chart, the Market Profile chart, showed true to form, that is, if the market had found *support*, but there was not enough. Please recall the double thickness of the tail.

Was there any possible chart pattern or formation that could be used to negate the bearish implication of #2 Chart? I found a leftmost congestion area formed on the daily bar chart (#5) that lasted for about 11 days. I bet that the S&P Index futures would attempt to find support at this area. Even with the bearish implication of the downtrending profile objective of lower prices, I bet that prices would find support around the lower range of the congested area, which is around the 340–341 area.

Wait, you say. If there is support to be found around the 340–341 area, isn't that about 5–6 points away from the initial entry level? Can the trader afford so much risk to find support levels? *This is where it is effective to properly place stop-sell orders closer to entry price levels to get rid of poorly priced longs.* My philosophy is that winners must be viewed from the perspective of long-term charts, whereas losses must be evaluated from shorter-term charts: I inspect the 5-minute and 15-minute charts to discover important stop-sell points.

Upon inspection of #1 and #3 Charts, 5-minute and 15-minute bar charts, respectively, I assess that placing stop-sell orders at slightly below the last low swing (stop point 1 of #1 Chart, which is equivalent to stop point 2 of #3 Chart) would be warranted. This was around the 346.25 level, the exact price level that initial longs were instituted. I reasoned that going long at 346.25 and getting out at 346.25 on stop sell orders would limit losses: a prospective wash trade. Say, has anyone you know been successful 100 percent of the time? Success is more a function of how to manage the losers more than a question of taking profits! Let's see what happened as the day progressed.

I was disturbed at the apparent weakness of this possible reversal to the upside. Could my analysis have been wrong?

I pulled out Figure C8.3, created at 3:08 of the same day. This chart was a 5-minute bar chart of the actual cash index.

What is the purpose of this exercise? The first purpose, because we are all humans, is to study charts that will act as placebos. Yes, even I am vulnerable to the need for crutches. My purpose in viewing the cash chart was to possibly find support for my bullish conclusions. Notice that the stop-sell order that had been placed

Figure C8.3

Corresponds to
346.25 on the
front-end S&P futures

earlier at the 346.25 price level for the S&P Futures Index had been taken out to the downside. The price of the futures at 346.25 corresponded to 342.25 in the cash, or a difference of about 4 full points. This confirmed the initial bearish conclusion drawn from the first periods of the Market Profile chart!

Figure C8.4 was created immediately after Figure C8.3 was printed. Figure C8.4 is a 5-minute bar chart of the March S&P futures contract that I had been initially long at 346.25 and was now stopped out at around the same price level. What a tough way to get back to even!

Figure C8.4

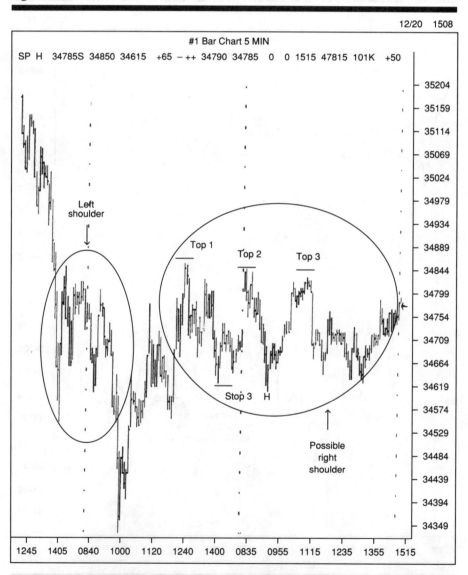

For the trading day of 12-20, I was stopped out right on the low of the next lower swing. In fact, price, once it touched the stop sell order, stopped going down at point H and proceeded to go straight back up to top out at around the third top of a possible triple stop formation (top 1, top 2, and top 3)! Multiple tops have a tendency to be broken violently. Because the market had the strength to rally to top 3, despite the fact that each later top was lower than the previous ones, I suspected that the next time there would be no top 4 formed, but rather prices would just punch through to the upside.

Jokingly, I have said of my trading at certain times that had I had no bad luck I wouldn't have had any luck at all! Humor is very important at critical junctures like these, as the seasoned trader is well aware.

As if to add insult to my injury, prices then sold off to slightly *above* point H and reversed direction to the upside! Had it gone lower, I would have at least felt somewhat vindicated that I was stopped out at a price that proved to be higher than the next swing low! But no, there was no such reprieve for heroism. I was stopped out of my long at the low! It appeared as if a tight congestion range was forming between the low of 346.25 and the high of 348.50, a rather narrow 2.25 points of congestion in the futures contract.

I then inspected the chart from a larger perspective and observed that the congestion to the left could be a possible left shoulder of a yet-to-be-completed Head-and-Shoulder bottom chart formation. The problem with this prognosis is the obvious fact that the right shoulder was about five times longer in duration than the left shoulder. In trying to find conforming patterns, the analyst would like to really see theoretically perfect formations, but failing appearances of such formations, the analyst uses quite a bit of subjective judgment to find somewhat theoretical formations. Bending the analysis quite a bit, I concluded that the right congestion area could be classified as the right shoulder of a reversal head-and-shoulder bottom pattern in a 5-minute bar chart! The spike to the downside, which could be the head of the head-and-shoulder bottom formation, shouldn't be tested again in this move. Was I correct in my assessment?

The night of 12-20 turned out to be another sleepless night, filled with constant ruminations about the markets. Figure C8.5 was created on 12-20 @ 7:07 P.M. and is the same as Figure C8.2 with the exception that #2 Chart contained five additional patterns from previous days' market actions.

Inspecting #2 Chart, I observed that day 5 and day 6 profiles were mildly bullish. If I would have been able to see the day 5 activity as a partially completed profile with the lower tail and the Value Area formed, implying that the upper tail had to be formed eventually, then a bullish case could have been made. Also, day

Figure C8.5

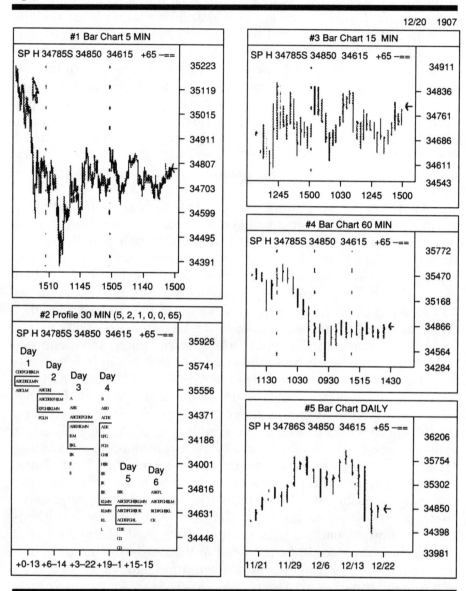

6 was further development of the Value Area formed on day 5. This implied that day 5 and day 6 would eventually lead to the formation of an upper tail!

In retrospect, the conclusions did not indicate that this possible bottom was a clean bottom: There were too many mitigating factors that could warrant *bottoming action* only and not a reversal to the upside. The bottoming action only allows one to consider going long, but not to profit from longs. The reversal to the upside allows the longs to be profitable. This fine distinction must be made. Buying at the bottom is fine but does not make any profits. Profits to be made from long positions are made only when prices do move up! The only firm conclusion that I could draw was that prices were not in a continuation pattern to the downside.

How did I play this?

The next chart, Figure C8.6, was created on 12-21 @ 9:06 A.M., shortly after the next day's opening.

Prices gapped up and traded slightly higher. The play was to go long. The problem with this trade, however, was the possibility

Figure C8.6

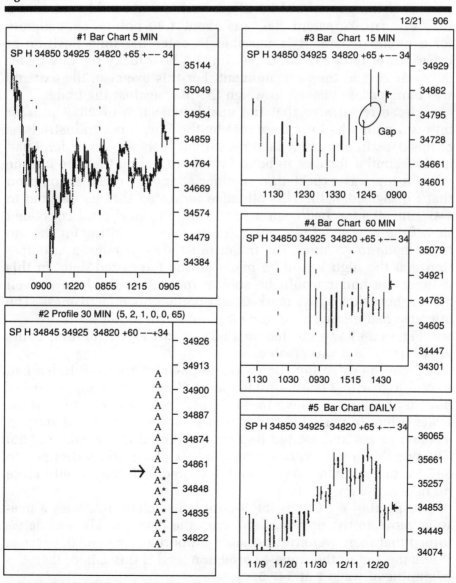

that the Market Profile chart (#2 Chart) showed a possibility that prices would sell off. Inspect the profile chart and note that the A range was extensive, from 349.25 on the high end to 348.20 on the low end. Even though this was only a one-point range, the second period showed a possibility that the Value Area would be developing in the lower half of the range. The implication? Prices had to work lower if the Value Area continued to develop in the lower half of the day's trading range.

Let's see what happened after the trade was placed at around the 348.50 level. I bet that #3 Chart, the 15-minute bar chart, would show prices holding above the 347.20 level. In fact, it didn't appear as if the gap would be filled. Perhaps it would turn into a runaway gap. Apparent risk was about 1.30 points. Let's digress for a moment here. It is possible to enter the long position at prices lower than 348.50, depending on how lucky the day trader is in entering at the right moment. For this exercise, the extreme was more or less chosen to weigh the play against the trader.

Please recall also that the upside objective of 2836 plus or minus 5 points had not been met by the Dow Jones Industrials as of this date. In one of my lectures several years ago, in which I had made a similar forecast in bond futures, revealing the date in time when a top was expected, a seminar attendee voiced an opinion that I disagreed with. This attendee indicated that he decided to wait until the top had been made in order to go short. I countered that if the forecasted top was valid, instead of waiting for the top to be made to go short, the trader must also go long in anticipation that the high would be made on the forecasted date. In this manner the trader would be able to trade from the long as well as the short side of the markets and double his effectiveness. The attendee had missed a possible 5-point move to the upside.

Figure C8.7 was created on 12-21 @ 1:02 P.M., about four hours after Figure C8.6 was created.

From the price four hours earlier, 348.50, the S&P Index had moved higher to 349.40, or 0.90 point. What is very supportive of bullish positions is shown in #2 Chart. The profile chart did show lower prices in period C and period D; however, it found support at these prices and rotated higher. The period D low was 347.55. The possible low I expected was 347.20. Once prices dropped to 347.55, prices rotated higher and appeared as if they would close on new highs for the day!

Inspecting #1 Chart, the 5-minute bar chart, one sees a five-wave move to the upside. I analyzed the data quickly and determined that there were two possible support areas: 348.70, because it was the end of the wave 4 correction, and if this failed, then the beginning of wave 1 at 347.55.

Figure C8.7

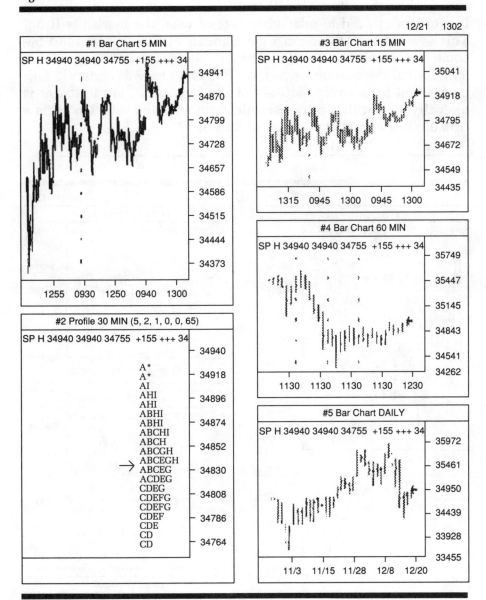

I instituted stop-sell orders initially around the 347.50 level. The plan was to move the stop-sell orders to the 348.65 level once prices took out new highs! Here is where the trader allows the market to make money for him or her; it is rather effortless work.

At this point I would like to digress and discuss managing positions and controlling situations. I entered positions at lower prices and the market proved me right. Now, no matter what I do, the market will do what it wishes to do. If it goes up, I have no control over the situation; if the market goes down, I have no control over the situation either. What I can do is guide the stop loss orders upward to take advantage of what the market will do! This is what the trader must get through his head if he is to become a successful trader. If the trader decides to arbitrarily sell his longs out at the current price level of 349.40 he will certainly take profits, but by actively selling out the long position the trader is basically saying that prices should drop after his sale. Isn't this a ridiculous assumption on the trader's part?

Figure C8.8

Figure C8.8 was created on 12-21 @ 1:50 P.M., before the market closed.

The #1 Chart, the 5-minute bar chart, showed a correction that went past the first support price of 348.65 and bottomed out at 348.20. I did not feel good about giving up about 1.20 points of profits if I could sell on the high of the move to 349.40.

The original stop was placed at 347.55. Thank goodness the selloff did not take this price out!

You will probably want to know my reasoning as to why the stop was placed at the lower of the two stop-sell prices. You might reason that had the stop been placed at the higher stop price, the trade would have been taken out at about a 0.50 point additional profit. Here is where it is important to have a larger-scale perspective of the market's move in the back of your mind. It was my analysis that the low made at the 334.60 level would eventually prove to be a very important bottom. Recall that the left congestion area was correctly analyzed to be a left shoulder and the right congestion area was a longer-duration right shoulder. The completed pattern was a Head-and-Shoulder bottom. With this type of valid prognostication it didn't make sense to worry about a small profit.

Fortified with this information, I believed that the market must be given a bit of leeway in working itself into first a supportive stage and then into a runaway stage. The supportive stage, basically a trendless market bound tightly in a trading range, would not hurt the position by much, but it also had a very good possibility of retracing as much as it could without losing the bullish feel of the market. The runaway stage is where the money is really to be made. For the additional half-point profit that the long could have been stopped out at the higher stop price, I did not consider it worth the effort to make the play then. Why worry about 0.50 points profit when it appears to be possible to make over 5 full points of profits?

Figure C8.9 was created after the close of 12-21 @ 10:52 P.M. Needless to say, the market closed at 349.45, or about 0.60 points higher.

What is important to note is that the market charged higher in the last 25 minutes of the trading day. It moved 1.75 points higher in that time period. Assessing what the total range of the day was (349.75 high to low of 347.55), 2.20 points, the last 25 minutes gave us about 80 percent of the range! Bullish indeed.

The profile chart (#2) also showed strength by a remarkable absence. Please recall that day 3 developed a lower tail, which I reasoned had to be balanced by the development of a future higher tail. Day 4 was basically a reworking of the Value Area created on day 3; also, day 4 did not have a higher tail formation. Are we ever going to get the higher tail? Day 5, remarkably, showed additional Value Area development, but at slightly higher prices.

Figure C8.9

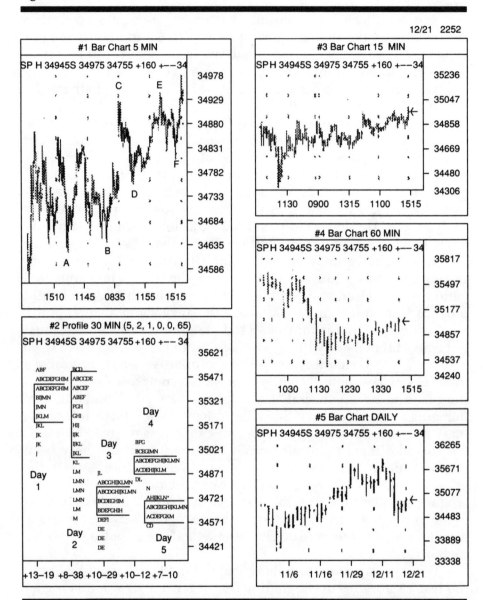

12/21 2252

What is absent is the fact that day 5 did not develop a higher tail! Are we to expect a tail to the upside to form? Logic would warrant so. Perhaps on day 6 or day 7?

Figure C8.10 was created several minutes after Figure C8.9 and is a 5-minute bar chart of the cash S&P Index.

This chart is presented as further confirmation that prices were not that weak in the cash index. The only problem is that prices in

Figure C8.10

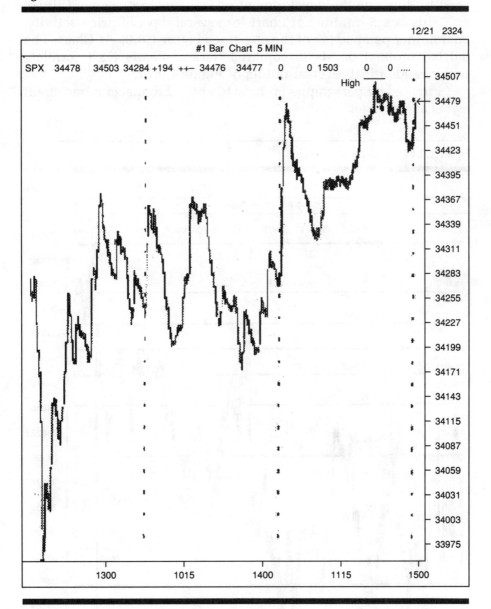

the cash index did not make new highs for the day toward the end of the day, but slightly after the halfway mark. It would have been soothing to my long positions had the highs been made toward the very end of the trading day. This gives the conclusion that longs and trapped shorts wanted to enter the market then and not even bother waiting for the next day. This need to rush things is important in analyzing the psychology of the markets.

Figure C8.11 was created on 12-22 @ 9:08 A.M. and will now be used to illustrate the development of Fibonacci retracement lines.

This is a 5-minute bar chart for several days of price activity. For another perspective of the chart, see Figure C8.9, #1 Chart. The labeled reversal points in capital letters of Figure C8.9 correlate with the identical reversal points of Figure C8.11.

First, a few paragraphs on how to apply Fibonacci retracement levels are in order.

Figure C8.11

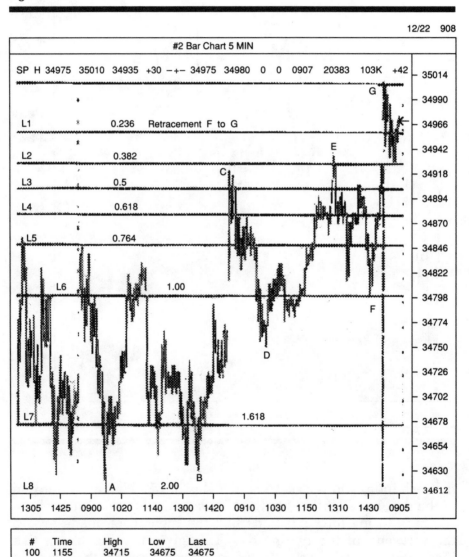

#	Time	High	Low	Last
100	1155	34715	34675	34675
>101	1200	34690	34650	34680
102	1205	34690	34675	34685

From points F to G, I first calculated what the absolute distance traveled was. In this case, price moved from the 348.00 level to the 350.10 level, an upward move of 2.10 points.

Fibonacci retracements are functions of ratios. Leonardo di Pisano de Fibonacci discovered the importance of the ratio in the early fifteenth century.*

The important ratios are 0.236, 0.382, 0.500, 0.618, 0.764, 1.00, 1.618, and 2.00. Figure C8.12 contains lines labeled L1, L2, L3, L4, L5, L6, L7, and L8. Each line correlates with the above retracement ratios. The retracement is based on the move made from Point F to Point G. You can overlay this ratio retracement anywhere on the chart. You can take the distance traveled from Point A to Point G and create retracement overlays.

The inference is that prices, when they reverse direction, will find support levels around the significant Fibonacci ratio lines. This approach does not purport to show absolute support; it is to be used as a guideline to a possible support area.

With the advances in microcomputer technology, I have found a significant improvement in applying Fibonacci ratios for retracements. In Figure C8.11, the lines drawn were based on points F to G. Additionally, I can find retracement levels from points A to G, points B to G, and points D to G. My software can create only four sets of Fibonacci ratios on each set of charts; this prevents me from looking at additional starting points. However, even with the four possible studies, I use the sets of lines that appear most often; these lines have more credibility in indicating support levels in retracements. For example, line L5 in our chart example may represent a 0.764 retracement of points F to G. If, in a second Fibonacci ratio analysis, points B to F caused a line L10 to be imposed on line L5, for example, then the L5 line becomes that much more important because there are two separate starting points that converge on the ending point (point G) that created it.

In this example, price appeared to be arrested from a continued selloff at around the 0.382 retracement, line L2. Because the market did not drop back to the 0.500 level retracement, line L3, before it started to resume its upward move, it appears to be stronger than expected. I bought more positions based on this type of market action. Price was at 349.75.

Let's see what happened next. I consider it part of an intellectual puzzle that must unfold according to my analysis.

Figure C8.12 was created about an hour later @ 10:24 A.M..

---

*For an important discussion of Fibonacci ratios, see *The Technical Analysis of Stocks, Options and Futures.*

Figure C8.12

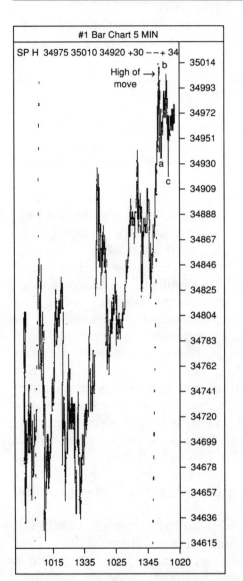
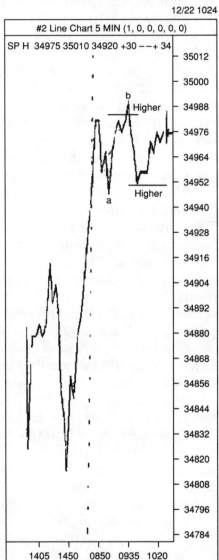

The price had hardly changed; I created Figure C8.13 to document the price action.

The #1 Chart is a 5-minute bar chart. The #2 Chart is a magnified portion of the day's action in line chart format. I needed to observe the wave formation in greater detail to see whether or not the correction that was obviously unfolding was going to be a normal zig-zag correction or a running correction (this is Elliott wave terminology).

Figure C8.13

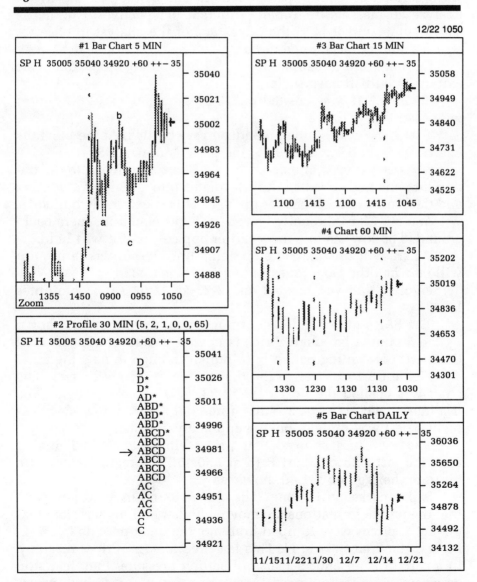

From the magnified #2 Chart, it appeared as if the correction was turning out to be a running correction. Point B of the line chart (#2) took out the previous high and then sold off to above the low point A. Point C remained above point A before it resumed its upward move. This is extremely bullish.

Please note that I applied my analysis to the closing line chart. If you inspect #1 Chart you will notice that the correction, analyzed from the perspective of the 5-minute bar chart, showed that the C wave correction took out the A wave low. Also, you will observe that the high of the move was never taken out by the B wave correction to the upside. This is one of the reasons why I analyze all markets from many different perspectives: Nothing is set in stone, and it is to the advantage of the analyst to observe, observe, and observe some more.

I did not find it justified to buy additional positions, but I was extremely bullish nevertheless.

Figure C8.13 was created on 12-22 @ 10:50 A.M., 26 minutes later than Figure C8.12.

The S&P Futures Index is indeed very bullish. At the previous chart's last sale price of 349.75, the price is now at 350.05.

Observe the type of market the #2 Chart is showing to the trader: it opens higher, sells off, then rotates into a higher Value Area and then makes new highs for the day! This is extremely bullish!

The #5 Chart the daily bar chart, is presented for mere background. The low made 4 days earlier appears as if it will hold.

Where will this market stop going up? One initial stop point will be when the Dow Jones Industrials reach 2836.

Figure C8.14 was created on 12-22 @ 11:07 A.M., 17 minutes later.

The S&P Futures Index continues its upward move as shown by the 5-minute bar chart. Price is now at 350.45. It appears as if the market is waiting patiently to punch through to new highs.

Figure C8.15 proves to me that my analyses are correct. The chart was created the next day, 12-23, @ 19 past midnight. The last trading day was 12-22. This turned out to be another sleepless night, and I was up late looking and analyzing charts.

The #1 Chart showed that prices closed at 351.05, higher than the last sale of Chart 8.15 at 350.45. The market sold off a bit from the high of 351.80, however.

Is the market still strong? The clue is found in #2 Chart. Note that the profile formations are moving higher and higher. Note that on day 4, prices were stopped from moving up at periods I, J, K, L, M, and the final ticks at N. This is called a *ledge*. Prices reach up to a certain level and, because of selling pressure, they just stop going up...for the moment. Once the supply is absorbed, prices charge up with a rush.

Figure C8.14

Figure C8.15

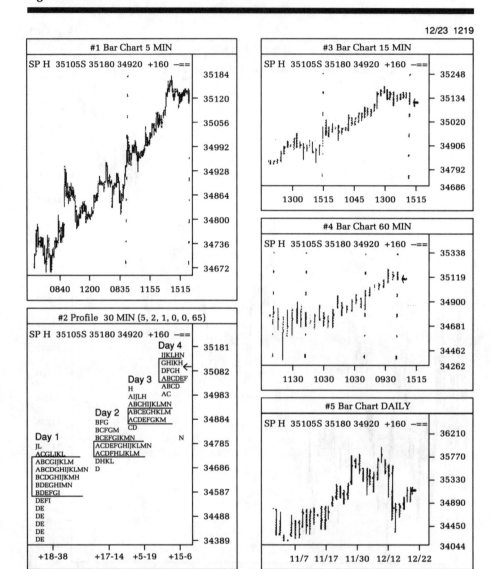

No other clues were found to show continued movement of prices upwards in the 15-minute, 60-minute, or daily bar charts.

Now look at Figure C8.16. This little chart said it all. It was created on 12-27 @ 10:42 A.M. Prices had now moved up to 352.15, or about a full point higher than the last price of Figure C8.15 at 351.05.

My analysis continued to prove correct.

An aside is warranted here. This little campaign started eight days ago with prices at around 345.00. Prices are now a full 7

Figure C8.16

12/27 1042

#2 Line Chart 15 MIN (1, 0, 0, 0, 0, 0)

SP   H   35215   35250   35050   +170   +--   35210   35215   35220   0   0   1042   15275   +37

points higher. The first long position was stopped out at a scratch price and I lost commissions. The second position was instituted with stop-loss orders at about a full point lower. The risk of this trade was one full point. In retrospect, because I was long multiple positions, each position fully guarded against damaging losses, I was playing from a position of power. With this type of trading approach, you will find that losses are disproportionate to the gains that can be made, but only if you can handle your *winners*.

Figure C8.17

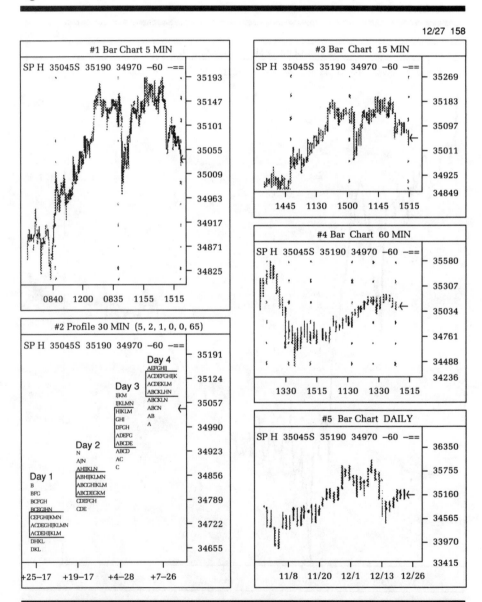

Figure C8.17 was created after the closing of the trading day on 12-27 @ 1:58 A.M. Here was a bit of pain had the trader watched the market sell off on a tick-by-tick basis.

From #2 Chart, it seemed as though the market had met a stone wall at the 351.80 level. There is a huge ledge that spanned across seven time periods: A, E, F, G, H, I, and J. In the whole trading day, there are only periods A to M, or thirteen periods. Seven periods take up more than half of the trading day. There is a lot of selling going on here.

Bring in the fact that day 3 had a similar ledge that spanned four time periods. We're talking resistance over 11 time periods in a total of 26 periods. This is selling.

What should I do? Because the market had already closed and I had already placed stop-loss orders to protect my positions, what could I do but wait for the market's opening the next day?

Recall also that the Dow Jones Industrials hadn't reached 2836 yet, either. Sometimes the best decisions are those that don't have to be made.

Figure C8.18 was created on 12-27 at 3:28 P.M., after the cash had stopped trading.

From #1 Chart, prices closed on this day at 353.25. Our initial long was made at 348.50. There's about a 5-point profit on the initial position and several points additional on the rest of the long positions. This is turning out quite well.

The profits were being made without any efforts! Please note that no matter what I did, I could not force the market higher or lower. My profits were made in following the movement of the markets. You must let this sink in; otherwise, you will forever be fighting the markets.

The #2 Chart is a point and figure chart based on 30-minute bar data. When I start to analyze, looking for potential reversal points, I will always look at the bigger picture first. From the larger scale, I will narrow my focus to more discrete time frames.

The point and figure chart showed obvious strength. What it also showed was the fact that the 356.00 level might prove to be a resistance level. At this price level, 353.25, price had broached the left congestion area. It would require tremendous strength to clear the 356.00 level to the upside.

Looking for other areas and analyses that might disclose strength or weakness, I created Figure C8.19 for the same day's trading data, 12-27 @ 6:58 P.M. Why do I get the feeling that this is going to be a longer day than expected?

It appears from a brief analysis of #1 Chart the 5-minute bar chart, that the S&P Futures Index is on its way to new highs! What gave this indication?

Figure C8.18

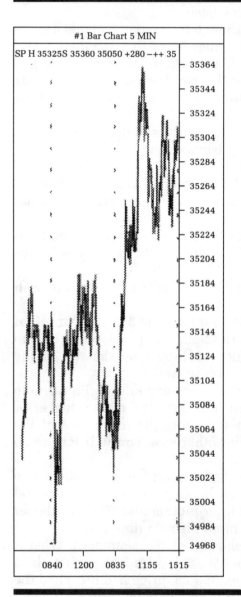
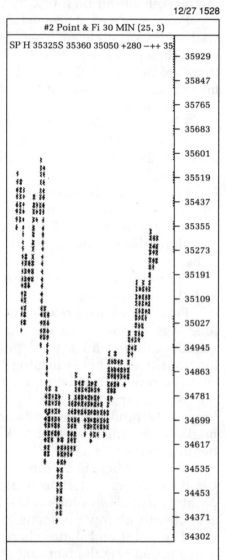

Figure C8.19

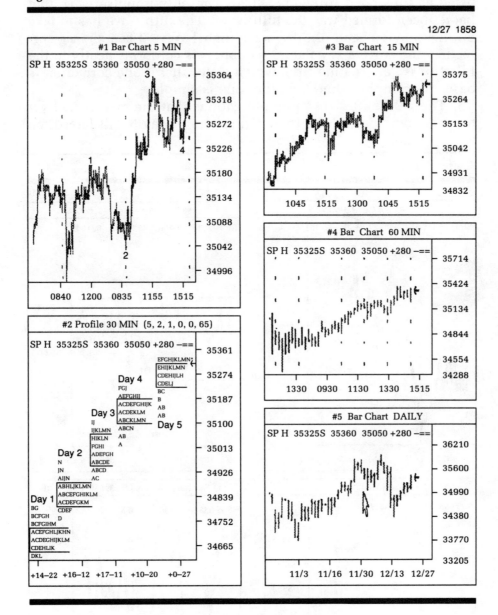

The #1 Chart, after a quick Elliott wave theory analysis, is labeled as illustrated in Figure C8.20. The only impulse wave that hadn't been formed was the fifth wave. The fifth wave has to take out the previous end of third wave highs! Wave 2 is a zig-zag correction and wave 4 is a flat correction; this conforms neatly to the Elliott wave alternation rule, which states that if one correction is basically complex, then the other one is simple.

The #2 Chart gives more indications that the market had yet to make new highs. Note the auction line of day 5. All later time

Figure C8.20

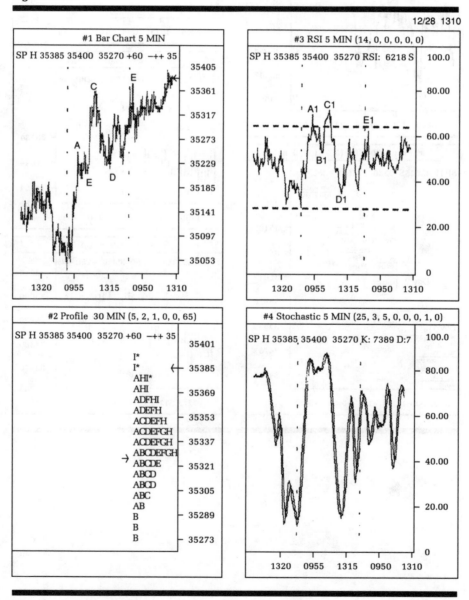

12/28 1310

periods are higher priced. Also, the ledge formed from periods E to the close showed that there was a seller at around the 353.00 level, but that the buying was just as strong. All I needed was a slight tipoff to the upside and the market would be running into new highs.

Prior to this series of plays in this bullish campaign, I did not pull out a single momentum study. I now want to see how price behaves in overbought terrritory, but as I pointed out, earlier momentum studies, as a general rule, will give false overbought signals in bullish markets. However, the one time that the one overbought signal does disclose that the market is topping out is the one that I don't want to miss.

Because there is only one valid overbought signal in bull markets to effectively act on, I rely on using other technical indicators to filter out all the other overbought indications.

Figure C8.20 was created on 12-28 @ 1:10 P.M., several hours before the close of trading. Needless to say, the S&P futures punched through new highs to 354.00. However, is this the real high?

The #2 Chart, the profile chart, showed period A opening half an hour of activity and then period B going into lows for the day to 352.70, even below the previous day's settlement. However, there was strength enough for the index to make new highs in period I, and then rotate to the downside. What is the prognosis of this type of activity? The only conclusion I can make is based on the fact that there is definite price rotation. Is there strength? Is there weakness? A bit of both, but not enough to justify any decision to enter *new* positions, either on the long side or on the short side. Is there enough information to make a decision to rid oneself of long positions? Yes, but even here there isn't enough data to make a valid decision, because there isn't really any topping-out action. So what am I to do? Hang on to the positions.

Why is this the case now? Isn't it true that if one is in doubt about the market, one should stay out? Yes, but one isn't trying to initiate new positions, but trying to maintain previously existing positions. If you had placed proper stop-sell orders to protect profits, the price activity, which is now vacillating from an "iffy" buy to an "iffy" sell, would not have the anxiety-producing effect that it might be having on you.

The #3 Chart is a Relative Strength chart created with 14 5-minute data bars. Fourteen bars of data is the conventional time length to input into this formula. I have labeled the points on this chart as A1, B1, C1, D1, and E1. The alphabets correlate with the price extremes found in the 5-minute bar chart (#1). Points A1 and C1 indicated overbought, but prices eventually moved beyond these two points. This was another case of falsely using momentum studies to enter positions. Can you use these momentum peaks to get rid of preexisting positions? Yes, to the degree that closing out of preexisting positions will not make money, but will remove the reader from potentially profitable moves. The philosophy behind this is based on the belief that if you don't know that you could have had more profits, then you won't be upset.

The #4 Chart is a 5-minute stochastic chart with 25 data blocks compared between crossover activities of a 3-bar moving average against a 5-bar moving average. Again, I must warn you that using overbought signals based on this technique is barely acceptable for getting rid of longs, but definitely not acceptable to initiate short positions.*

Figure C8.21 was created immediately after the market closed @ 3:32 P.M. on the same day as Figure C8.20.

Note that price is now at 354.85, a full point higher than two hours earlier. This is the beauty and simplicity of making profits in the markets. In the two hours that I waited patiently for the market to move, I exerted no effort in making profits. I watched the market make money for me! This is the real reason why we all trade: Trends make money.

The #2 Chart shows additional strength. The profile chart, toward the end, punched through to new highs! Where is the market going to stop? Please note that if the profile was going to develop into a normal chart and close in the middle of the day's range, it had about 90 percent of the day to do it. Yet, at the end, overriding buying forced the pattern away from a pattern that would normally occur 70 percent of the time—a normal profile—into that of a trending market, and a trending market of tremendous strength.

Why would I want to sell out longs now?

The only warning that a possible top could be in the making is based on the #5 Chart, the daily bar chart. Please recall what I had determined as a possible resistance point in the market's upward move in the explanation in Figure C8.18. The point and figure chart showed a left congestion area that had to be cleared to the upside before the market could challenge new highs. The uppermost price in Figure C8.19 was around the 356.00 level. However, because this was a daily bar chart analysis, I was fully aware that there would be shorter-time-frame warnings flagging me to get rid of longs at or near the top of the market.

Figure C8.22 was created on 12-30 @ 1:19 A.M. This set of charts was actually derived from all the price action of 12-29 but was created in the morning of the thirtieth.

My analysis was correct. The S&P Futures Index had to go higher. Initial resistance should be around the 356.00 level. How-

*For actual formulas to calculate these studies manually, refer to *The Technical Analysis of Stocks, Options and Futures.*

Figure C8.21

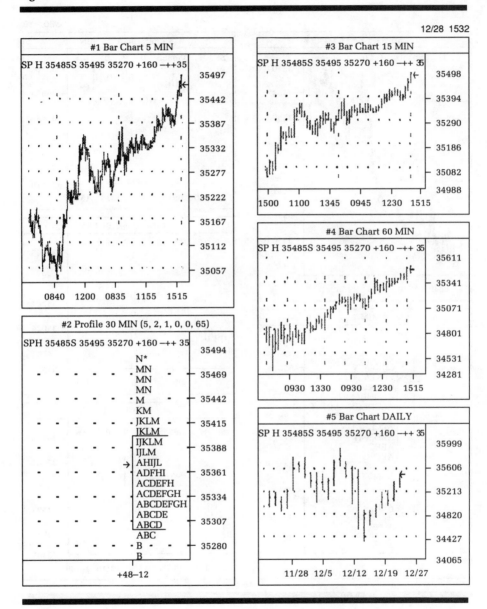

12/28 1532

The market was going up, and I did not have the analytical techniques to assess whether or not the market had topped out or was going to top out. The only forecasted reversal area was the initial forecast of the Dow Jones Industrial averages to hit the 2836

Figure C8.22

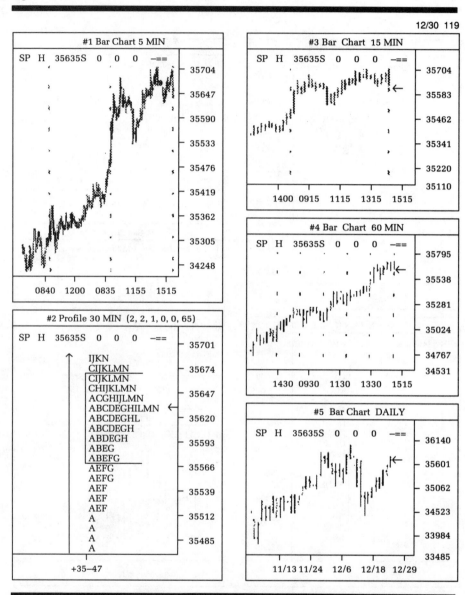

level. The 2836 level had not been reached as of the twenty-ninth of December. It was close, but not there yet.

The only indication that prices hadn't found a top was based on the set of charts in Figure C8.23 (#2), the profile chart. The profile chart once again proved its usefulness in helping me determine whether or not the market had found a top. Note that the auction line was progressively higher. The strength at the top range was not very great, but it did show strength. The Value Area de-

Figure C8.23

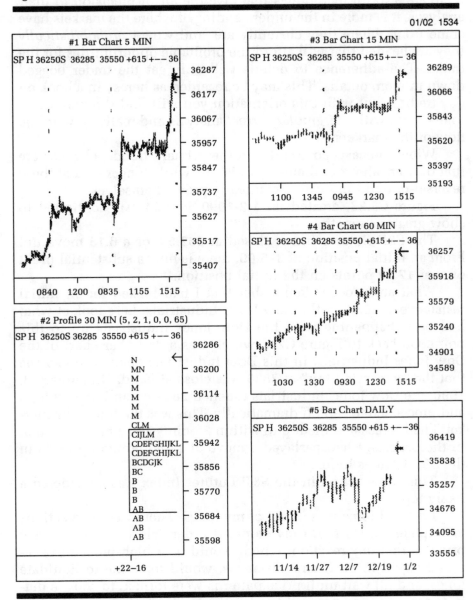

velopment showed progressively higher moves to the upside. The expectation was that prices should open higher the next day! The market closed on this day at 356.35, about a point and a half higher from the previous close.

Here I would like to discuss how I apply trading techniques. As you have already gathered from previous sections on analytical techniques, I don't adhere strictly to the very fine details of my analysis. Most students of Market Profile theory will adhere to the precise details. My own experience has shown me that even though there are a lot of techniques that give the air of precision to their analyses, it is more in the understanding of where the markets have come from, where they currently are, and where *probabilistically* they are headed that will afford the profitable opportunities for the trader. The adherence to details will only get the trader bogged down in more details. This may be regarded as heresy in a book on day trading, but with this orientation you will find it much easier to dispense with *marginally correct* analysis and really go with the flow of the markets.

When forecasts go counter to the primary trends, chances are that they are ahead of themselves. Wait a while longer so that these reversal-of-trend indicators can really prove themselves.

Figure C8.23, created on 1-2-1990 @ 3:34 P.M., continued to show greater strength.

The S&P Futures Index closed at 362.50, or a 6.15 move up! From an initial position of 345.00, there is now a substantial profit of over 17.50 points on the initial position.*

What am I to do? Remember that I had looked for an initial resistance at 2836 on the Dow Jones Industrials. Let's look at what had been happening with the Dow Jones Industrials up to this point. Go back to Figure C7.4, which was a daily bar chart of the Dow Jones Industrials. In this Dow Industrials chart, you can see that the "forecasted top" at 2836 was close at hand. On January 3, 1990, the Dow Jones Industrials touched 2834 on an intraday high and proceeded to sell off dramatically. This was the top to the market. I had forecasted the top to within 2 points a full month earlier. In the process, I had parlayed a move of 17.50 points upwards in the S&P Futures Index.

This price action in the S&P Futures Index was considered a likely top!

I did not force myself out of my longs. There were two actions to implement: (1) move my stop-sell orders closer to the market price so that *any* reaction, which would be a high-probability reversal signal in such circumstances, would force me to liquidate longs; and (2) wait until price patterns were formed to show a definite top and then proceed to play the market from the short side.

On January 3, 1990, when the Dow Jones Industrials touched the forecasted high, the S&P Futures Index hit a high of 364.80.

---

*The trader could have added more positions by pyramiding. See my book *Trading Rules: Strategies for Success*(Chicago: Dearborn Financial Publishing, 1990) for complete details on how pyramiding could have been accomplished correctly. With a 17.50 point profit on the initial position, properly pyramiding could have easily created over 100 full points of profits for a much larger position.

Figure C8.24

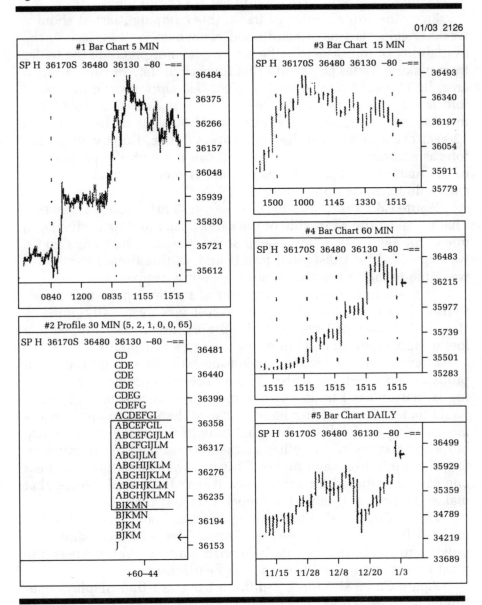

01/03 2126

The high was a move of 19.80 points up, from the initial entry of 345.00. However, I wasn't able to capture the exact high. In fact, my trading got very sloppy.

Figure C8.24 was created on 1-3 @ 9:26 P.M. During the trading day my remaining positions were stopped out. Be advised that the only indication that I used to unload the balance of my positions was the forecasted price of 2836 on the Dow Jones Industrials. No other indicators, such as momentum studies or moving average downside crossovers, were used to get rid of the longs.

From the initial series of trade, this campaign lasted about 3 weeks. Again, as I have mentioned elsewhere in this Case 8, the availability of forecasts into the future does not preclude the trader from making trades going into that forecasted date or time reversal area. In *The Technical Analysis of Stocks, Options and Futures*, I forecasted a bond reversal date to occur on August 2, 1989. The manuscript was given to the publisher 660 days earlier. I used a 12-year cycle to forecast the bond reversal date. Don't wait for the forecasted date to initiate trades. You can trade on the proper side of the market until the forecasted date is met, at which time you can trade from the opposite side!

Figure C8.25 was created on 1-4 @ 4:50 P.M. I admit freely that I hadn't taken the short side of the selloff. As I told an audience in one of my seminars, I "fell asleep at the wheel." The campaign up was squeezed for substantial profits and, at this time, I decided it was time to take a respite from the grueling campaign.

At the time, I made the decision to lighten up on trading activities; I had no idea where the market was eventually going to stop. In February of 1990 the S&P Futures Index had dropped to a low of 320.50, or an erosion of well over 24 full points.

I have seen tremendous market moves of this magnitude; you probably have seen them also. The unfortunate problem with trading is that unless I trade all the time, I will miss some very profitable trades. On the other hand, because there are so many, many moves being made all the time, not only in the S&P Futures Index, but also in many of the other markets, there isn't really much to fear about missing major moves. This one was missed, but the next one can be prepared for adequately. It isn't the actual trading that makes the profits; it is all the preparation and planning.

Figure C8.25, #2 Chart, along with my conclusion that the top had been made, showed weakness. The #2 Chart showed a downward Auction Line that is bearish, and two Value Areas, the most recent one being lower than the earlier one.

Figure C8.26 showed a 5-minute bar chart that displays continued price weakness. The low of the move since the top had been made is now 355.05.

Because the markets are now bearish, I found it hard to initiate any large position with the view of pyramiding to the downside. Weak bear markets do not provide the opportunities to add positions because price floors do not hold up long enough for this to be accomplished. Instead, I chose to pick at certain market rally points to initiate small-sized positions.

Figure C8.25

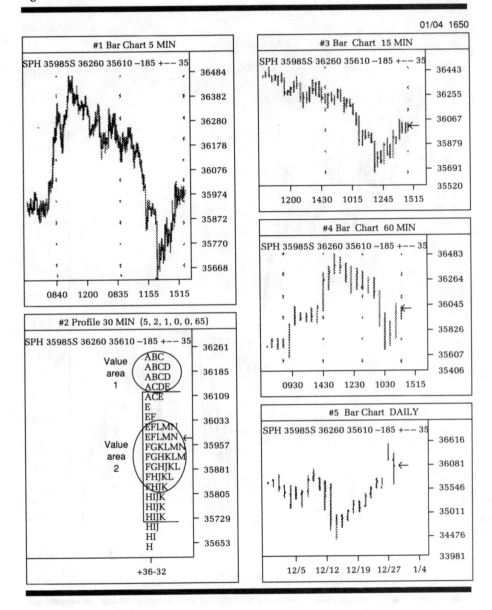

01/04 1650

#1 Bar Chart 5 MIN

SPH 35985S 36260 35610 −185 +−− 35

36484
36382
36280
36178
36076
35974
35872
35770
35668

0840   1200   0835   1155   1515

#2 Profile 30 MIN (5, 2, 1, 0, 0, 65)

SPH 35985S 36260 35610 −185 +−− 35

36261
Value
area
1

ABC
ABCD
ABCD
ACDE   36185
ACE   36109
E
EF
EFLMN   36033
EFLMN
FGKLMN   35957
FGHKLM
FGHJKL   35881
FHJKL
FHJK
HIJK   35805
HIJK
HIJK   35729
HIJ
HI   35653
H

Value
area
2

+36-32

#3 Bar Chart 15 MIN

SPH 35985S 36260 35610 −185 +−− 35

36443
36255
36067
35879
35691
35520

1200   1430   1015   1245   1515

#4 Bar Chart 60 MIN

SPH 35985S 36260 35610 −185 +−− 35

36483
36264
36045
35826
35607
35406

0930   1430   1230   1030   1515

#5 Bar Chart DAILY

SPH 35985S 36260 35610 −185 +−− 35

36616
36081
35546
35011
34476
33981

12/5   12/12   12/19   12/27   1/4

Figure C8.27, created on 1-9 @ 2:06 A.M., shows the very reason why I am not amenable to shorting huge positions in bear markets.

Bear markets do not behave in the same way that bull markets do. Selloffs in bear markets are dramatic. Rallies in bull markets can be dramatic, but often they go up gradually. Bear market selloffs thus do not allow the trader to add more positions as the price

Figure C8.26

erosion continues. Bull market rallies, however, because they move up relatively slowly and gradually, allow the trader ample opportunities to add to his or her longs.

Countermoves are the market actions that are damaging. The #1 Chart of Figure C8.27 shows the precise reason why shorting, as a general rule, must be limited in size: The countermoves are

Figure C8.27

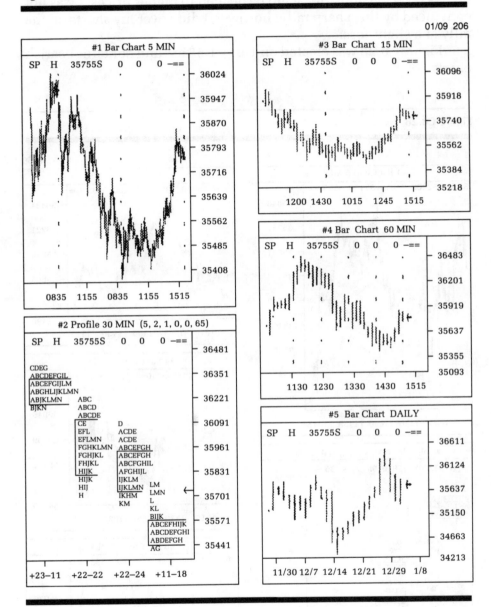

sharp and quick! When countermoves start, it doesn't take a genius to figure out that if the poorly positioned trader can't get out with a handful of positions, trying to get out with a 50 lot isn't going to be much easier. Does this mean that the trader can play counter-moves in bear markets for good profits? Yes, but it is beyond my scope and knowledge to play markets such as these.

The market action on this day gives the impression that the sell-off has reversed and appears to be headed to higher prices. I was not convinced by this sharp rally; however, I did cover my shorts on the rally at a slight loss.

Figure C8.28 was created on 1-9 @ 1:58 P.M. and contains bearish charts.

Figure C8.28

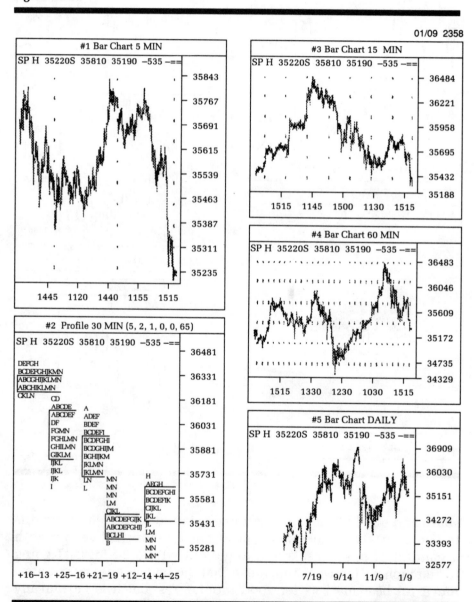

As indicated in the previous charts, I had missed the start of the campaign to the sell side. Despite the initial miss, I continued to sell the move to the downside, in much smaller lots. Even though I was able to capitalize on part of the move with smaller lots, the fact that I could have really parlayed larger, initial positions into large profits represented missed opportunities.

You must not allow yourself to feel like this. There isn't any way to buy at the very bottom, then wait to sell at the very top, and then buy at the very bottom again. This is all theory. When one is trading in the real world, there is the element of psychology. In order to play the long side of the market, I had to muster all the technical analytical techniques that I knew to reinforce my bullish scenario. Once the market had topped out, there was still the residual bullishness that I had psyched myself into accepting. To have gone immediately short after taking profits on bullish positions is next to impossible.

I mitigated this potential problem of not being able to partake of both the long and short side to their fullest potential by tracking more than one market. Even though I could not psychologically come to terms with going short in the S&P futures, I had prepared myself to go short in other markets. This is one of the mental games that I have implemented to allow myself to trade both the bullish side and the bearish side at the same time. I track many markets. It would be wise for you to implement this type of strategy also.

Figure C8.29 was created on 1-10 @ 1:17 P.M. and is a daily bar chart.

To show you that I was still mildly bullish, at this point in time I had drawn upward sloping trend lines with points B and C. I ignored point A, dismissing it as an extreme oversold price point. The Trend Line formed from connecting points B and C gave support at point D.

It appeared as if there was some support at this price level. However, from a mere Elliott wave count analysis, it appeared as if this upward move from point A failed to take out the high made in the early part of October (10-7-1989). The possibility that this upward move was a fifth wave that failed to take out the previous impulse wave 3's high was great based on this analysis. If this was a fifth-wave failure, then the weakness based on this weakness would eventually take out the upward sloping trendline support! Play the market bullishly, but don't even risk $2\frac{1}{2}$ percent of your equity on it. Take a flyer, but don't expect to pat yourself on the back if money is made: Money made on going long here is based purely on luck and not on strategy.

Figure C8.29

Figure C8.30 was created on 1-12 @ 12:01 P.M., a minute after noon. It is a 5-minute bar chart.

In this analysis, I basically used the breakdown of three fan lines to indicate continued weakness. Fan lines are drawn from a common low or high point. The first line drawn is the sharpest-angled line. Once this line, L1 on the chart, is taken out to the downside, then the market attempts to find the next level of sup-

Figure C8.30

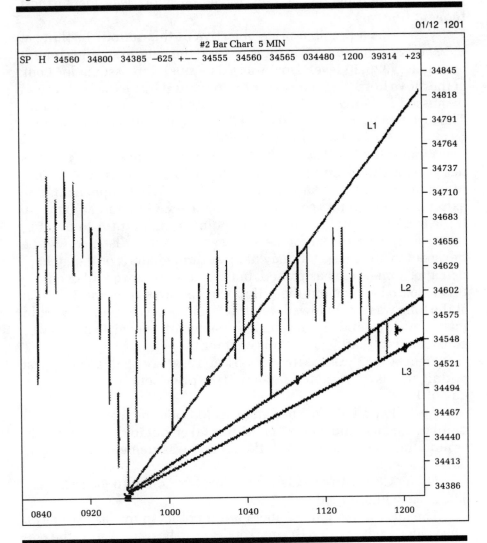

port. Finding the second level of support, as evidenced by a price reversal to the upside, warrants the drawing of a second trendline, L2 in this case. Once L2 is taken out to the downside, then comes the very important third fan line, L3, which is the least sloped of all three trendlines. If line L3 is taken out to the downside, look out below, because all the price supports, based on this analysis, would be gone.

I looked for the breakdown of price past L3. In this case, the price was around the 345.50 level. Once prices took this out, it was a definite short sale. I don't have the charts that actually showed the breakdown, because I was actively trading the markets from the short side and missed the opportunities to document this. At the time, documenting the reasons for going short was the furthest thought from my mind.

What was a possible price objective of this selloff? Looking at #5 Chart of Figure C8.31, it appeared as if the bottom should come at around the 326.50 level. How was this eyeball forecast made? Look at the move from the high at point A to point B (the extreme low was dismissed as being tremendously oversold and not a valid point). The distance from point A to point B should be equal to the distance from point C to whatever point D will be.

What is the justification for this? My experience in the markets has given me the feeling that the markets, like most aspects of daily living, have a kind of karma going for them. What happens in one extreme will happen again in the same degree in another extreme. If the market dropped X number of points from point A to point B, then somewhere in the market's moves, the same distance will be traversed by the market. It may happen immediately, or it may happen after some time has passed, but the countermove will occur. In this case, to balance out the selloff from point A to point B, which at the time was a new low, the selloff from point C to point D should make new lows and also be about the same price level. (This may be considered the "art" part of this chapter.)

Figure C8.32 was created on 1-17 @ 12:30 A.M., half an hour past midnight. It is a 5-minute bar chart of the price action for the trading day of 1-16.

Again I applied fan lines analysis to find where a possible sell point could be found. Once line L3 was taken out to the downside at around the 343.75 price level, the market was tremendously weak. Sell some more.

Figure C8.33 was created two days later on 1-18 @ 10:24 A.M. The price had dropped to 337.50.

The market had eroded about 6 full points in the last two days. The velocity with which the market drops in bear markets is the reason why professionals like to play the short side. They don't have to hang on a long time for their positions to make money on the short side. This is the exact reverse of bull markets, where the professional would have to build up positions and leave them open for a longer time period.

Figure C8.34 is the final chart of this trading example. I created this daily bar chart on 2-21 @ 8:37 A.M. as a matter of record. The S&P Futures Index had dropped to the 320.50 level from the last short of 343.75. Even though there wasn't a substantial opportunity to be made on the short side because the opportunities to pyramid large positions weren't there, there were quick profits to be made!

Figure C8.31

01/15 1108

#1 Bar Chart 5 MIN

SP H 34050 34170 33905 −45 −++ 34

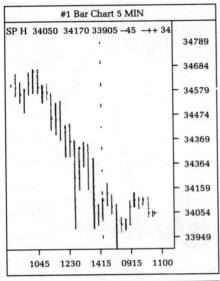

34789
34684
34579
34474
34369
34364
34159
34054
33949

1045   1230   1415   0915   1100

#2 Profile 30 MIN (5, 2, 1, 0, 0, 65)

SP H 34050 34170 33905 −45 −++ 34

	34171
A	
A	34140
AD	
AD	34109
ADE	
ACDE	
ABCDE	34078
ABCDE	
ABCE*	34047
ABCE*	
BC*	
BC	34016
BC	
BC	
BC	33985
BC	
B	
B	33954
B	
B	
B	33923

#3 Bar Chart 15 MIN

SP H 34050 34170 33905 −45 −++ 34

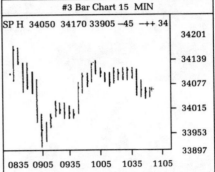

34201
34139
34077
34015
33953
33897

0835 0905 0935 1005 1035 1105

#4 Bar Chart 60 MIN

SP H 34050 34170 33905 −45 −++ 34

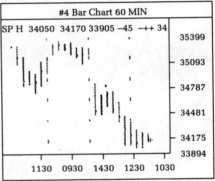

35399
35093
34787
34481
34175
33894

1130   0930   1430   1230   1030

#5 Bar Chart DAILY

SP H 34050 34170 33905 −45 −++ 34

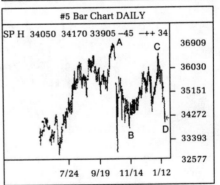

36909
36030
35151
34272
33393
32577

7/24   9/19   11/14   1/12

Figure C8.32

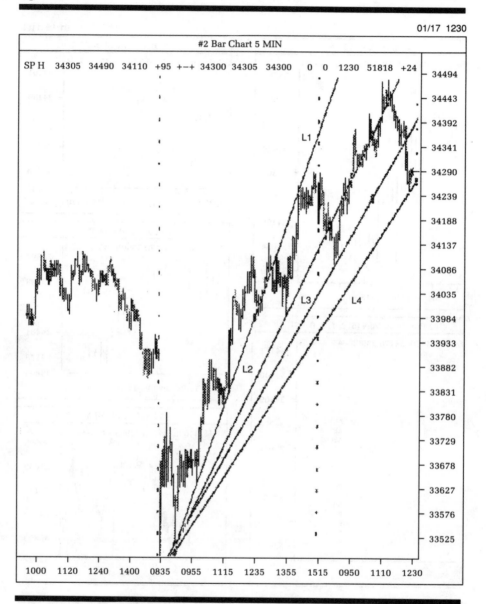

Figure C8.33

#4 Bar Chart 60 MIN

SP H 33750 33960 33600 −125 +++ 33745 33740 33735 0 0 1024 56680 +22

Figure C8.34

This ends the trading campaign using the S&P Futures Index. As lengthy as this example was, the ways I used and applied various technical analysis techniques illustrate that there is an element of artistry in successfully trading a campaign. As much as you can know about various trading techniques, it's more in knowing when to apply these techniques, and then determining which signals generated are acceptable and which ones aren't acceptable, that will make you a more effective trader.

CASE 9   Fibonacci Ratios and the S&P Index

After the lengthy explanation of the previous case, this case deals solely with analyzing the Fibonacci ratios to determine most likely price reversal points.

I have not yet found a valid way to trade the markets using Fibonacci ratios, either in terms of price or time traversed. However, there are times and prices that coincide perfectly with price and time reversals in market action. The underlying cause behind this type of "hit" is not known. My book *The Technical Analysis of Stocks, Options and Futures* contains several references that you may wish to investigate for further information.

Figure C9.1 was created on 5-22 @ 10:51 A.M. and contains a 60-minute bar chart of the June S&P futures contract. You will notice that a trend line has been drawn and is identified as line L1. Please note that the trend line is rather accurate in showing support every time prices retrace to the support levels.

In Figure C8.12, we looked at another study using the Fibonacci ratios. The ratios are as follows:

0.236
0.382
0.500
0.618
1.000
1.618
2.618
4.236

These ratios are derived from the Fibonacci summation series. The summation series, in turn, is derived from the primary starting number, 1. Because the "sum" of 1 is still 1, the second number is also 1. If you take the number 1 and add the previous number, 1, you create the next number in the series, 2. The next step is to take the number 2 and add it to the previous number, 1, to obtain the third number, 3. Adding the third number, 3, to the previous number, 2, you obtain the number 5. This continues onward to infinity. The summation series appears as follows:

$$1, 1, 2, 3, 5, 8, 13, 21, 34, 55, 89, 144, \ldots$$

One interesting characteristic of the summation series is that each number is related to the other numbers with a different set of ratios. If you were to take any number and divide it by the *preceding* number of the summation series, you would find a ratio

Figure C9.1

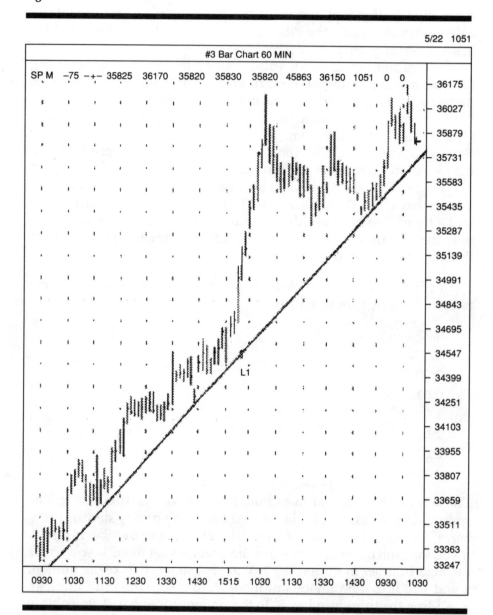

that approached 1.618. If you took one number and divided it by the *following* number, the approached ratio would be 0.618. This simple summation series contains within it a tremendous amount of significance.

Going back to Figure C9.1, my task was to find an approximate retracement level and add more long positions. I looked at the latest move to the upside—in this particular example, from point A, with a value of 353.40, to point B, with a value of 361.70. The move was a little over 8 full points. Where would I have found support levels? See Figure C9.2 for an exact hit!

Figure C9.2 was created about three hours later on the same trading day, 5-22. Instead of looking for a viable retracement support area using a 60-minute bar chart such as Figure C9.1, I retrieved a shorter duration chart (a 5-minute bar chart) and then analyzed the movement to the upside on a more discrete time frame.

Figure C9.2

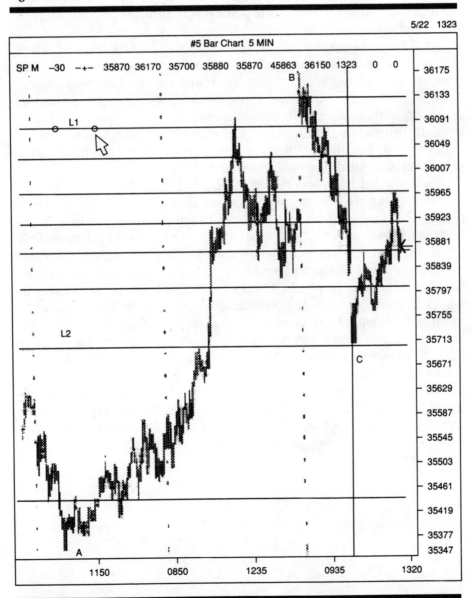

Line L1, as marked by the arrow on the solid horizontal line, is not a part of the Fibonacci retracement analysis. This is a line that I drew for a separate analysis. (You will have to forgive me for not recalling an exact explanation of the analysis.)

As you can see, the S&P futures contract arrested its sell-off at price point C with a value of 357.00 and rallied up to the 359.50 level, or a move of about 2.50 points. When I created the chart I superimposed several sets of Fibonacci retracement lines and tried to determine which ones would prove to be the critical support price points. At this writing, I cannot identify line L2. It was a critical support line based on some start and stop of a major swing study. I did not make any major plays at this price point, otherwise I would have kept detailed records.

It is important for you to understand that the number of ratios used in Fibonacci ratio analysis can be extensive and that the price reversal points created might be too many for the exacting trader to reverse his trades. However, if you were to focus on those potential reversal points and apply momentum studies (for example, relative strength indicators, stochastics, and other overbought/oversold indicators) you would be better equipped to see that a possible major price reversal point has been reached.

You should be aware that the Fibonacci numbers and their ratios that are applied to price points can also be applied to length of time. All examples till now have been based on price analysis. If the bottom had been made 12 days earlier and the market had moved off the lows, then you could expect a reasonably good sell-off after the highs were made on the thirteenth day. Thirteen is a Fibonacci number. Fibonacci numbers can be applied not only to days, but also to weeks from major tops or bottoms, and, on an even larger scale, to months and years. Conversely, the application of the numbers from the summation series can be applied to shorter time frames: hours from short-term tops or bottoms, and minutes from even shorter time reversals.

In all cases you are advised that this type of analysis cannot stand by itself. It must be used as part of some major type of mathematical technique: It could be a technique as simple as moving averages or as complex as the moving average convergence/divergence method!

CASE 10   Applying Momentum to the S&P Index

The previous case dealt with possible price reversal points. Unfortunately, the software that I used did not allow for Fibonacci studies of time. (I have suggested this to the software developers, and they are studying the need for such a method. At the present time, there is no software that contains this approach.) Because there was no Fibonacci study to apply to time, I applied the next-best approach to discover the creation of intermediate tops or bottoms.

Figure C10.1 contains four charts derived from the basic moving average. The #1 Chart is a 5-minute stochastic chart of the S&P Futures Index.

The #2 Chart comprises three moving averages of a 5-minute bar chart: a moving average of the highs only, a moving average of the lows only, and a moving average of the closes only. This chart does not use momentum studies, but does use the basic moving averages from which momentum studies are initially generated. I have always found it helpful to inspect the basic studies generated from moving averages when I rely on *momentum* studies; I want to know whether or not any major momentum reversal corresponds to a normal moving average study. It is important to be cautious—the exceptions to the analyses are the ones that might provide you with wrong conclusions.

In #2 Chart the price has dropped with great velocity from the bulk momentum as represented by the bracketed moving averages. There is an element of elasticity in the marketplace. Just as with a rubber band, if external forces stretch prices too far, there will be a *reactionary* spring to the other side. This type of price action, relative to the bulk momentum, indicates oversold conditions. For the day trader, it could pay to go long at these levels—not for a sustained reversal, but for a quick flip for a five lot or so.

The #3 Chart is a 5-minute relative strength indicator (RSI) study. The RSI study shows that there is a possible oversold price level, but this is contrary to #1 Chart, which shows no crossovers to the upside from the lowest oversold area.

The #4 Chart is a 5-minute oscillator study. Oscillators are indicators that are the next level above moving averages—very primitive and basically showing overbought/oversold conditions independent of where the markets are at. I inspect such charts because they can give the general feeling of whether or not a reversal area will be *sustainable*. It is apparent that there will be at least minor reversals on these reversal signals, but there is a need to know

Figure C10.1

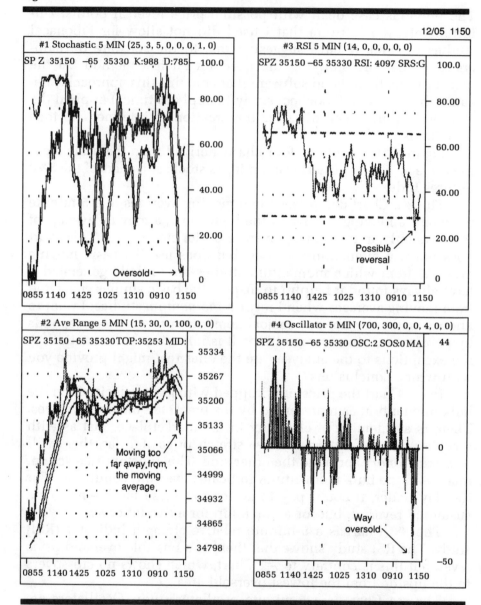

whether or not there is any strength to the reversals. Considerably oversold levels and quick rebounds, as shown in #4 Chart, are warning flags that the reversal is more a technical rebound—which is more vulnerable to a continuation of the move just as abruptly— than a rebound with substantive buying power.

CASE 11   A Possible Reversal Pattern in the S&P Index

Figure C11.1 was created on 9-4 @ 8:40 A.M., ten minutes after the S&P Futures Index opened. This figure shows possible reversals to the downside.

Please note that the #1 Chart, a daily bar chart with three moving averages of length—5, 13, and 21 days—superimposed on-to it, shows no gap formations to the downside. You must look for

Figure C11.1

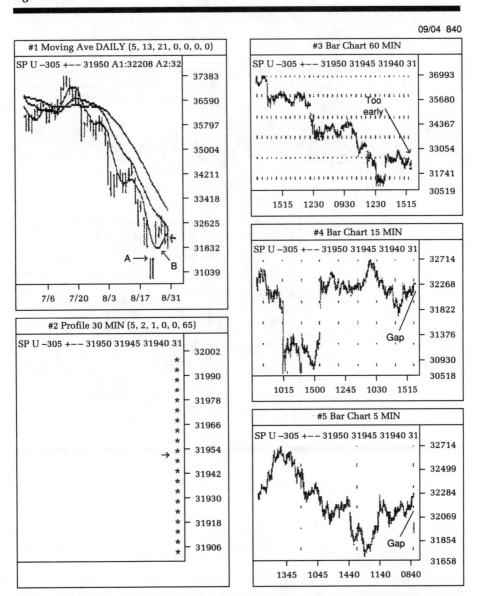

Figure C11.2

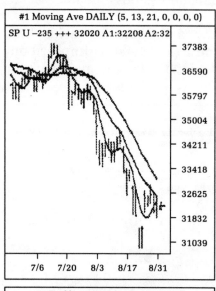

#1 Moving Ave DAILY (5, 13, 21, 0, 0, 0, 0)

SP U −235 +++ 32020 A1:32208 A2:32

37383
36590
35797
35004
34211
33418
32625
31832
31039

7/6   7/20   8/3   8/17   8/31

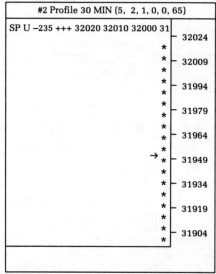

#2 Profile 30 MIN (5, 2, 1, 0, 0, 65)

SP U −235 +++ 32020 32010 32000 31

32024
32009
31994
31979
31964
31949
31934
31919
31904

#3 Bar Chart 60 MIN

SP U −235 +++ 32020 32010 32000 31

32714
32268
31822
31376
30930
30518

1030   1330   0930   1230   1515

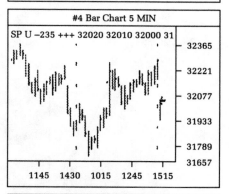

#4 Bar Chart 5 MIN

SP U −235 +++ 32020 32010 32000 31

32365
32221
32077
31933
31789
31657

1145   1430   1015   1245   1515

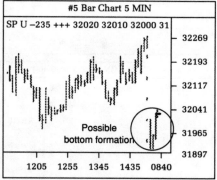

#5 Bar Chart 5 MIN

SP U −235 +++ 32020 32010 32000 31

32269
32193
32117
32041
31965
31897

Possible
bottom formation

1205   1255   1345   1435   0840

gap formations within the context of the charts observed. In this particular situation the 5-minute bar chart (#5) and the 15-minute bar chart (#4) show the formation of gaps within the context of the charts. It was too early to observe any formation of gaps in the 60-minute bar chart (#3): The first 60 minutes of trading activity hadn't yet passed when Figure C11.1 was created.

What I look for in the formation of gaps is the possibility that those gaps will be filled on the day of trading activity. It is not widely known that, if gaps are not filled, the direction of the gap formed shows the intermediate moves to come. This does not mean that those formed gaps will never be filled at any point in the very near future. It merely means that—if a 5-minute bar chart, a 15-minute bar chart, a 60-minute bar chart, and a daily bar chart all show a gap—the gap is of *major* significance. If such a gap is not filled, market action will further confirm that the gap is valid for forecasting an intermediate move. If such a gap is filled, despite all indications otherwise, the counter strength move will be extremely strong and the implication is to look for a massive buying!

Note that in #1 Chart, the daily bar chart, points A and B show gaps formed to the left and the right of the two-day reversal formation. Because the two days were set off on the daily bar chart, it is presumed that all the other more discrete scale charts would show gaps also! However, the reverse situation is not likely. If the larger scale chart doesn't show a gap, but the more discrete time frame charts show the gap, you should not conclude that this is a continuation of the breakdown. However, the first sign of significant gaps formed is based on the existence of gaps in charts having more discrete scales.

Figure C11.2 was created four minutes later on 9-4. It appears the gaps formed in the smaller scale charts will be closed! Without the larger-scale chart showing any gap formation, it is not valid to infer that the closed gap of the smaller-scale chart is a possible breakdown. These are the innuendos and nuances that a capable market trader can pick up easily.

The #5 Chart, a 5-minute bar chart, is already showing a possible reversal pattern because the last bar of the chart is one of three bars in a possible "three bar" island reversal. The other two bars show lower prices than the third bar.

The Market Profile (copyright Chicago Board of Trade) chart (#2) of both Figures C11.1 and C11.2 showed nothing of significance since the first half hour of trading hadn't been completed. Instead of using profile or momentum studies, this reversal from the bottom was more accurately forecasted by studying gaps in different time frames and comparing their relative strengths.

CASE 12   A Secondary Bottom for the S&P Index

You can see that Figure C12.1 is a line chart created by connecting the closing prices of each bar of the 5-minute bar chart. The chart was created on 12-11 @ 10:48 A.M. This trade encompassed only one trading day, but served to give the general direction of the next several day's trading bias.

Figure C12.1

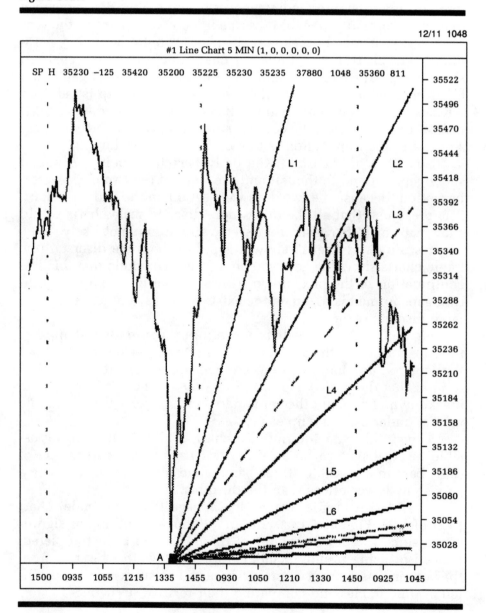

In this example, I applied the Gann lines to the low of the swing, which may or may not have been the bottom of the move. Only after price moves away from the low of the swing to the upside can it be shown that the bottom has been made.

For practical purposes, I applied the Gann lines after L2 had been broken to the downside. I examined the sell-off to get a general idea of whether some uptrending lines—Gann lines or not—had been broken to the downside. In this case, it appeared that at least one line had been broken to the downside, most likely line L1.

Once the Gann lines were applied to the chart, the price action since the bottom had been made became clearer, relative to some base. Lines L1, L2, L3, and even L4 had been broken to the downside. I had to observe how prices behaved around L5, L6, and so on, all the way to the parallel line that runs straight across the bottom, which contains Point A.

For a quick analysis of the market, I pulled out the previous three days' profiles (Figure C12.2). The 30-minute profiles show a general weakness in the market. Three of the four days' (the first, third, and fourth days') profiles show eroding auction lines. (The second day doesn't show this, but it shows even more weakness than the eroding auction lines because an attempt in period C to take out new highs was met with selling that took the price down to period L at 350.25).

Judging by the price action on the fourth day, the S&P futures did indeed show weakness. Also, price had dropped to 350.95, very close to the support line L6 from Figure C12.1. Breaking this line, L6, would warrant continued weakness.

With puzzlement over trying to find a possible support level, I created Figure C12.3 an hour later.

Price had moved off the low with decisive strength. In #2 Chart , the profile chart, prices had rotated around the second lower value area and moved sharply off the lows. Would prices rotate higher to form a normal day? That is, would prices fill in the one period gap in the neck area (period F)? If price were to do this, then the only negative analysis of the profile would be negated and a possible low would have been made. In this case, the problem with double–value area distributions was that they showed continued weakness.

The #3 Chart, the relative strength index chart, shows a possible bottom. The #4 Chart, the stochastic chart, shows a similar signal. The #5 Chart, however, shows an oscillator that is sharply overbought. This is still not convincing enough proof that a bottom had been made.

Figure C12.2

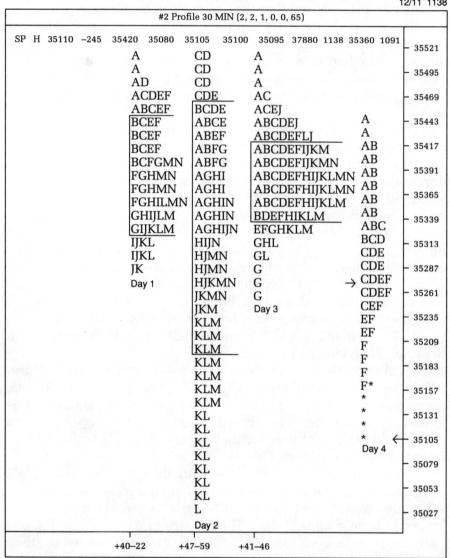

Figure C12.3

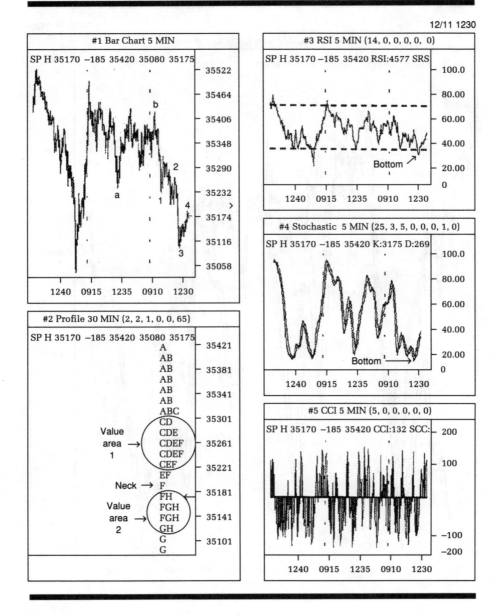

12/11 1230

Figure C12.4

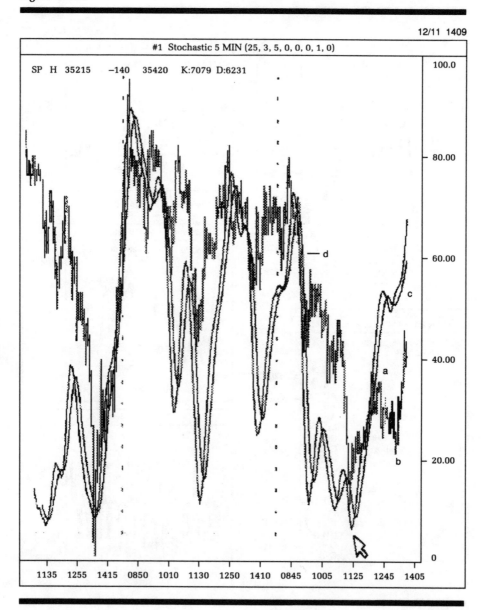

Figure C12.4 was created 1 ½ hours later. It is a stochastic 5-minute bar chart and shows good upside strength. The bottom made at point A, as identified by the arrow, shows confirmation of the bottoming action by the stochastic oversold signal.

Price had moved up about half a point.

Go back to Figure C12.3 and inspect #1 Chart. I was aware of the possibility that this sell-off into secondary lows might be the C wave of an A-B-C correction in Elliott wave terminology. Why was this possible? From point B of #1 Chart, prices had dropped into a nice 4-wave formation, with the possible fifth wave yet to form. The *rule of alternation* showed that the second wave of the c wave was a running correction to the downside; this meant that the fourth wave of the c wave had to be sharp and to the upside. The second wave eventually created the fourth wave. Now, all I had to observe was the possibility that the fourth wave was a 3-wave correction—an A-B-C wave—and the C wave would have been completed.

Figure C12.4 shows the possibility that the fourth wave would be a 3-wave correction. Where was a possible resistance level going to come in? Around point D, or 353.00, would be the most likely maximum level. Would this be the case? Could I have sold short around the 353 level and expected prices to drop to new lows?

Figure C12.5 shows more ambivalent signals that confused me even more. This chart was created on 12-11 @ 2:59 P.M.. What I had been looking for was a possible rally to the upside after new lows had been made. What did I find?

First, the S&P Futures Index rallied to new highs for the move—not quite high enough to take out the highs of the day that had been made in the first hour of the trading day. I interpreted the new to secondary highs beyond the 353.00 initial resistance area as a warning flag that new lows having yet to end the fifth wave might not be possible.

I drew a downtrending line L1 connecting the first high, point A, and the second high, point B. At point C, price broke above it to the upside! Where was the correct analysis?

The #2 Chart of Figure C12.5 is another chart that I pulled out to analyze. This chart is a 30-minute bar chart of the Dow Jones Industrial Averages. What was shown on this chart? I created a downtrending line L2 by connecting point A2 and point B2. This line is similar in concept to line L1, the line drawn in #1 Chart. I noted that, even at point C2, the Dow Industrials had taken out the line at point C. This confirmation of the downtrending line break to the upside of point C1 on line L1 was all I needed to reanalyze the possibly incorrect Elliott wave count.

Note that, in #1 Chart of Figure C12.3, I had thrown together a possibly valid Elliott wave count with a fifth wave yet to form. Well, I studied the corrective waves more precisely and noted that I had counted the corrective waves incorrectly. In #1 Chart of Figure C12.5 the correction in the second wave was between 353.40 and 353.90 and not as labeled in #1 Chart of Figure C12.3, which showed it to be between 352.00 and 353.00. With this corrected count, the upside move to take out downtrending resistance lines could be accepted within the framework of Elliott wave analysis.

Figure C12.5

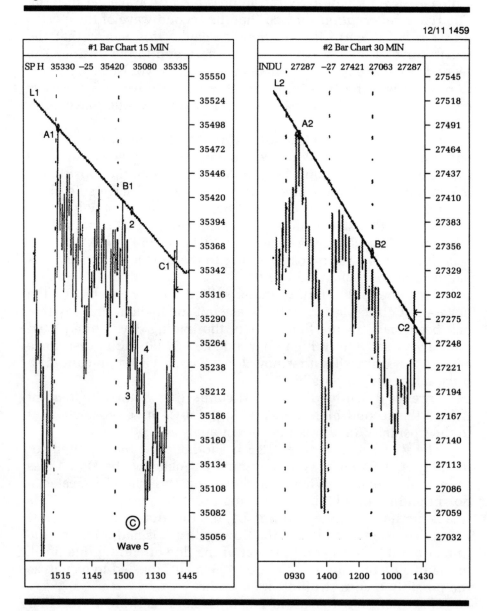

One of the discouraging indications, that of the profile showing a double–Value Area distribution, was eventually negated because the F neck was filled in and prices eventually created a trending day—after the lows had been made in period G (see #2 Chart of Figure C12.3). This development suggested very good strength.

I made no trades and lost no money on this set of trades. There were initially too many divergent signals. Some analysts said to buy; others said to sell. Some said the bottom had been made; others said the top had to be made. In spite of such disagreement, I eventually analyzed the market correctly. Without experience the trader can only apply the technical analysis techniques blindly, but with more experience the trader can reanalyze data that had been incorrectly analyzed before and come up with better conclusions. As the market proved, prices went considerably higher.

CASE 13   Which Chart, Which Index?

There are times when the day trader needs to determine which chart should be used in his or her analysis. This section will illustrate the importance of taking several charts and analyzing them for different perspectives. If the trader can get to the point of taking several charts and keeping the analyses open on them until some very good conclusions can be drawn, then he or she will be on his way to a *gestalten*, a study and understanding of the market as a whole picture and not as its individual parts.

Figure C13.1, created on 8-28 @ 8:40 A.M., clearly shows the differing signals generated from different charts. The #1 Chart is a line chart of a 5-minute bar chart of the S&P Futures Index; #2 Chart is a line chart of a 5-minute bar chart of the Major Market Futures Index. The relative price actions match exactly at points A1 and A2, points B1 and B2, points C1 and C2, points D1 and D2, points F1 and F2, points G1 and G2, and points H1 and H2. All these points corresponded with each other in the sense that highs or lows were made for the respective swings.

The diverging points were at points E1 and E2. In market analysis, what is often most important is not the similarity in patterns, but rather the dissimilarities, or the divergences. When markets behave according to expectations, then profits can be made easily, because there are previous models of expected price behaviors the trader can apply to current price actions. However, when markets don't behave according to expectations, then either market conditions are not as they seem or previous expectations will eventually not be met; this approach also provides profitable opportunities, albeit with greater risk and entirely different trading strategies, which can even minimize market risk.

In Figure C13.1, you can see everything going according to plans—each index confirms the other. However, at point E1, which was eventually superceded by point G1, and at E2, which was never superceded by point G2, you can garner significant information. One obvious conclusion is that the Major Market Index is much weaker than the S&P Futures Index; a way to play this relative weakness would be to enter spread positions: Go long the S&P Futures Index and short the Major Market Index.

What is the advantage to this? First, the position the trader takes in this situation is a spread position. The spread position is available because there is an observable relative strength in the S&P Futures Index and an observable relative weakness in the Major Market Futures Index. The spread position will not produce as much profit as an outright position in either market, but the subjective risk judgment indicates that the probability of a profit is much higher. As a professional, these are ideal situations to play: low risk of loss and high probability of profit.

Second, the trader can take advantage of features that spreads provide: lower margin requirements, more added positions, facilitating the trade conclusion through the implementation of option spreads, and so on. This set of answers to the relative weakness is much better than an outright position that you could have decided

Figure C13.1

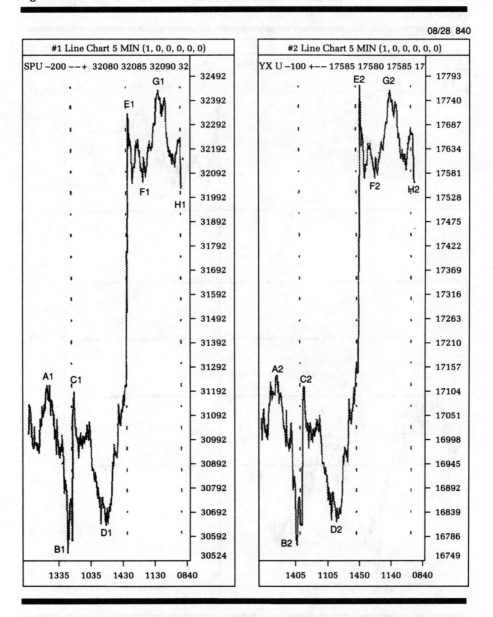

to enter after you had concluded that an Elliott wave impulse wave had ended and the market was headed into a correction.

Figure C13.2 was created on 8-28 about 20 minutes later and is a 5-minute bar chart of the Major Market Futures Index. Please note that there is huge gap from the previous day's closing price of 171.55 and the current day's opening price of about 177.00, about a 5.45 point gap opening.

Note also that the gap is very evident in the bar chart but was not shown on #2 Chart of Figure C13.1. The simple lesson here is

Figure C13.2

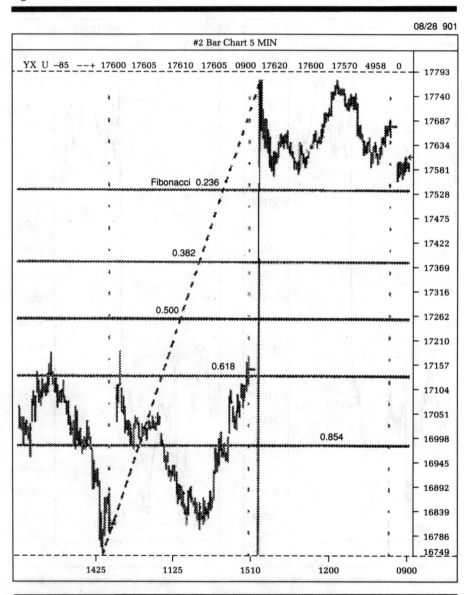

that viewing the bar chart showed a gap, while viewing the line chart (#2) showed no such gap.

For a quick Fibonacci analysis, observe that the ratio retracements are as posted on Figure C13.2. In most market moves, retracements of 50 percent are expected. Anything less than that indicates strength and the trader should buy on any dip; anything more than that indicates weakness and that the upmove is suspect. The placement of the 50 percent retracement at around the 172.65 price level indicates strength. How was this observed? By the simple fact that if price were to sell off to a 50 percent retracement and then were to resume its upward trend, the gap formed from the close to the open would *not* be filled. From one simple tenet of Elliott wave analysis, you must be aware that unfilled gaps are indicative of wave 3 formations and herald much stronger moves in the direction of the impulse wave.

So, from basic inductive reasoning you can gather that even though the Major Market Futures Index (#2 Chart of Figure C13.1) shows weakness at Point G2, the fact that a Fibonacci analysis indicates the good probability that a mild retracement is in store, the trader must be very willing to cover on any rebound attempts. The conclusion: Short the Major Market, but be ready to cover quickly. Why is this so important to know in this situation? When I cover shorts, I know that I can cover quickly or cover at my leisure. This is one short that will have to be covered quickly, because the probability of a strong selloff is not great. Be aware that this weak selloff is not reflective of the weak top at G2 of #2 Chart in Figure C13.1.

Figure C13.3 shows two 5-minute bar charts created on 11-20 @ 1:04 P.M.: #1 Chart is of the Dow Jones Industrials, and #2 Chart is of the S&P Futures Index.

Again we have divergence, but this time not at high prices as in Figure C13.1, but at low prices. Divergences in markets can occur anywhere, but they often occur at the least likely places. Note that in both charts, points A1 and A2 and points B1 and B2 match the relative weaknesses and strengths.

The divergence shows up at points C1 and C2 and points D1 and D2. Whereas in #1 Chart point C1 holds above point A1, #2 Chart point C2 takes out point A2. The evident weakness of point D2, compared to point D1, confirms the weakness. Once C2 showed weakness, the day trader should have been able to short this market readily, instead of shorting the Dow Jones Industrials through the use of the similar, but not identical, Major Market Futures Index.

I have one word of caution to traders who are looking for this type of divergence: these opportunities to trade divergences must be done over time, but exited quickly. It must be done over time because the trader is looking at pervasive strength or weakness relative to another market; and it must be exited quickly because often the one market that is the weakest or the strongest will effect countermoves sharply to the upside or to the downside, respectively. Because the trader is looking at relative strengths and weaknesses, the total position must be entered through the execution of multiple trades; exiting must be done in one trade.

Figure C13.3

11/20 1304

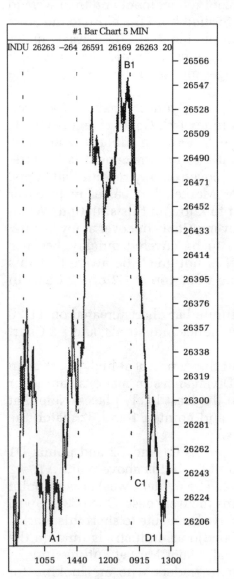
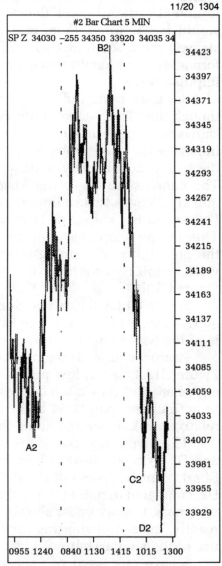

CASE 14   Elliott Wave and the S&P Index:
A Near-Perfect Trade

The following trade was made on October 20, 1989 and shows how a melding of various trading approaches can create ample trading opportunities with minimal risk.

There are six sets of charts used to illustrate this particular trade, which generated approximately 3.40 S&P futures points, or a profit potential of $1750 per contract.

This example was created solely for my records before I decided to write this book, so if you find the charts to be incomplete, please remember that I was trading from my own experience and for my own account. At the time, I was not trading and documenting my trades with the intention of teaching readers and students the techniques of day trading.

The first chart, Figure C14.1, illustrates the bottom price of approximately 341.00, which was made two days before, October

Figure C14.1

18, 1989, through to the current action of October 20, 1989. In toto, there were about 2 1/2 days of market action of 5-minute bars. The chart was created at 11:05 A.M. on the twentieth. On the eighteenth (the leftmost price action of Figure C14.1) the market bottomed and started its first leg up. At the time that the first leg was started, it was not discernible as to whether or not this move would be sustained.

Let's take some time out and review some tenets of Elliott wave analysis:

> In using Elliott wave theory, the practitioner is searching for repeatable patterns. In the case of the Elliott wave theory, price action moves upward in waves of uptrends and waves of downtrends. In Elliott wave terminology the upwaves are impulse waves and the downwaves are correction waves. There are a total of five waves that make up a larger impulse wave, and this larger impulse wave is itself part of a series of longer-duration wave sequences.

Because the market supposedly bottomed out at the 341.00 level, we are looking for the development of a series of impulse-correction waves. The first impulse wave ended on the same day that it began, October 18. At around the 346.40 price level, the futures stop going up and go into a corrective wave. From the bottom of this first impulse wave to its top, price traveled about 5.40 points.

The first corrective wave, labeled in Elliott wave terminology as the second wave, stops going down at about the 343.55 level, a retracement of about 2.85 points. This correction was approximately a 52.1 percent retracement. There is no significance in this percentage because there is no correlation with known ratios.

The bottom of the next impulse wave, labeled as wave 3, starts at 343.55. The price then moves up to 351.95, an impulse wave that moves about 8.40 points.

To this point in the analysis of Figure C14.1, I had not decided to execute any trades. However, because I was looking at an overall impulse wave I tried to lean to the buy side. Hence, I looked for any possible entry point to purchase the S&P futures contract.

At the completion of wave 3, the futures price drops. The first correction appears to be a flat correction, as much as flat corrections can be discerned from the pattern. It could be argued that the correction is a muddled zig-zag correction. There is a clue to what this correction is all about, though.

The third wave was 8.40 points in length. This, compared to the 5.40 points that the first wave took, was about 1.55 times greater in length. This third wave satisfied one of the precepts of the Elliott wave theory: The third wave has to be longer than both wave 1 and wave 5.

The third wave, to this point of the analysis, is the longest. Because it is the longest, the higher probability correction that ensues must now have a greater retracement than the wave 2 correction. In other words, we have reduced the precept of alternating corrective waves (if wave 2 is zig-zag, wave 4 has to be flat, and conversely if wave 2 is flat, then wave 4 must be zig-zag) to the following: If wave 2 travels less distance, then wave 4 must travel a greater distance, or if wave 2 travels a greater distance, then wave 4 must travel a smaller distance. We had a problem discerning whether wave 2 was flat or a zig-zag. However, we have less of a problem forecasting that wave 4 must be of longer duration correction than wave 2 because (1) wave 3 moves such a price distance that a correction would most likely be of greater length than the previous correction, and (2) we had great difficulty figuring out whether wave 2 was zig-zag or flat. We now conclude that wave 4 will contain a much greater distance to be covered than wave 2. As market action did prove, the distance traveled by wave 4 moved from a high of 351.95 to a low of 346.35, a distance of 5.60 points.

However, prior to this actual market move to the 346.35 reversal area, the analysis pointed to a very likely entry point for a very profitable trade.

Wave 4 corrections should not correct into wave 2; that is, this correction should end above the end of wave 1 and definitely not below the end of wave 2.

Figure C14.2 was created several minutes later and contains a right descending trendline from the 351.95 high. I decided to draw this trendline because I needed a sensitive point to initiate any buy orders.

I also drew a horizontal line to mark off the top of wave 1. My strategy at this point had now materialized to the point that told me to buy at around the 346.80 level. Here I had to go long, with the expectation that the wave 5 impulse wave should then go above the previous wave 3 high, or 351.95. I reasoned that if I could buy at 346.80 and was able to sell around the 352.00 level or higher, I should make at least approximately 3.20 points, or about $1600 per contract.

When price reached the 346.80 level I initiated a purchase. The price bottomed out at exactly 346.35, offering me a risk of 0.45 S&P futures points, or $225. I did not expect the price to go much below this level, because I expected prices to stay above the ending of wave 2.

Where do I enter stop orders to limit my losses if I turn out to be wrong in my analysis? First, I had to define when the analysis could be considered as incorrect.

Figure C14.2

Figure C14.3 was created on the same day at 1:37 P.M., local time. The chart was used to assess what the stop-sell point was to be.

The analysis to enter the long side at around the 346.80 level will be considered incorrect if price obviously continues to go down. However, there was a glimmer of a valid stop point to limit the losses: the gap that was formed on the opening of trade on October 19, 1989. The price gapped up at around the 345.80 high and the low of 344.50. I used the bottom of the gap, 344.50, as a possible stop-loss point. This would limit my risk to about 2.30 points (346.80 entry and 344.50 stop loss).

To be even safer, however, in limiting my losses, I could also have used the previous support level, which was made within the first two hours of the trading made on October 19: around the 346.10 level. If I used this as the stop-loss limit, my loss would then be limited to a maximum of 0.70, or exactly $350. This risk is much better than the previous risk of 2.30 points, or $1150.

Figure C14.3

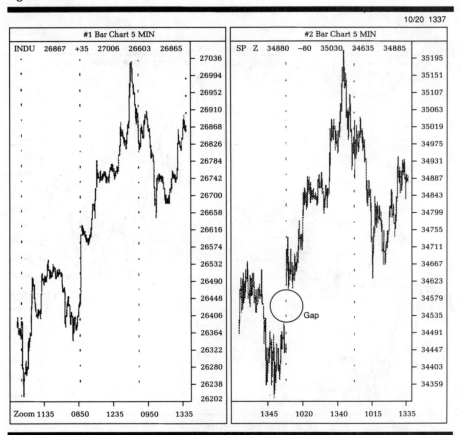

Figure C14.4 was created to continue the analysis.

At the end of the fourth wave, I entered long positions at around 346.80.

Now I apply the basic concepts of chart patterns and trend lines to fortify and confirm my analysis even more. In Figure C14.2, created at 11:09 A.M., I drew a trendline down from the top 351.95. The downward-sloping line will provide a confirmatory signal once price breaks it to the upside. If price is capable of breaking the downward-sloping line to the upside, then I had a better confirmation that wave 5 is in force and that the top of wave 3—351.95—will be surpassed.

Now look at how the other markets are acting by inspecting Figure C14.3. Specifically, I analyzed the Dow Jones Industrials Averages. Please note that Figure C14.3 contains two charts: the Dow Jones Industrials and the S&P December futures contracts. Please note that the Dow Jones Industrials contains a cleaner chart: The lines are more defined and are not muddled with other prices

Figure C14.4

that are scattered all over the December S&P 500 futures. At least there are better series of impulse and corrective wave formations on the industrials charts.

From the upside breakout, I am now satisfied that wave 5 is forming and that I was correct in positioning to the long side. In Figure C14.4 you should note that the downward-sloping trendline was broken to the upside at around the 347.50 price level. This further confirms the analysis that wave 5 is forming.

Figure C14.5 was created on the same day at 3:32 P.M. Trading had concluded for the day.

As the day continues to a close, price moves up to 350.30. Price jiggles up and down while it moves upwards. When I positioned at around the 346.80 I expected price to move above 351.95 before the move was considered to be finished. At this point I could cash

Figure C14.5

10/20 1532

in the position, which would have given me a profit of 3.50, or $1750.

If I had wanted to take the added risk of carrying a position over the weekend, I can hope to squeeze at least an additional 1.70 points.

Figure C14.6 was created several hours after the market had closed. I had a feeling that I should check another indicator to confirm my conclusion that I should carry positions into the next day.

On a whim, I checked out one of the price-sensitive momentum studies. In this particular case, I looked at the stochastics chart. Figure C14.6 showed that at around the price level where I did go long, 346.80, a definite oversold signal was reversing to the buy side.

Figure C14.6

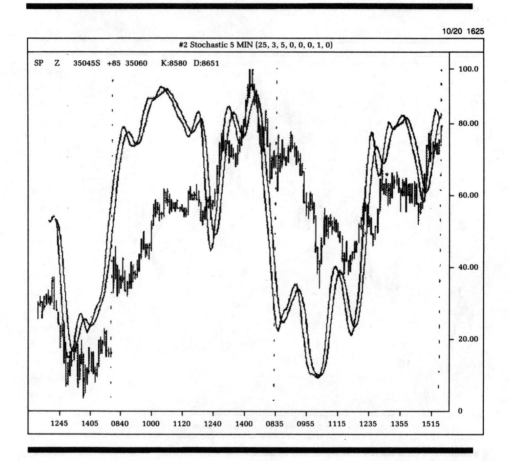

10/20 1625

| #2 Stochastic 5 MIN (25, 3, 5, 0, 0, 0, 1, 0) |

SP   Z   35045S   +85 35060   K:8580 D:8651

Had I looked at this study at the time I actually decided to go long at the 346.80 level, I would have had further confidence of positioning to the long side.

In conclusion, this trade was a virtually riskless trade, which allowed me to make the maximum allowable swing points: The actual high of the day, 350.50 and the second selloff low of 346.35, showed a range of 4.15. My trade gave me 3.50 points, or exactly 84.33 percent of the day's total range!

APPENDIX
Datafeed Vendors and
Software Reference Guide

Through the various data vendors, the day trader has access to unprecedented amounts of data for analysis. The following two lists are composed of datafeed suppliers and software developers. Datafeed suppliers have also become software developers to facilitate the use of their own datafeeds. In their efforts to become vertically integrated financial information suppliers, some companies who have traditionally been sources of financial information have purchased software development houses. The two lists attempt to separate the two functions, but it is possible that, by the time you decide to obtain more information on these companies, the developers with innovative ideas will be acquired by larger datafeed vendors.

DATAFEED SUPPLIERS

ADP Brokerage Information Services Group
2 Journal Square Plaza
Jersey City NJ 07306
800–237–6683
Supplies data for Videcom quotes and graphic analyses

ANYWHERE, Inc.
8280 Greensboro Drive No 320
McLean VA 22102
800–321–8425
Real-time quote systems

Bonneville Telecommunications
19 W South Temple
Salt Lake City UT 84101
801–532–3400 or 800–255–7374
Real-time futures, stocks, options, news, weather

Bridge Information Systems
717 Office Parkway
St. Louis MO 63141
314–567–8100 or 800–251–3282
Real-time datafeed for futures; charts, graphs, news, research

CMA, Inc.
151 W 46th St
New York NY 10036
212–382–1822 or 800–262–4127
Specializes in real-time quotes for South American stocks and
futures

Commodity Communications Corporation (FutureSource)
955 Parkview Lane
Lombard IL 60148
708–620–8444 or 800–621–2628
Real-time quotes; technical, analytical, historical and news for
in-house software

Commodity Information Services (CIS), part of the S&P group
1221 Avenue of the Americas
New York NY 10020
212–512–6110 or 800–437–3725
Real-time market information systems covering futures,
financials, and cash markets

Commodity News Service (now owned by Knight-Ridder)
2100 West 89th St 6053
Leawood KS 66206
303–945–7373
Commodity and financial news, real-time quotes, charts

Commodity Quotations, Inc. (and Commodity Quote Graphics)
PO Box 758
Glenwood Springs CO 81602
303–945–8686 or 800–525–7082
Real-time quotations and technical decision support systems
for futures and options

Comstock
670 White Plains Rd
Scarsdale NY 10583
914–725–3477 or 800–431–5019
Real-time quote systems for futures, stocks, options, and
foreign exchange

Dow Jones & Company, Inc.
PO Box 300
Princeton NJ 08543
609–520–4900 or 800–345–NEWS
The premium data provider; they have everything a trader
could need

FNN Data Broadcasting (Signal Division)
1900 S Norfolk Street
San Mateo CA 94403
800–367–4670
Signal and Quotrek delivery systems, real-time quotes for fixed
fees; largest datafeed distributor with support from third-party
software creators

Knight-Ridder Commodity News Service
2100 W 89th St
Leawood KS 66206
913–642–7373 or 800–255–6490
Future and financial news, real-time quotes, charts

Market Data Corporation
3910 FM 1960 West Ste 230
Houston TX 77068
713–586–8686 or 800–433–7068
Hand-held, PC-based live quote system

Market Vision Corporation
40 Rector Street
New York NY 10006
212–227–1610
Datafeed provider

MJK Associates
122 Saratoga Ave Ste 11
Santa Clara CA 95051
408–247–5102
Time-sharing futures database service available worldwide

MMS International
1301 Shorway Road
Third Floor
Belmont CA 94002
415–595–0610 or 800–227–7304
On-line fundamental, technical coverage of debt, equity, and
currency markets

National Computer Network Corporation
223 W Jackson Blvd No 1202
Chicago IL 60606
312–427–5125
Real-time and end-of-day options analysis valuation, CBOE,
futures indexes

The Options Group (TOG)
50 Broadway Ste 2000
New York NY 10004
212–785–5555
Real-time option analytics for all non-equity markets, both
listed and over-the-counter

P.C. Quote
401 S LaSalle St Ste 1600
Chicago IL 60605
312–786–5400 or 800–225–5657
Real-time stocks, options, futures quotes delivered to IBM AT
via satellite

Quotron Systems
12371 W Jefferson Blvd
Los Angeles CA 90066
213–827–4600 or 213–302–4621
On-line, real-time price, market information, all U.S., 25
international exchanges

Reuters Limited
200 Liberty St
New York NY 10281
212–493–7100

Telemet America, Inc.
325 First St
Alexandria VA 22314
703–548–2042 or 800–368–2078
Quotation services

Telerate International Quotations
1 World Trade Center
New York NY 10048
212–938–5400
Instant access to real-time financial quotes and analysis
worldwide

Track Data, Dial/Data Division
61 Broadway
New York NY 10006
718–522–6886 or 212–943–4555
Daily and historical data

Trans-Lux Corporation
110 Richards Ave
Norfolk CT 06854
203–853–4321 or 800–243–5544
Large-scale electronic posting displays

Wang Financial Services (now owned by FNN Data
Broadcasting)
120 Wall Street
New York NY 10005
212–208–7700 or 800–423–2002
Real-time coverage, all markets, on-line options analysis,
strategies, decision support

The day trader may also use real-time software to apply market analyses proficiently. The following list of software developers includes a wide range of companies with different degrees of support. Because the software programming business is essentially a one-person operation (the actual programmer), anyone who has some degree of understanding of the markets and mathematical techniques can be a software developer. However, they will not always be able to service and market their products. This list has been culled from other lists; to the best of my knowledge, these companies will be around to support users in the future.

INTRADAY ANALYSIS SOFTWARE DEVELOPERS

ADAPTi Inc.
2124 Kittredge St Ste 500
Berkeley CA 94704
415–549–2026
Multi-user Apple Macintosh charting, analysis, alerts, and
portfolio pricing

Applied Technology Services
25-10 Thirtieth Rd
Astoria NY 11102
718–204–1999
Multi-user intraday charting and analysis

Aspen Research Group, Ltd.
201 Centennial St, Ste 209
PO Box 1370
Glenwood Springs CO 81602
303–945–2921
Apsen Graphics software accesses a 10-year daily historical
database of over 100,000 markets.

Bristol Financial Services, Inc.
23 Bristol Pl
Wilton CT 06897
203–834–0040
Intraday software (My experience with these developers
in 1985 left a bad taste; there was no support and no
upgrades without additional fees; however, in all fairness to
these developers, it is my understanding that they have
developed better software and upgraded client
servicing.)

Coherent Software Systems
772 Anthony Rd
Portsmouth RI 02871
401–683–5886
Portfolio management, historical and real-time charting, and
electronic quote retrieval

Commodity Quote Graphics (CQG)
PO Box 758
Glenwood Springs CO 81602
303–945–8686 or 800–525–7082
Real-time quotations and technical decision support systems
for futures and options

Comtrend (ADP Comtrend)
2 Journal Square Plaza
Jersey City NJ 07306
800–237–6683
Supplies data for Videcom quotes and graphic analyses

CTS Trend
139 South St
New Providence NJ 07974
201–771–0060
IBM-based analytical software with six separate modules

Econometrix
10841 Deborah Dr
Potomac MD 20854
301–299–2319
Intraday charts

Ensign Software
2641 Shannon Ct
Idaho Falls ID 83404
208–524–0755
Software plots real-time technical analysis for the IBM-PC

Foley Financial, Inc.
McCormack Station PO Box 4535
Boston MA 02101
617–237–3001 or 800–662–7355
Intraday and historical technical analysis for stocks, options,
and futures

Futuresource; a division of Oster Communications
955 Parkview Ln
Lombard IL 60148
708–620–8444 or 800–621–2628
On-line software for their own datafeed

MasterChartist
(Most of the illustrations from this manual are from this
software; this does not, however, serve as an endorsement
of their products or services.)
750 N Freedom Blvd Ste 3018
Provo UT 84601
801–375–6847 or 800–433–4276
One of the largest independent producers of third-party
technical analysis software

Multex, Inc.
254 W 31st St
Ninth Floor
New York NY 10001
212–629–7994
Real-time software quotation and analysis operating under Windows and Excel software for the IBM-PC

Northfield Trading Company
4877 S Everett St
Littleton CO 80123
303–972–1433 or 800–648–2232
Licensed buy-sell signal generator

$Link
1335 Rhode Island St
San Francisco CA 94107
415–641–0721
Real-time
technical analysis software for the IBM computer

Telerate Systems Inc.
1 World Trade Center
New York NY 10048
212–938–5400 or 800–872–3400
Developed, among other products, the Teletrac real-time technical analysis system

Bibliography

Achelis, Steven B. *Market Indicator Interpretation Guide Using the Technician Program.* Salt Lake City, UT: Computer Asset Management, 1986.

Angas, L. L. B. *Investment for Appreciation: Forecasting Movements in Security Prices, Techniques of Trading in Shares for Profit.* New York: Somerset Publishing, 1936.

Angle, Kelly. *100 Million Dollars in Profits: An Anatomy of a Market Killing and a Realistic Trading Plan.* Brightwaters, NY: Windsor Books, 1989.

Bayer, George. *Stock and Commodity Trader's Hand-Book of Trend Determination: Secrets of Forecasting Values, Especially Commodities Including Stocks.* Carmel, CA: Author, 1940.

Beckman, Robert C. *The Downwave: Surviving the Second Great Depression.* New York: E.P. Dutton, 1983.

Beckman, Robert C. *Into the Upwave: How to Prosper from Slump to Boom.* 3rd ed. Horndean, England: Milestone Publication, 1988; distributed in the U.S. by Seven Hills Books, Cincinnati, OH.

Beckman, Robert C. *Supertiming: The Unique Elliott Wave System: Keys to Anticipating Impending Stock Market Action.* Los Angeles: Library of Investment Study, 1979.

Belveal, L. Dee. *Charting Commodity Market Price Behavior.* Wilmette, IL: Commodities Press, 1969.

Bernstein, Jacob. *The Handbook of Commodity Cycles.* New York: John Wiley & Sons, 1982.

Bernstein, Jacob. *Short-Term Trading in Futures: A Manual of Systems, Strategies and Techniques.* Chicago: Probus Publishing, 1987.

Bernstein, Jake. *Facts on Futures: Insights and Strategies for Winning in the Futures Markets.* Chicago: Probus Publishing, 1987.

Bobin, Christopher A. *Agricultural Options: Trading, Risk Management, and Hedging.* New York: John Wiley & Sons, 1990.

Caplan, David. *The Professional Option Trader's Manual.* Malibu, CA: Opportunities in Options, 1987.

Chicago Board of Trade Options on Futures: Members' Manual. Chicago: Chicago Board of Trade, 1984.

Cleeton, Claud E. *Strategies for the Options Trader.* New York: John Wiley & Sons, 1979.

Coninx, Raymond G. F. *Foreign Exchange Dealers Handbook.* New York: Pick, 1982.

Crane, Burton. *The Sophisticated Investor: A Guide to Stock Market Profits.* New York: Simon & Schuster, 1959.

Davis, Gary A., and M. Allen Jacobson. *Stock Option Strategies.* Cross Plains, WI: Badger Press, 1976.

Dremen, David. *The New Contrarian Investment Strategy.* New York: Random House, 1982.

Edwards, Robert D., and John Magee. *Technical Analysis of Stock Trends.* 5th ed. Springfield, MA: John Magee Publishing, 1973.

Eng, William F. "Behavior of Technical Indicators in Market Stages." In *High Performance Futures Trading: Power Lessons from the Masters,* edited by Joel Robbins. Chicago: Probus Publishing, 1990.

Eng, William F. *Options: Trading Strategies That Work.* Chicago: Dearborn Financial Publishing, 1992.

Eng, William F. *The Technical Analysis of Stocks, Options and Futures: Advanced Trading Systems and Techniques.* Chicago: Probus Publishing, 1988.

Eng, William F. *Trading Rules: Strategies for Success.* Chicago: Longman Financial Services Publishing, 1991.

Engel, Louis, in collaboration with Peter Wyckoff. *How to Buy Stocks.* 6th rev. ed. New York: Bantam Books, 1977.

Evans, D. Morier. *Speculative Notes and Notes on Speculation, Ideal and Real.* 1864. Reprint. New York: Burt Franklin Publisher, 1968.

Fong, H. Gifford, and Frank J. Fabozzi. *Fixed Income Portfolio Management.* Homewood, IL: Dow Jones-Irwin, 1985.

The Fortune Investment Information Directory: Stocks, Bonds, Funds, & Options. 1st ed. Guilford, CT: The Dushkin Publishing Group, 1986.

Foster, Orline D. *The Art of Tape Reading: Ticker Technique.* Revised and edited by Robert H. Persons, Jr. Palisades Park, NJ: Investors' Press, 1965.

Foster, Orline D. *Making Money in the Stock Market*. New York: Doubleday, Doran and Company, 1930.

Gann, William D. *The Tunnel Thru the Air or Looking Back from 1940*. New York: Financial Guardian Publishing, 1927.

Gastineau, Gary L. *The Stock Options Manual*. 2d ed. New York: McGraw-Hill, 1979.

Gay, Gerald D., and Robert W. Kolb. *Interest Rate Futures: Concepts and Issues*. Richmond, VA: Robert F. Dame, 1982.

Gehm, F. *Commodity Market Money Management*. New York: John Wiley & Sons, 1983.

Gleick, James. *Chaos: Making a New Science*. New York: Viking Penguin, Inc., 1987.

Goodspeed, Bennett W. *The Tao-Jones Averages: A Guide to Whole-Brained Investing*. New York: Penguin Books. 1984.

Granville, Joseph E. *Granville's New Strategy of Daily Stock Market Timing for Maximum Profit*. Englewood Cliffs, NJ: Prentice Hall, 1976.

Hadady, R. Earl. *Opening Price Statistical Data on the Futures Markets*. Pasadena, CA: Key Books Press, 1984.

Hagin, Robert L. *The Dow Jones-Irwin Guide to Modern Portfolio Theory*. Homewood, IL: Dow Jones-Irwin, 1979.

Hansen, Duane C. *The Globalization of the International Financial Markets: Implications and Opportunities*. Chicago: Arthur Andersen, 1988.

Hawk, William A. *The U.S. Government Securities Market*. 3rd rev. ed. Chicago: Harris Trust and Savings Bank, 1976.

Hill, John, Jr. *Gold Bricks of Speculation: A Study of Speculation and Its Counterfeit, and an Exposé of the Methods of Bucketshop and 'Get-Rich-Quick' Swindles*. Chicago: Lincoln Book Concern, 1904.

Hill, John R. *Scientific Interpretation of Bar Charts*. Hendersonville, NC: Commodity Research Institute, 1979.

Hill, John R. *Stock & Commodity Market Trend Trading by Advanced Technical Analysis*. Hendersonville, NC: Commodity Research Institute, 1977.

Homer, Sidney. *A History of Interest Rates*. 2nd ed. rev. New Brunswick, NJ: Rutgers, 1977.

Howard, B. J. *The Price Spiral Method*. Brightwaters, New York: Windsor Books, 1988.

The Individual Investor's Guide to Investment Publications. 1st ed. Chicago: International Publishing Corporation, 1988.

Jiler, Harry, Seymour Gaylinn, Walter L. Emery, Milton W. Jiler, William L. Jiler, and J. Roger Wallace, eds. *Commodity Year Book 1975*. New York: Commodity Research Bureau, 1975.

Jiler, William L. *How Charts Can Help You in the Stock Market*. New York: Trendline, 1962.

Johnson, Robert W. *Financial Management*. 6th ed. New York: Allyn and Bacon, 1971.

Jones, Donald L. *Applications of the Market Profile: A Trader's Guide to Auction Markets*. Chicago: CISCO, 1988.

Jones, Eric T., and Donald L. Jones. *Hedging Foreign Exchange: Converting Risk to Profit*. New York: John Wiley & Sons, 1987.

Kallard, T. *Making Money in Commodity Spreads*. New York: Optosonic Press, 1974.

Kaufman, Perry J. *Commodity Trading Systems and Methods*. New York: John Wiley & Sons, 1978.

Kaufman, Perry J. *The Concise Handbook of Futures Markets: Money Management, Forecasting, and the Markets*. New York: John Wiley & Sons, 1986.

Kerr, Joseph H., Jr. *Methods in Dealing in Stocks: A Practical Guide and Handbook for Recording and Interpreting the Daily Action of the Stock Market*. Burlington, VT: Fraser Publishing Company, 1978.

Koch, Harvey. *Fastest Way to Get Rich: Trading in Financial Futures*. New York: Stein & Day, 1981.

Kroll, Stanley, and Irwin Shishko. *The Commodity Futures Market Guide*. New York: Harper & Row, 1973.

Krow, Harvey A. *Stock Market Behavior: The Technical Approach to Understanding Wall Street*. New York: Random House, 1969.

Kuehl, Edward C. *Things I Learned in the Stock Market*. Appleton, WI: C.C. Nelson, 1960.

Labuszewski, John W., and Jean Cairns Sinquefield. *Inside the Commodity Option Markets*. New York: John Wiley & Sons, 1985.

Labuszewski, John W., and John E. Nyhoff. *Trading Financial Futures: Markets, Methods, Strategies, and Tactics*. New York: John Wiley & Sons, 1988.

Labuszewski, John W., and John E. Nyhoff. *Trading Options or Futures: Markets, Methods, Strategies, and Tactics*. New York: John Wiley & Sons, 1988.

Langley, Russell. *Practical Statistics for Non-Mathematical People*. New York: Drake Publishers, 1971.

Levine, Sumner N., ed. *The 1988 Dow Jones-Irwin Business and Investment Almanac*. Homewood, IL: Dow Jones-Irwin, 1988.

Lindow, Wesley. *Inside the Money Market*. New York: Random House, 1972.

Loeb, Gerald M. *Your Battle for Stock Market Profits: How to Make Money and Keep It in Today's Market*. New York: Simon and Schuster, 1971.

Lofton, Todd, ed. *Trading Tactics: A Livestock Futures Anthology*. Chicago: Chicago Mercantile Exchange, 1986.

Longstreet, Roy W. *Viewpoints of a Commodity Trader*. New York: Frederick Fell Publishers, 1973.

Lorie, James, and Richard Brealey, eds. *Modern Developments in Investment Management*. New York: Praeger Press, 1973.

Lowell, Fred R. *The Wheat Market*. Edited by Chester W. Keltner. Kansas City: Keltner Statistical Service, 1968.

Luskin, Donald L. *Index Options and Futures: The Complete Guide*. New York: John Wiley & Sons, 1987.

Mader, Chris, and Robert Hagin. *The Dow Jones-Irwin Guide to Common Stocks*. (Previously published under the title *What Today's Investor Should Know about the New Science of Investing*.) Homewood, IL: Dow Jones-Irwin, 1976.

Magee, John. *Wall Street—Main Street—and You*. Springfield, MA: John Magee, 1972.

Martin, Ralph G. *The Wizard of Wall Street: The Story of Gerald M. Loeb*. New York: William Morrow, 1965.

McEvers, Joan, ed. *Financial Astrology for the 1990s*. St. Paul, MN: Llewellyn Publications, 1989.

McKinzie, Jeff L., and Keith I. Schap. *Hedging Financial Instruments: A Guide to Basis Trading for Bankers, Treasurers and Portfolio Managers*. Chicago: Probus Publishing, 1988.

McMillan, Lawrence G. *Options as a Strategic Investment: A Comprehensive Analysis of Listed Option Strategies*. 2nd ed. New York: New York Institute of Finance, 1986.

Morgan, E. Victor, and W. A. Thomas. *The London Stock Exchange: Its History and Functions*. 2nd ed. New York: St. Martin's Press, 1969.

Murphy, John J. *Intermarket Technical Analysis: Trading Strategies for the Global Stock, Bond, Commodity, and Currency Markets*. New York: John Wiley & Sons, 1991.

Murphy, John J. *The Technical Analysis of the Futures Markets: A Comprehensive Guide to Trading Methods and Applications.* New York: New York Institute of Finance, 1986.

Natenberg, Sheldon. *Option Volatility and Pricing Strategies: Advanced Trading Techniques for Professionals.* Chicago: Probus Publishing, 1988.

Nelson, S. A. *The ABC of Stock Speculation.* Wells, VT: Fraser Publishing Company, 1964.

Peck, Anne E., comp. *Selected Writings of Holbrook Working.* Chicago: Board of Trade of the City of Chicago, 1977.

Peritt, Gerald W., and Alan Lavine. *Diversify: The Investor's Guide to Asset Allocation Strategies.* Chicago: Longman Financial Services Publishing, 1990.

Plummer, Tony. *Forecasting Financial Markets: Technical Analysis and the Dynamics of Price.* New York: John Wiley & Sons, 1991.

Powers, Mark J. *Inside the Financial Futures Markets.* 2nd ed. New York: John Wiley & Sons, 1984.

Prechter, Robert Rougelet, Jr., and Alfred John Frost. *Elliott Wave Principle: Key to Stock Market Profits.* Chappaqua, NY: New Classics Library, 1978.

Prechter, Robert Rougelet, Jr., ed. *The Major Works of R. N. Elliott.* Chappaqua, NY: New Classics Library, 1980.

Pring, Martin. *How to Forecast Interest Rates.* New York: McGraw-Hill, 1981.

Rhea, Robert. *The Dow Theory: An Explanation of Its Development and An Attempt to Define Its Usefulness as An Aid to Speculation.* New York: Barron's, 1932.

Rolo, Charles J., and George J. Nelson, eds. *The Anatomy of Wall Street: A Guide for the Serious Investor.* New York: J. B. Lipincott, 1968.

Rowley, Anthony. *Asian Stockmarkets: The Inside Story.* Homewood, IL: Dow Jones-Irwin, 1987.

Sarnoff, Paul. *Jesse Livermore: Speculator-King.* Palisades Park, NJ: Investors' Press, 1967.

Schabacker, R. W. *Stock Market Profits.* Burlington, VT: Fraser Publishing Company edition, 1970 (originally published in 1934).

Schwager, Jack D. *A Complete Guide to the Futures Markets: Fundamental Analysis, Technical Analysis, Trading, Spreads, and Options.* New York: John Wiley & Sons, 1984.

Seaman, George. *This is the Road to Stock Market Success.* 2nd ed. Chicago: Seamans-Blake, 1946.

Sepharial. *The Silver Key: A Guide to Speculators.* Unknown publisher and date. The author believes this volume was written between 1920 and 1930.

Sheldon, Michael U. *Successful Speculation.* New York: Grossett & Dunlap, 1969.

Smith, Courtney. *Option Strategies: Profit-Making Techniques for Stock, Stock Index, and Commodity Options.* New York: John Wiley & Sons, 1987.

Smith, Keith V. *Portfolio Management: Theoretical and Empirical Studies of Portfolio Decision-Making.* New York: Holt, Rinehart and Winston, 1971.

Spalding, William F. *The London Money Market: A Practical Guide to What It Is, Where It Is, and the Operations Conducted in It.* 4th ed. London: Sir Isaac Pitman & Sons, 1930.

The Spicer & Oppenheim Guide to Securities Markets Around the World. New York: John Wiley & Sons, 1988.

Steidlmayer, J. Peter. *Chicago Board of Trade Market Profile: A Time Distribution Analysis that Explains Market Behavior.* Chicago: Chicago Board of Trade, 1984.

Steidlmayer, J. Peter. *Steidlmayer on Markets: A New Approach to Trading.* New York: John Wiley & Sons, 1989.

Steidlmayer, J. Peter, and Shera Buyer. *Taking the Data Forward: Analyzing Long-Term Trends with Chicago Board of Trade Market Profile.* Chicago: Author, 1986.

Steidlmayer, J. Peter, and Kevin Koy. *Markets and Market Logic: Trading and Investing with a Sound Understanding and Approach.* Chicago: The Porcupine Press, 1986.

Stigum, Marcia. *Money Market Calculations, Yields, Break-Evens, and Arbitrage.* Homewood, IL: Dow Jones-Irwin, 1981.

Stigum, Marcia. *The Money Market: Myth, Reality and Practice.* Homewood, IL: Dow Jones-Irwin, 1978.

Strong, Robert A. *Speculative Markets: Options, Futures and Hard Assets.* Chicago: Longman Financial Services Publishing, 1989.

Teweles, Richard J., Charles V. Harlow, and Herbert L. Stone. *The Commodity Futures Game: Who Wins? Who Loses? Why?* New York: McGraw-Hill, 1974.

Thomas, Conrad W. *Hedgmanship: How to Make Money in Bear Markets, Bull Markets, and Chicken Markets while Confounding Professional Money Managers and Attracting a Better Class of Women.* Homewood, IL: Dow Jones-Irwin, 1970.

Thomsett, Michael C. *The Mathematics of Investing: A Complete Reference.* New York: John Wiley & Sons, 1989.

Thorp, Edward O. *Beat the Dealer: A Winning Strategy for the Game of Twenty-One.* New York: Blaisdell, 1962.

Thorp, Edward O. *The Mathematics of Gambling.* Secaucus, NJ: A Gambling Time Book distributed by Lyle Stuart, 1984.

Thorp, Edward O., and Sheen T. Kassouf. *Beat the Market: A Scientific Stock Market System.* New York: Random House, 1967.

Tso, Lin. *Complete Investor's Guide to Listed Options: Calls and Puts.* Englewood Cliffs, NJ: Prentice Hall, 1981.

Tso, Lin. *How to Make Money Trading Listed Puts.* New York: Frederick Fell Publishers, 1978.

Whitrow, G. J. *The Nature of Time.* (Originally published as *What Is Time?*) London: Thames and Hudson, 1972.

Williams, Frank J. *If You Must Speculate, Learn the Rules.* Burlington, VT: Fraser Publishing Company edition, 1970 (originally published in 1930).

Wong, M. Anthony. *Trading and Investing in Bond Options: Risk Management, Arbitrage, and Value Investing.* New York: John Wiley & Sons, 1991.

Wyckoff, Peter. *The Psychology of Stock Market Timing.* Englewood Cliffs, NJ: Prentice Hall, 1969.

Zahorchak, Michael G. *Favorable Executions: The Wall Street Specialist and the Auction Market.* New York: Van Nostrand Reinhold, 1974.

Zwieg, Martin E. *Understanding Technical Forecasting: How to Use Barron's Market Laboratory Pages.* Chicopee, MA: Dow Jones, 1980.

Index